D1320038

FREDERICK TAYLOR

The MIT Press Cambridge, Massachusetts, and London, England

Sudhir Kakar

FREDERICK TAYLOR
A STUDY IN PERSONALITY AND INNOVATION

Set in Linotype Baskerville and printed by The Heffernan Press Inc.
Bound in the United States of America by The Colonial Press, Inc.

ISBN 0 262 11039 3 (hardcover)
ISBN 0 262 61011 6 (paperback)

Library of Congress catalog card number: 79-122260

To my parents and Kamla,
in part repayment
of a generational debt

CONTENTS

Frederick Winslow Taylor, the "father of scientific management" invented new techniques of factory management and along with time and motion study, an ideology of authority in organizations. No single figure in the history of industrialization did more to affect the role of the manager than Taylor and, in fact, those who came after him had to take Taylor's work into account in the application of their theories and techniques. As Professor Kakar points out in this study, Taylor's work applied across cultural boundaries and appealed to the interests of those concerned with increasing productivity independently of political beliefs governing the distribution of wealth.

Until now, Taylor's place in industrial history depended upon the outcome of controversies between his disciples and critics, the latter being for the most part humanists and trade union leaders. His official biographer, Copley, admired Taylor and tried to fit him into the conventional patterns of the gentleman of the late 19th century. This gentleman happened to turn to industrial management but never really left his birthright as a Philadelphian and a Quaker, according to Copley. Copley could dispose of Taylor's critics by shrugging off disputes as the inability of narrow-minded men to understand a gentleman genius. Taylor's behavior characteristics could be considered charming eccentricities but certainly of no relevance to Taylor's work and life style. With today's knowledge of personality dynamics, and particularly with the application of this knowledge to biography, Professor Sudhir Kakar presents a new interpretation of Taylor's innovations which emphasizes the relationship between Taylor's personal conflicts and the development of his system of scientific management.

One of the problems in writing a psychological interpretation of Taylor as an innovator is to go beyond the classical symptoms of the obsessional neurosis and consequently to avoid making a clinical case out of the man. As Professor Kakar recognized early in his work, it is pointless to ignore the obvious symptoms. Taylor indeed tried to control his instinctual life by mechanistic means, by activity and attention to external detail. He was very ambivalent toward authority, and his own potential as an authority figure, and he tried to solve this problem by looking for the loved and hated father in his real relationships at work.

These defenses worked no better for Taylor than they do for most obsessional individuals. But Taylor had the means for escalating his conflict from the management of symptoms within himself to the control of work and the regulation of conflict between management and labor or, if you will, between fathers and sons. Taylor could use his aggression to "show up" existing managers and management practices (and they did not love him for this aggression) just as he could expose soldiering on the job as a reflection of what children will do if left to their own devices. His aggression had content and purpose that went well beyond his personal conflict and that could be objectified and used by others quite apart from the motivations of their founder.

The limitations in Taylor's theories, as Professor Kakar shows, were precisely in the limitations of his defenses: his theories could not account for people's behavior anymore than his defenses could permit him a range of flexible responses and object ties of a tender type. Taylor's moralistic approach to work relationships could not encompass the potential for new responses when individuals and groups secure power. In the politics of work, self-interest and group formations develop beyond the simple exchange of money for effort expended. The terms of the conflict also escalate to include one's sense of identity and autonomy; or, to put it another way the struggle people engage in to feel like a man and not as a child in their occupations. Taylor's inner struggle between the child and the man never resolved itself. In Taylor's life he tried to bypass this issue in the search for a higher attachment to morality and God. The extent to which he fell short of the resolution is a legacy for our times in the dilemmas of work in modern organizations.

This is the era of the computer, of automation, of sophisticated management control techniques, and of competing ideologies of authority. Taylor's personal concerns and the broader questions he addressed himself to are as real today as they were in his time. The main difference now, however, is in the tendency, especially among young people, to reject any form of rational control externally imposed. They reject technology and the constraints of authority implicit in technology. Where in Taylor's time the favored solution was to ignore one's self, the tendency today is to overestimate one's self in gaining power and control over reality. In either case, the terms of the conflict are still in the balance of instinctual life, reason, and morality.

The broad problem Professor Kakar asks us to consider in his psychohistorical study of Frederick Taylor is the relationship of the innovator to his personal development and his society. No more timely problem could come before us in a period of history where technology solves everything in theory and far less in practice. We have yet to come to terms with the human and political nature of man and whether he is to be the controller or the one controlled by technology.

Abraham Zaleznik

Cahners-Rabb Professor of Social Psychology of Management
Harvard University

Affiliate Member
Boston Psychoanalytic Society and Institute

Cambridge, Massachusetts
March 1970

This study was initiated and completed during the one-and-a-half years of my stay as a Research Fellow on Social Psychology of Management at Harvard University's Graduate School of Business Administration. The greatest debt I owe is to Professor Abraham Zaleznik who throughout the course of the study has been intimately associated with it, giving generously of his time in the discussion of various drafts, clarification of what was first puzzling, and in suggestions that were to prove fruitful.

Parts of this study were presented as papers at the meetings of the Boston Group for Applied Psychoanalysis and the seminar on Psychoanalytic Psychology and Management Theory at the Harvard Business School. I wish to thank members of both the groups for their helpful suggestions and comments. The primary research was carried out at the Taylor Archives in the Stevens Institute of Technology, Hoboken, New Jersey. I am grateful to Professor Williams and his assistants who gave me the fullest access to the Taylor Collection. I also wish to thank the publishers Harper & Row for their permission to quote from Taylor's *Principles of Scientific Management* and Frank B. Copley's official biography of Taylor.

The study was supported by a financial grant from Harvard Business School's Division of Research. I am most grateful to Dean George F. F. Lombard, Professor Bertrand Fox, and Dean Lawrence F. Fouraker for their support. I am especially indebted to Pamela Daniels, for her encouragement and her editing which did infinitely more than just take the kinks out of the language and to Ann Beale, who so patiently and skillfully typed the various drafts.

And finally, for my *guru* Erik Erikson, *srigurave namah*— homage to my honored teacher—the traditional Sanskrit phrase with which good Hindu students liked to begin their work. In its approach and method, his influence is clearly evident throughout the study.

Ahmedabad, April 1970.   Sudhir Kakar

FREDERICK TAYLOR

The inscription on his gravestone in the Chestnut Hill cemetery in Philadelphia reads simply:

FREDERICK WINSLOW TAYLOR
Born 1856—Died 1915
Father of Scientific Management

In the popular mind his name, as well as the system he "fathered," is associated with the efficiency craze that gripped the United States in the decade before the First World War, a craze which has been called a "normal American madness." His name is thus associated with those of other "eccentrics" produced by the efficiency movement, such as Frank Gilbreth, humorously portrayed in *Cheaper by the Dozen*. The movement itself is supposed to have quietly disappeared, as many fads do, leaving behind only those ripples that are of interest to social historians and to the older generation of trade unionists who still remember the union battles against the introduction into the factories of the hated "Taylor System." Even those memories, however, are considered to have the quality of fading photographs—quaintly interesting, in a nostalgic way, but without contemporary relevance.

Taylor and scientific management, however, cannot be dismissed so lightly. To his followers, of course, Taylor's greatness was an accepted fact. Their tributes not only endowed him with genius but surrounded him with a messianic aura. "Invariably when I have thought of Mr. Taylor and attempted to value his services to mankind," says one admirer, "an impelling desire to compare him with Darwin has seized me."[1] This may seem farfetched today to those for whom Taylor's name means only a few lines in American social and intellectual history; yet not only his followers but also eminent contemporaries held Taylor and his contributions in very high regard. Dean E. F. Gay of the Harvard Business School said, in 1911, that he regarded "the development of Scientific Management as promising to be the most important advance in industry since the introduction of the factory system and power machinery";[2] while Justice Brandeis, who with Walter Lippmann was one of the earlier champions of scientific management, wrote that Taylor was ". . . a really great man—great not only in mental capacity, but in character, and that his accomplishments were due to this fortunate combination of ability and character."[3]

Taylor's ideas have had an enormous influence on the industrial life of almost all countries. Many of his ideas are now looked upon as being so self-evident as to be part of normal industrial practice. The development of these ideas in relation to Taylor's personality and to the particular needs of his historical era has, however, for the most part been ignored.

Already in 1918, Taylor's system was taking on the trappings of an international movement independent of particular economic systems of political ideologies. In France, a circular of the Ministry of War, dated February 26, 1918, and signed by Georges Clemenceau, pointed out the imperative necessity of the study and application of methods of work according to the principles of "Taylorism" and ordered the establishment in each plant of planning departments— a central feature of the Taylor system. The Ministry recommended that the heads of the plants make themselves familiar with Taylor's principal writings, including his magnum opus, *Principles of Scientific Management*.[4] At the opposite end of the ideological spectrum, *Pravda*, in its issue of April 28, 1918, published an article of Lenin's on "The Immediate Tasks of the Soviet Government." Under the heading, "Raising the Productivity of Labour," Lenin wrote:

We must raise the question of piece-work and apply and test it in practice; we must raise the question of applying much of what is scientific and progressive in the Taylor system; we must make wages correspond to the total amount of goods turned out, or to the amount of work done by the railways, the water transport system, etc., etc.

The Russian is a bad worker compared with people in advanced countries. It could not be otherwise under the tsarist regime and in view of the persistence of the hangover from serfdom. The task that the Soviet government must set the people in all its scope is—learn to work. The Taylor system, the last word of capitalism in this respect, like all capitalist progress, is a combination of the refined brutality of bourgeois exploitation and a number of the greatest scientific achievements in the field of analysing mechanical motions during work, the elimination of superfluous and awkward motions, the elaboration of correct methods of work, the introduction of the best system of accounting and control, etc. The Soviet Republic must at all costs adopt all that is valuable in the achievements of science and technology in this field. The possibility of building socialism depends exactly upon our success in combining the Soviet power and the Soviet organisation of administration with the up-to-date achievements of capitalism. We must organise in Russia the study and teaching of the Taylor system and systematically try it out and adapt it to our own ends.[5]

The fact that both a conservative bourgeois regime in France and a revolutionary regime in Russia propagated Taylor's system should not be a surprising one. To them, Taylor's work was a part of technology with its implications of *universality* and *neutrality*. What Taylor had done was to extend, or rather to enlarge, the concept of technology, which had hitherto been restricted to mechanical and chemical—in other words, nonhuman—processes. His effort was to bring human work and the organization of work into the realm of technology.

Taylor's system was directed to the following ends:
1. Standardizing work, which meant the determination of the "one best way" of working; and
2. Controlling so extensively and intensively as to provide for the maintenance of all these standards.

The implications of Taylor's work thus go beyond mere industrial management technique to the broader issues of the very nature of *work* and *control*. And his work becomes increasingly relevant to the philosophical-ethical complex of problems subsumed under the heading technology and society (or, in popular terms, the relationship of man and machine) which today is so much in the center of discussion all over the world.

Taylor was thus the founder of a system that stated the relationship of man—workers and managers—to the new technology. To him, "scientific management" was completely free of value judgments; it was simply the discovery of technological imperatives as they applied to men at work. The only implicit moral "commandment" was that of increasing productivity. Persons or groups of persons, workers, management, owners of capital who transgressed against this law were all equally sinners. It is no wonder that he was attacked from all sides. His statement of the relationship between men and technology seemed to leave everyone unfree, stirring up anxieties at a deeper, unconscious, psychic level. For if a man is to maintain his own particular individuality in the midst of other individualities, there are certain prerogatives he cannot afford to lose—he would fight against the perceived danger of such a loss with all the resources at his command, conscious and unconscious, collective and individual. Some of these prerogatives have been called a sense of *wholeness,* a sense of *centrality* in time and space, and a sense of *freedom of choice.*[6]

In the new, regimented work patterns, Taylor's system, with its goal of increased productivity, seemed to deck technology with the mantle of determinism and thus to threaten one of the essential prerogatives: *freedom of choice.* The comparison of him with Darwin now seems to become at least more understandable, for Darwin, of course, threatened another prerogative: a sense of *centrality* in time and space.

It is not being claimed here that Taylor's system is the only form of industrial organization, the only "true statement" of the relationship of man and technology in an industrial culture. Rather, since the momentum of industrialization continues to increase and the technological morality of increased productivity has universal acceptance, careful examination of the problems of work and control is unavoidable and Taylor's seminal contributions to these problems take on new priority. Since work constitutes an important part of human life, Taylor's ideas and the reaction to his ideas have subtly—and not so subtly—influenced the quality of human life more than the work of many famous men in other spheres of human activity, whose names may be household words in their countries. Take, for example, the standardization of tools, one of the smallest elements of scientific management.

Until the advent of machines in the industrial revolution, the typical Western workman, even in firms with a relatively large subdivision of labor, had made a given article entirely with his own tools. Since every operation was primarily performed by a worker and not by a machine, the tools he used were considered an extension of his own organism—they did not seem to have an independent existence. The tools were thus highly personalized, with a great "irrational" diversification of design. Often they had been in the family for generations and had been decorated with patterns, floral or otherwise, which some would consider a useless elaboration, as somehow not "functional." The modifications of a tool were not the outcome of an exclusive technical logic but often of aesthetic considerations. The search for efficiency in the design of a tool was only one factor among many. It was the industrial revolution, bringing independent sources of power and semiautomatic operations of the machine, that seemed to give the machine an existence independent from the worker. With increasingly rapid industrial development, machine tools, along with the cutting tools and costly gauges, had to be supplied to the workman. And yet, the old relationship between the worker and his tools was not completely obliterated. The worker personally took care of the lathe tools and the milling cutter that were supplied him, keeping them in good shape, grinding them as he thought fit; in addition, he himself provided and owned such tools as monkey wrenches, scribers, and calipers. Taylor's standardization of tools wiped out these last vestiges of an almost emotional relationship that had existed between the worker and his tools, and, as will be seen later in the study, the workers, feeling impoverished, explicitly protested a dimly perceived sense of loss.

Taylor's impact, important as it was, is thus not confined to the field of management alone. He is an equally significant, though neglected, figure in an ongoing historical process—the formation of a universal, technological identity. Furthermore, though his contribution was related to the solution of his personal conflicts, as the following pages attempt to show, this solution transcended the personal realm insofar as it also provided an answer to an acute social problem brought about by the changing factory culture. That this answer may be a mistaken one and that subsequent schools of thought have revised or even completely reversed some of his postulates are immaterial. An answer is rarely final, its importance consisting not only in the quantum of truth it contains but also in its influence on the formation of a world image, in this case the relationship of man as a worker to the technology he uses.

The structure of this study utilizes what has come to be called the psychohistorical method, which traces the interdependence of an historical movement with the personality of its founder and the needs of a particular period of history. It does this by identifying the personality themes which recur constantly throughout the "great man's" life, symbolically and literally, though they may be expressed in a form that is applicable to a specific stage of life. In Taylor's case, whatever their several manifestations, these personality themes are seen to possess an underlying pervasive quality which finally matured in his historic work—the development of "scientific management." It is only through an identification of these themes that one recognizes the unconnected episodes of Taylor's life, which on surface seemingly changed its direction, to be, in fact, supportive of a persistent inner direction, and that the varied facets of his personality, sometimes contradictory, had a core of psychological consistency. The recognition of these recurring personality themes and the demonstration of how they matured in his work is, however, only a *part* of the psychohistorical inquiry. By itself, it is not sufficient to explain how "scientific management" also developed into a historical movement with such great importance for the organization of modern work. For a study which fulfills the requirements of psychohistory, the emphasis on both sides of the hyphen has to be an equal one; the relationship between biography and history has to be considered as one of *interpenetration*.

The psychohistorian as a biographer shares with the clinician the problem of his own reactions to his subject. For though the biographer may be far removed in time—and in this particular case, also in culture—from his subject, he does not approach his subject without preconceived ideas and emotional predispositions, ideas, and predispositions that are themselves liable to radical change as the biographer probes his subject's life and entrusts himself with his intimate journals and private correspondence.

These changing emotional responses, often unconscious, have a capacity to interfere with the objectivity of the writing in the most subtle of ways, for example, in the choice between two words with the same meaning but quite different nuance. Thus, the cause of objectivity is unfortunately subject to betrayal in the mere choice of an adjective. Objectivity then does not lie in its silent assumption by the writer and the reader but in the writer's effort to be aware of and to spell out his very subjectivity.

It is therefore not out of immodesty, but in line with what I believe to be an essential part of the psychohistorical method, that I would briefly like to trace my own exposure to Taylor and scientific management. At the very least, such a statement constantly reminds the writer to guard against the impulse to influence the reader; and should such an impulse slip through, it permits the reader to judge it in perspective.

I first came across scientific management as a young engineering student in India, where Taylor was presented to us as a great engineer (his book on reinforced concrete was well regarded) who, in addition, was the founder of the science of management. The only nonengineering course in our final year, Factory Organization and Business Management, was based largely on Taylor's *Principles of Scientific Management*. My next contact with Taylor was as a student of economics in Germany, where, in a seminar as well as in a book dealing with industrial psychology, Taylor was vigorously denounced by our professor. The professor, as a follower of the German idealism of Fichte and Schelling and as a representative of the "universal" school of economics, maintained that Taylor had been on the wrong track and had done incalculable harm to the cause of management. Taylor's greatest lacuna, one was taught, lay in his complete ignorance of human nature as it related to the problem of work. Compared to this shortcoming, his distaste for philosophy and the arts, though considered deplorable, was not held against him. He was—and there are few words in the language of a classically educated scholar which have worse connotations —a *mere technologist,* a man whose work was passé, even in a "country receptive to this sort of thing," America!

Having thus been exposed to two diametrically opposite evaluations, I became aware, during the course of this study, of the temptations that beset the biographer. One is apt to find oneself oscillating between a denunciation of Taylorism or a self-prescribed mission to rescue his reputation and rehabilitate him—between seeing his single-mindedness as Puritan narrowness or as Faustian drivenness. It is thus in many biographers that the cynic and the evangelist jockey for position.

For the purpose of this study, I have divided Taylor's life

into three periods. The first concerns his life until the critical episode at Exeter, which I have taken as the central incident of this period. This first section describes his parents, his early childhood, and the social and economic milieu in which he grew up. It attempts to identify those themes and conflicts in Taylor's personality that were to recur throughout his life.

The second period, from his apprenticeship until the end of his career at Midvale, covers those years of his life in which he was able, at least temporarily, to resolve the conflicts of authority and control, and in which most of his innovative work, in engineering as well as in scientific management, was done. It deals with industrial conditions of the period, Taylor's personal conflicts in his work life, and how his attempts to confront these conflicts were expressed in the formulation of scientific management. In addition to discussing the nature of innovative and creative work, it attempts a theoretical treatment of two general problems: work motivation and work restriction. It examines Taylor's contributions in these two areas, influenced as they were both by his inner conflicts and by prevailing ideology.

The third period can be divided into two parts: first, the years of work in various companies until his dismissal from the Bethlehem Steel Company; and second, from Bethlehem until his death—those years in which he abandoned paid work to become a prophet and preacher of his system, devoting his own resources to the training of his disciples. The first part considers the failures and frustrations of this period as well as Taylor's attempts to meet them and takes up the general theme of the mastery of disappointments in midcareer. The second part then deals with the slowly spreading recognition accorded to scientific management and the sudden public fame of Taylor's last years.

Personality can best be studied when it is in a state of acute conflict and its lines are etched in sharp relief. More important, if the conflict spills out into an open crisis in the form of symptoms or in actions incongruous with a trusted or characteristic life-style, an individual becomes more accessible to his biographer whose task of recording as well as interpreting a critical moment or event thus becomes some what easier. The crisis in Frederick Taylor's life at the end of his school period in the Phillips Exeter Academy was one of this nature.

A bare recounting of the facts of this crisis, without any embellishing asides or interpretive attempts, is dramatic enough. Fred (to use a biographical convention) had entered Exeter in 1872 at the age of sixteen to prepare for Harvard College and a future career as a lawyer. He came from an old and respected family of Philadelphians, members of the American "Establishment" of that period. If the word "proper" had not become popularly associated with the Boston aristocracy, the Taylor family would certainly have been called "proper Philadelphians." The young Fred had already traveled widely in Europe with his parents, had been to school in Paris and Berlin, and spoke French and German fluently—a rare accomplishment for an American boy of that period. At Exeter, in his senior year, he led his class, and diligently studied Virgil's *Bucolics, Georgics,* and *The Aeneid,* Books VII, VIII, and IX, for Latin; *Memorabilia,* Plato, and Herodotus in Goodwin's *Reader,* for Greek; Geometry and Chauvenet's Books III, IV, and V, for mathematics.[1] He passed his entrance examinations for Harvard with honors, and then, complaining of failing eyesight, he abruptly returned to his parents' home in Germantown, one of the most exclusive neighborhoods of Philadelphia and the stronghold of the Quaker elite. We can not know about the discussions that took place between his parents, family friends, and the eighteen-year-old Fred on the unusual step he was taking, but in 1874, he joined the Enterprise Hydrau-

2

THE CRISIS AT EXETER

lic Works as an apprentice worker to learn the trades of patternmaker and machinist.

In spite of his "strong distaste for manual labour"[2] and though his eyesight was very early "restored,"[3] he persisted in working in the factory as a journeyman machinist, earning nothing in his first year, $1.50 a week in the second and third years, and $3.00 in his fourth year,[4] after which he went to work in another factory as a common laborer. He was perhaps the only factory worker in America who was a member of the Philadelphia Cricket Club! This then is the "event" that we have chosen to start our study of Frederick Winslow Taylor.

Whether Taylor was consciously aware of the psychological import of his apparently somatic illness is a moot point. There is enough evidence to show that the story of his entry into industry—namely, the leaving of Exeter because of impaired eyesight—was very important to him. Though the details in the autobiographies he wrote for the *Who's Who* from 1906 to 1914 varied, this story was repeated every time. Since a simple catalog of facts, without any *why's* and *wherefore's,* is the accepted form for autobiographical entries in *Who's Who,* this item tends to stand out even more prominently.[5]

To extract a "meaning" from such an event in an individual's life, Erik Erikson has suggested that it be considered in the four-fold complementarity of the individual's developmental history (psychosexual and psychosocial), his present state and stage of life, the present state of the individual's communities, and the history of these communities.[6] This search for meaning in four interacting "co-ordinates," this search for a configuration of meanings rather than simple (and often oversimplified) causations, is the method used in this study.

Frederick Taylor was the fifth generation of his family to be born in America, descending from an English Quaker who had settled in the region of the Lower Delaware River in 1677. The family had steadily prospered, and Fred's grandfather, Anthony Taylor, had been a leading merchant who had amassed a fortune in trade with the East Indies. This enabled him to retire at the age of thirty-eight to a country estate of four hundred acres. He invested his money in land and by the time of his death was the largest landowner in Bristol County. Further, he was a banker and one of the original organizers of the Farmers' National Bank of Bristol. Fred's father was the youngest of Anthony Taylor's eleven children. To describe him in one sentence, one would say that Franklin Taylor was a gentleman of leisure, the Philadelphia counterpart of the English "squire," a pillar of the Quaker community in Philadelphia which was concentrated around Rittenhouse Square and in Germantown.

Though the Quaker elite had lost political control of Pennsylvania after their refusal to support the Indian Wars of the 1750s, they still formed a "solid" upper class parallel to the "fancy" Episcopalian upper class that lived on the Main Line. The dominant characteristics of this Quaker upper class were seclusiveness, simplicity, moral fervor, and clannishness, characteristics which had become intensified by the Revolutionary War and its aftermath. As the Quaker historian, Rufus M. Jones, wrote:

The Revolutionary War left the Philadelphia Yearly Meeting more moral internally, more devoted to moral reforms, more conservative of ancient tradition, custom and doctrine, more separate from the world, more introversive in spirit than it found it. Had the active public-spirited Friends, who went off with the revolutionary movement, remained to mould their generation, a type more outward, more progressive, more intellectual, would have resulted. . . . As a result of the narrowing and uniting processes combined Friends are what they are. What they would have been with a wider outlook upon life and a looser standard of conduct we can only conjecture.[7]

The Quaker aristocracy was more intellectual and introspective than its Episcopalian counterpart but had the same strong sense of family tradition and of caste. Franklin Taylor was a member of this caste, sharing and accepting its norms; and it may be, in fact, unreasonable to describe him as a gentleman of leisure with the present connotations of the term. Of course, one did not work in the sense of holding a job, to make money, or to get ahead. On the other hand, the Quaker ideal frowned on "one-who-did-not-work," on the wastrel. This resulted in a few of the professions being considered worthy of a gentleman—medicine, law, banking, and running the family firm. The first two, medicine and law, were the two "sacred professions."[8] A lawyer in Philadelphia, using *Esq.* after his name while everyone else had a *Mr.* before his, was accorded the same reverence as a Divine in Puritan Massachusetts or as a Herr Professor in Germany. The dilemma of how to get around the "job-aspect" of the profession was resolved by not being a practicing lawyer for any great length of time. There were nonpracticing doctors; however, as one historian describes it:

Much more common is the non-practicing lawyer and it is almost routine for a gifted young man, especially one with literary tastes, to study law, practice a year or two, then go into whatever he pleases, his duty done. But at least a gesture towards work, and preferably towards the two Sacred Professions, is mandatory.[9]

In keeping with his position and the values of *his* times, Franklin Taylor was graduated from Princeton in 1840, took his M.A. from the same university, settled down in Philadelphia studying law in a law office, and was admitted to the bar in 1844. His practice of law, perfunctory at best, was soon given up, and the only work that took up any amount of his time was his position as secretary to the Board of Managers of the Pennsylvania Training School for Feebleminded Children. He thus fulfilled the Quaker ideal of combining "work" with "good works." Franklin Taylor was a cultivated man who loved poetry, history, languages, especially the classical ones, and spoke highly of Cicero's *Orations*. Most of his life he suffered from dyspepsia and was often irritable in a mild way. Fred's recollection of him is "of his soft, mild manner and a gentleness which is almost that of a woman . . . of very unusual bravery and strength."[10] The picture we get of him from his letters to Fred is of a reserved father who hides his affection for his son behind the high ideals of the kind of gentleman he wants his son to become. He himself had a strong sense of rights and obligations and placed high value on the inner control of conscience rather than on any external laws or prohibitions as regulators of man's conduct. A letter he wrote to Fred at school reads:

There is no written law that men should not smoke in drawing rooms or come with muddy boots or soiled clothes or should not read when in company or very many other cases. . . . Now no one has any moral right to violate any of these proprieties and whosoever does so does what is unbecoming a gentleman. Whether one agrees with the doctrines taught or not has nothing to do with the matter, or if it affects it at all should lead one to be more careful of offending their feelings than if one was in unison with their beliefs. . . . My dear boy, I have written a good deal on this subject as I have felt very much about it and I trust when you come to think on the matter you will take a juster, truer view. Do not do violence to your better, truer self and seek to justify sophistically anything which your inner conscience doubts—walk carefully and slowly and remember tis better to follow the doubt than to violate your inner light. Good-by my dear boy, be good, be true and faithful in little things and you will be true in larger ones.[11]

Of Emily Winslow Taylor, Fred's mother, we are told that she had the "stronger character." She was descended from a long line of New England Puritans and Quakers. The women in the Winslow family were reputed to have been strong, self-reliant, and willful, believing in the power of private inspiration. Emily Taylor's grandmother, Thankful Hussey, had acquired some fame as a Quaker woman preacher who often traveled unattended and on horseback from Maine to Rhode Island, preaching en route. Her father, Isaac Winslow, had accumulated a large fortune through his whaling vessels. Emily Taylor was said to be an accomplished linguist in her own right, though her interest lay primarily in modern languages. She was fluent in French, Italian, and German, and had a working knowledge of Spanish. Frank Copley, Taylor's official biographer, writes of her: She was not a demonstrative woman. The English ideal of keeping all one's emotions properly and decently suppressed had in her an excellent exponent. It may be, as the poet says, sweet to dance to violins when love and life are fair, and to dance to flutes and dance to lutes may be delicate and rare; but the time to which life went for Emily Taylor mainly was sounded by the Spartan notes of the fife . . . . She never set much store on tact. Tact, she was inclined to associate with hypocrisy. She knew her mind and in season she spoke it, plainly and to the point. Hers was the Quaker ideal of language stripped of all flattery and purged of all dross.[12] Needless to say, she did not enjoy poetry.

This, then, was the family and the social milieu in which Frederick Taylor was born in 1856. The Taylor household, to which a younger sister Mary was an addition three years later, consisted of his parents, his older brother Edward, a maid, a cook, and a coachman. Their first house was a plain two-story stone structure, with attic and wings, on Willow Avenue. When Fred was one year old, the family moved to a new house called "Cedron," in the far western section of Germantown where they lived until 1869. "Cedron," the house in which Fred spent his childhood, was probably very similar to the other "solid" upper-class houses characterized by a certain demureness and conformity. They are described as having a large parlor downstairs, running the full length of the house and usually empty except for large gloomy furniture and pictures on the walls. Up the stairs at the front of the house was either a master bedroom or a library. Off another landing was usually the real heart of the house, the sitting room above the dining room. The impression was generally one of sober solemnity, reinforced by the ticking and striking of clocks, the whispering of servants, and the glow of furniture polish on dark mahogany.[13] The house and the garden were the center of family life, and here Fred grew up, carefully guarded from contact with what was called the "world"—the dangerous world of wickedness which a child vaguely knew lay all about him and especially beyond Germantown.

The principal issue of child rearing in the America of this period, roughly from 1800 to 1875, seems to have been the problem of parental authority. In one form or another all the books of child-rearing advice imparted the same message: an infant's nature is depraved, willful, and intensely selfish. This must be suppressed by strict obedience training. The authority of the parents must be established early in the child's life and firmly maintained throughout the years of growth. As one writer melodramatically stated it, "The bloodiest pirate that infests the seas, was in childhood susceptible of easy control, and his present horrid position and prospects result almost exclusively from the fact that he did not receive it."[14] Indulgence on the parents' part was not a sign of love but of carelessness; what was demanded was a "thinking love."

In order to save the depraved infant and to form in the child religious habits of mind, founded on Christianity, it was essential that the child submit to the will of the parents, and thus any obstinacy was severely punished. A single lapse was seen as a permanent setback. In part, the child-rearing advice from ministers, educators, and medical doctors was a reaction against what was perceived as a growing laxity in the social order and in child-training methods. From the evidence we have of Emily Taylor's family tradition and character, it seems legitimate to see in her a "defender of the old order" who did not at all partake of this growing "laxity."

Emily Taylor was then representative of her time if her child-rearing methods were based on the foregoing assumptions about a child's nature. However, whereas a "lesser" woman might have been tempted to relax her vigil because of sentimental maternal feelings, we can be reasonably sure that there would be no lapses by a woman with an "independent, strong-willed character" such as Emily Taylor is reputed to have possessed. Copley tells us that her system of child training was all "work, drill, and discipline" where "child was remorselessly pitted against child." It made no difference to her if, in the spelling bees she organized for her children and others who might be present, a child was put to open shame; and we should add here that Fred's spelling abilities until the age of fourteen were decidedly poor. Thus, when we read in young Fred's journal of his mother's reactions to a gift of "sossage" from a German lady—"when she presented it to mother there was quite a crook perceptable in her nose which is mothers sighn of disgust"[15]—we can surmise that from his earliest years Fred was often made aware of the "crook perceptable in her nose which is mothers sighn of disgust." As in the severe Exeter discipline later on, where "no excuse was taken for any delinquency whatever, and in which every boy had to toe the mark in all respects,"[16] Emily Taylor permitted no lapses:

As to her household, it truly was a thing ruled, regular. . . . To one member of the family was assigned the duty of seeing that all the match receptacles were kept filled; and when, after two years, the mistress of the household one day found a receptacle that had not been filled, the important thing with her was, not that all receptacles had been kept filled for two years, but that on this day there had been a lapse.[17]

She was particularly concerned about the boys, so much so that people thought that her anxiousness in this respect "robbed her of the joys of motherhood." She was determined that her boys should grow up "pure in mind and body." When the family was in France and the boys were being drilled in French under her strict supervision, it was her habit to go over the texts first and then pin together pages that she considered unfit for young eyes.

Often a very strict early training, especially when the child is learning the rudiments of muscular control, can result in the child's carrying within him a sense of inner badness and a sense of doubt and shame, which are intensified by the "shaming" used by the mother. In such a case a child will . . . overmanipulate himself, he will develop a precocious conscience. Instead of taking possession of things in order to test them by purposeful repetition, he will become obsessed by his own repetitiveness. By such obsessiveness, of course, he then learns to repossess the environment and to gain power by stubborn and minute control, where he could not find large-scale mutual regulation. Such hollow victory is the infantile model for a compulsion neurosis. It is also the infantile source of later attempts in adult life to govern by the letter, rather than by the spirit.[18]

If, on the basis of the preceding clinical observations, one looks for elements of compulsive behavior in Taylor's life, the plethora of examples from early boyhood onward becomes an embarrassingly rich mine and almost too self-evident. Thus, Birge Harrison, who knew Fred almost all his life, writes in his recollections:

Fred was always a bit of a crank in the opinion of our boyhood band, and we were inclined to rebel sometimes from the strict rules and exact formulas to which he insisted that all of our games must be subjected. To the future artist [Harrison], for example, it did not seem absolutely necessary that the rectangle of our rounders court should be scientifically accurate, and that the whole of a fine, sunny morning should be wasted in measuring it off by feet and by inches.[19]

Fred was severe in his observance of each and every rule of the game, whatever the game might be. In a game of croquet he would carefully work out the angles of the various strokes, the force of impact, and the advantages and disadvantages of the understroke, overstroke, and so on, before he started to play. In cross-country walks he constantly experimented with his legs in an endeavor to discover the step which would cover the greatest distance with the least expenditure of energy. He suffered from insomnia all through his life. At the age of twelve . . . his sleep was not of the best and he was troubled with very fearsome and terrifying nightmares. Being of an observant nature he soon noticed that when he awoke from one of these obsessions he was invariably lying upon his back—and from this he argued that there must be some connection between the position in which he lay and the distressing mental disturbance. Thereupon he constructed for himself a sort of harness of straps and wooden points, the latter so arranged that whenever in his sleep he turned over upon his back the points in question would press the dorsal muscle and at once awaken him.[20]

Though this harness was his favorite—he used it at Exeter —he experimented with pillows of tufted hair cloth, or a pillow made from a board with uprights at each end and covered with a piece of canvas. He tried stretching strings across the uprights, and would then wake up with the marks of the strings covering his face. In later life he slept in a sitting position propped up with pillows. Spending a night at a hotel became an ordeal, both for him and for the hotel personnel, for there was a constant struggle to get enough pillows which he would then supplement with bureau drawers before he could go to sleep. Examples of this kind of behavior are scattered throughout his life. Before going to a dance he would conscientiously and systematically list the attractive and unattractive girls with the object of dividing his time equally between them.[21] Whether he reflected on the causes for his behavior or whether he accepted his friends' explanation that it was due to "his high nervous energy" or his physician's attributing it to his "extraordinary intense nature," we do not know.

The performance of these ritualistic acts, whether in walking, dancing, preparation for sleep, or in minute attention to the rules and regulations of boyhood games ("the letter rather than the spirit"), is akin to magical thinking; their common theme and purpose is to make amends, to propitiate the vindictive and wrathful gods who are within oneself. For one of the elements of neurotic "anality" is the presence of an unusually strong and demanding conscience. Taylor early spoke of such a conscience as one where "no excuse was taken for any delinquency whatever and in which every boy had to toe the mark in all respects," or what Taylor later called his "whale of a New England conscience." A feeling of guilt is often a dominant characteristic, and, faced with this harsh inner tribunal, Fred tried to turn the aggressive impulses into their opposite: he became a peacemaker. From his friend Harrison's recollections we learn that during the Civil War, when all the boys over six years old formed a juvenile homeguard which practiced a kind of fighting drill, Fred was conspicuous by his lack of enthusiasm, maintaining the universal brotherhood of man, "a proposition which was of course inconceivable to any of the rest of our company." He was distinctly uneasy at the witnessing of any hostile scene between two persons, even if they were man and wife.[22] Copley tells us that it was the same at Exeter. He hated quarrels among the boys even if he himself were not involved, and he played a leading role in bringing about peace between the town and the schoolboys, where "bad feeling" had existed before.[23]

Throughout his adult life, Taylor insisted that scientific management was the only system which would make for peace and harmony between the management and the workers and that this was its only *raison d'être*. With his honesty and literal-minded devotion to truth, he was perfectly sincere in the expression of his belief that scientific management was a doctrine of peace and harmony, and this, in spite of virulent attacks on it by both management and trade unions. Indeed, it was only for the cause of peace that he could let go of his hostility. As one of the workers who worked under Taylor during his early years at Midvale perceptively put it:

. . . His work, under the new Taylor System, seemed to be of the most contradictive character, that is he was working hard and quarrelling with many people to establish a system . . . the aim of which was to make permanent peace between employer and employee.[24]

He was passionately attached to his self-image as an industrial peacemaker and expressed this conviction again and again:

Scientific management is not any efficiency device, not a device of any kind for securing efficiency; nor is it any bunch or group of efficiency devices. It is not a new system of figuring costs; it is not a new scheme of paying men; it is not a piecework system; it is not a bonus system; it is not a premium system; it is not time study; it is not motion study . . . it is not any of the devices which the average man calls to mind when scientific management is spoken of . . . they are useful adjuncts to scientific management.[25]

What scientific management really was, was a great "mental revolution," a revolution of peace which took place in both the sides:

They come to see when they stop pulling against one another, and instead both turn and push shoulder to shoulder in the same direction, the size of the surplus created by their joint efforts is truly astounding. . . . This, gentlemen, is the beginning of the great mental revolution which constitutes the first step toward scientific management. It is along this line of complete change in the mental attitude of both sides; of the substitution of peace for war; the substitution of hearty brotherly cooperation for contention and strife; of replacing suspicious watchfulness with mutual confidence; of becoming friends instead of enemies; it is along this line, I say, that scientific management must be developed.[26]

Of course I do not wish to be understood that there are never any quarrels under scientific management. There are some, but they are the exception rather than the rule . . . . So I think that scientific management can be justly and truthfully characterized as management in which harmony is the rule instead of discord.[27]

He tried to carry out this in practice in his last years by inviting one or two workers and some employers to his Sunday luncheons in an exclusive Philadelphia hotel.

In an adult, compulsive behavior often manifests itself in the need for absolute order, cleanliness, punctuality, and thrift (monetary and emotional). But all these traits are conflicted ones, giving rise to ambivalent feelings. In light of the above observations, many items in Taylor's personality become clearer and fall into place as partial manifestations of a general theme. His habit of swearing, which so puzzles Copley and so shocked his Puritan relatives and friends, becomes more understandable—swearing is a way of getting rid of aggressive wishes and messy thoughts. It is less surprising to learn that Taylor not only abstained from smoking or drinking—even coffee or tea—but that he attributed this total abstinence to economic considerations, to *thrift*. It is less surprising to find that the inner disorderliness sometimes broke through and that the author of the time-study was notoriously unpunctual for his personal appointments, which he often "forgot" due to his "poor memory." It is less surprising to learn of his preoccupation with dirt and disorder and his use of their imagery.

Was Taylor aware of the fact that the many imperatives which guaranteed his personal restraints were at the same time autocratic attempts at controlling others? For it is the issue of control, inner and outer, which is one of the dominant themes of his life and, as we shall see later, also of scientific management.

Since we have little information on Taylor's childhood relationship with his father or his siblings, an impression may have been created that Emily Taylor should be cast in the role of the villainess of the piece. This would be doing her an injustice. She grew up in the confluence of Quakerism and Puritanism at a time when the Quakers were still overcome with wistful nostalgia for the "old days" when their small number, they liked to remember plaintively, lived in purity and innocence—a kind of original social paradise. Thus, in 1836 John Watson in his *Annals of Philadelphia* wrote:

In primitive days when culprits were few and society simple and sincere, what they aimed to impart was solid and substantial. . . . I can no longer employ my pen to illustrate the changing manners and times of our city. The traces of the past are wholly effaced. The former was an age of homely and domestic comfort . . . and this is now an entire age of luxury and cumbrous pomp . . . . Luxury produces its own downfall and ruin.[28]

A rapidly changing society exerts greater pressure on mothers to train their children to grow up with the older— known and tested—virtues deeply ingrained in their character. In mid-nineteenth century America, for example, an important maternal task was to combat sexual "sin" in young children; in fact, however, even the slightest hint of sensuality in a child might goad a mother into a harshness aimed at complete suppression. Things had to be "ruled and regular," and fearful parents sought to reproduce the mechanization of industry in all areas of a child's bodily living. Emily Taylor's system of child training was a combination of both her personality and Quaker mores.

After some years of schooling in the Germantown Academy, Fred left with his family in 1869 for a trip to Europe which was to last almost three years. He was then thirteen years old. In a diary which he kept during a part of this trip he recounts his unwilling visits to museums, art galleries, and places of historical interest that were considered part of the education of every cultivated gentleman, such as his father. The diary is written in "tight" little sentences, bare of any personal emotion, a characteristic and curious feature being the occasional listing of all stations that their train passed through with the exact times of arrival and departure. He went to school in Germany, which he hated, and in his later years the Germans were a part of his private chamber of horrors which included theologians, bankers, and professors. The family came back to America in 1872, and in the same year, along with his brother, he entered the Phillips Exeter Academy to prepare for Harvard. His father intended the brothers to follow the two "sacred professions": Edward was to become a doctor, and Fred, a lawyer.

The Exeter years were the years of Fred's adolescence, though the term itself is of a later origin. We use the term here in its full psychological definition according to which adolescence is the span of all attempts at adjustment to the new sets of inner and outer conditions that confront the individual in the stage of puberty.[29] Anna Freud has succinctly described the problems of this stage:

The physiological process which marks the attainment of physical sexual maturity is accompanied by a stimulation of the instinctual processes. . . . Aggressive impulses are intensified to the point of complete unruliness, hunger becomes voracity, and the naughtiness of the latency period turns into the criminal behavior of adolescence. Oral and anal interests, long submerged, come to the surface again. Habits of cleanliness, laboriously acquired during the latency period, give place to pleasure in dirt and disorder and instead of modesty and sympathy we find exhibitionistic tendencies, brutality, and cruelty to animals. The reaction-formations, which seemed to be firmly established in the structure of the ego, threaten to fall to pieces. At the same time, old tendencies which had disappeared come into consciousness. The oedipus wishes are fulfilled in the form of fantasies and daydreams in which they have undergone but little distortion. . . . There are very few new elements in the invading processes. Their onslaught merely brings once more to the surface the familiar content of the early infantile sexuality of little children.[30]

Adolescence then reawakens infantile conflicts, with the added impetus of an increase in instinctual drives and guilt feelings aroused by involuntary sexual phenomena. Here we come back to the harness Fred used while sleeping at Exeter, and let another sensitive adolescent, a contemporary of Taylor's, speak:

For a long time, if I had any physical excitation or nocturnal experience, I was almost petrified lest I was losing my brains and carefully examined the bridge of my nose to see if it was getting the least bit flat. I understood that anyone who swerved in the slightest from the norm of purity was liable to be smitten with some loathsome disease which I associated with leprosy and with the "unpardonable sin" which the minister often dwelt upon.

So great was my dread of natural phenomena that in the

earliest teens I rigged an apparatus and applied bandages to prevent erethism while I slept. . . .[31]

For Fred, who, as we have seen, had suffered from nightmares and terrifying dreams even in the relatively calm latency period, desperately using his available energies in coping with conflict, the advent of adolescence, trying at best, must have been especially perilous. The cultural mores demanded that one face the crisis alone, though in rare favorable circumstances one might be supported by benign, uplifting (and often confusingly irrelevant) parental advice. In the moral literature that period addressed to its youth, especially youth of Fred's social class, vigorous self-control and vigorous resolution were the advocated means of dealing with "passions," "internal revolutions," and "occult causes, probably of a physical nature."[32] Youth was seen to be a "pliant" and "formative" period, and the world to be full of seductive temptations. With firm resolve and the goal of excellence, there was no reason why temptations could not be mastered. "You may be what you resolve to be."[33]

Thus, at Exeter, though the students worked hard—they had to since half the class was dropped each year—Fred Taylor worked harder than the others and much harder than he was required to. Though he attributed his impaired eyesight to this hard study, in a later period of his life he wrote about the experience as follows:

Then two years of really very hard study, coupled with athletics, at Exeter and what I look back upon as perhaps the very best experience of my early life, namely the very severe Exeter discipline in which no excuse was taken for any delinquency whatever and in which every boy had to toe the mark in all respects.[34]

For Fred, then, this severe outer control was not enough, or rather it inspired an even harsher inner control. He pursued his studies relentlessly in spite of the frequent headaches and sleepless nights. It should be noted that there was no pressure from his parents that Fred stand first in his class—in fact, quite the contrary. His mother wrote:

Remember that it is never worthwhile to stand high in your class. . . . It will show much more good sense to retain your health for life than to study to be one of the first in your class.[35]

His father expressed a similar sentiment:

I want you to do what shall be best for you but I do not want you to suffer hereafter for your present ambition of standing higher in your class or because you desire to go to college.[36]

It was after he had passed the entrance examination for Harvard in 1874 that Fred complained of failing eyesight and returned home from Exeter. There are two suggestive facts about his illness which should be mentioned here as they shed some light on his relationship with his father: that the illness occurred after he had passed his entrance examinations and when he was seemingly set for a career in law, his father's profession. The form of illness he "chose" was the one from which his father had been lately suffering. In one of his letters, Franklin Taylor complained of

. . . a great weakness of my eyes . . . . Indeed I cannot read or write for any length of time without pain in my eyes and headache, but I think with time and care I shall entirely recover.[37]

If he was "rejecting" his father by refusing the lawyer's profession, then he still could not completely let go of him. We shall come back to this relationship in the following chapter.

So far we have attempted to delineate the central themes of Taylor's personality as they appear in his childhood and in the context of adolescence. Psychoanalytic psychology has, however, recognized that the emotional turmoil of this stage can be potentially beneficial—even creative, in the deepest sense—in that it offers the individual an opportunity to modify his earlier development and permits realignment of the psychic forces.[38] The study of adaptation complements that of the defenses and thus enlarges our perspective on personality. Erikson has called the adolescent crisis an *identity crisis*, which is characterized in part by the fact that a youth must forge a perspective and direction for his life, usually in the tangible choice of a "career," out of the remnants of his childhood and the hopes of his adulthood.[39] Some young men, finding that they are over-committed to a further course they themselves cannot accept, make a violent turn, repudiating the "old," which often means the perspectives intrinsic to the life-style of their parents. Fred Taylor was one of these persons. As Erikson has described such uncommon youth:

In some young people, in some classes, at some periods in history, this crisis will be minimal; in other people, classes, and periods, the crisis will be clearly marked off as a critical period, a kind of "second birth," apt to be aggravated either by widespread neuroticisms or by pervasive ideological unrest. Some young individuals will succumb to this crisis in all manner of neurotic, psychotic, or delinquent behavior; others will resolve it through participation in ideological movements passionately concerned with religion or politics, nature or art. Still others, although suffering and deviating dangerously through what appears to be a prolonged adolescence, eventually come to contribute an original bit to an emerging style of life: the very danger which they have sensed has forced them to mobilize capacities to see and say, to dream and plan, design and construct, in new ways.[40]

Frederick Taylor thus cannot be lightly dismissed as "just another neurotic." As one of the prophets of modern work and a decisive contributor to the social upheaval that made efficiency a way of life, let us suggest that he was an uncommon man with great conflicts.

Fred Taylor was eighteen years old when he came home from Exeter with his eyes ruined, or so he thought, for further study. He was, outwardly at least, a very disappointed young man, first, in his repugnance for this manifestation of physical infirmity in himself and for "not being able to stay the course," and second, in seeing all his future plans, Harvard, law, and so forth coming to nought. As one of his childhood friends writes, "At the time this appeared in the light of a veritable tragedy."[1] The few months he spent at home, supposedly resting, were in fact full of restlessness. He roamed about the house, unable to study and avid for the smallest jobs, such as carrying stones for his mother's hotbeds,[2] using activity of any and all kinds— obsessive activity—as a way of building up his inner defenses which had been so destructively breached in his last months at Exeter. The brooding months he spent at home were not only accompanied by disappointment but must have seen the resurgence of guilt in having disappointed and repudiated his parents. From the evidence we have, it seems that his parents showed sympathetic concern; at least there were no overt reproaches. If the study of the classics was detrimental to his health and had ruined his eyes, then he could rest, recover his health and—as his mother had once suggested—study engineering at the "School at Hoboken or in the school of technology at Boston."[3] Thus, if there were any reproaches for his "failure," for having "deserted" his father, they were made by Fred's "whale of a New England conscience." The struggle he was waging was on that inner frontier where his conscience and his father were close allies.

Fred did not go to engineering school or any other school. In late 1874, he joined Enterprise Hydraulic Works, a small firm which manufactured pumps, owned by the firm Ferrell and Jones (later Ferrell and Muckle), located on Race Street, down near the Schuylkill River, as an apprentice pattern-maker and machinist. In the circle of Fred's closely knit

3
THE YOUNG APPRENTICE

family there must have been much discussion of the unusual step he was taking, along with the proffering of much advice from the members of the older generation. The one piece of advice Taylor remembered vividly and which struck a responsive chord directly relating to his personal conflict was from his uncle, Caleb Taylor, a respected banker, who later was elected to the House of Representatives. The sum of the advice was that if Fred wished to succeed then he should learn to *obey*. In a lecture to students on success years later, Taylor recalled:

. . . [since] your success will depend mainly upon your ability to please the man whom you are serving, it becomes of the greatest importance to know exactly what will please. When I was about to begin to serve my apprenticeship, an old gentleman who had been very successful sent for me to come to see him. He lived some 20 or 30 miles away, and said that he had something very important to tell me. What he had to say took but three or four sentences. He said: "If you want success in your work, do what I say. If your employer wants you to start work at 7 o'clock in the morning, always be there at ten minutes before seven. If he wants you to stay until 6 o'clock at night, always stay until ten minutes past six. Now, if you haven't sense enough to know what I mean by this, you haven't sense enough to succeed anyway."

He also said: "Let me tell you one more thing. Whatever happens, however badly you may be treated, however much you may be abused, never give up your job until you have taken 48 hours to think it over; and if possible don't talk back to the man who is over you until you have time to cool off."[4]

The year in which Fred started his career in industry is almost squarely in the middle of the period of that very rapid industrial expansion that by the end of the century would make the United States the greatest industrial power in the world. This period brought the Industrial Revolution to its full flowering; by its end the United States had overtaken Great Britain and outraced Germany in industrial manufacturing.[5] Aided by revolutionary improvements in technology, vast natural resources, and a flood tide of immigrants (in 1882 alone, 789,000 were admitted) who provided the labor and increased the size of the internal market, the United States became an industrial state of the first rank, advancing rapidly on many fronts, in light manufacturing as well as in transport. Even a sampling of the statistics gives an idea of this tremendous increase in manufacturing and productivity. Whereas in 1840, the product per inhabitant was five pounds in English money, by 1875, with a vastly increased population, it had multiplied almost four times. Whereas in 1830, the consumption of cotton was about 52 million pounds, in 1870, it was almost ten times as much.[6] Between 1867 and 1873 alone, 3,000 miles of new railroad track were opened to traffic.[7] The statistics for other branches of industry—coal, steel, oil, electricity, mining, telegraphy, machine tools, and the like —show a similar rapid expansion. This change, however, was not only quantitative but also qualitative. For whatever else this period may have been—"the railroad age," "the coal age," or "the steel age"—it was certainly a factory age, with the factories steadily increasing in number and size and spelling the destruction of the old artisan handicrafts. Until the middle of the nineteenth century, America had been a nation of small and medium businesses, but in the second half of the century the situation changed radically. As late as 1850, one of the biggest plants in the country was an ironworks that employed about a thousand workers. In the early 1850s, the McCormick factory in Chicago, the country's largest producer of agricultural machinery, had fewer than three hundred regular employees and was managed by Leander McCormick and four foremen. The typical New England textile mill employed two to three hundred operatives.[8] No shop was so large that the manager did not know the older workers, and in most cases the manager was the owner or the active partner. The management style in most cases was a personal one. As Leland Jenks has put it:

. . . problems of organization and the use of labor force were solved *ad hoc,* empirically for each establishment. Knowledge about the solutions was transmitted by observation or word of mouth and had to be rediscovered by most new firms.

. . . Here management was an uncertain mixture of the traditional with the arbitrary or capricious—a personal autocracy of varying degrees of benevolence—and emanation of the personality of the owner-manager.[9]

With increasing factory size and increasing separation of owner and manager, the stresses on personal, autocratic management became correspondingly acute.

The problem was further complicated by the social upheavals of the period and by increasing labor unrest. Though it is generally agreed that from 1865 onward the standard of living of all classes increased, the relative distribution of the "cake" showed large disparities. There was a large increase in the incomes of the upper and middle classes, along with the rise of many "self-made" millionaires; the condition of the laboring classes was, however, not so bright. When the rate of physical expansion was high, "good times" and good jobs were available to all those able to do skilled work; when expansion lagged—and depressions were frequent—many jobs disappeared. Even in good times production was often seasonal in character, and few plants operated all the year around. Many workers were thus expected to live more than two months off work without pay. Since most of the factories were started in the urban areas—in Philadelphia alone between 1862 and 1872, three hundred new industries were begun[10]—new workers flocked from the farms and from abroad to the cities, greatly increasing city congestion and overcrowding the slums. Thus in the 1870s, New York was even more overcrowded than

Bombay, with 986.4 inhabitants per acre as compared to 759.7 per acre in Bombay.[11] Since the cities were governed by "businessmen in politics" for the benefit of the upper third of the population, social spending was more or less frowned upon and the condition of the laboring classes— housing, health, sanitation, schooling, etc.—was decidedly poor. In 1870, in New York, for example, the infant mortality rate was 65 percent higher than in 1810. Thus, when Mark Twain wrote *The Gilded Age* in 1874, he clearly realized that behind the bright facade and the dreams of sudden wealth, the metal was insubstantial: the age was gilded, not golden. In the summer of 1873, the Holyoke, Massachusetts *Transcript* wrote:

There is a pitiful and miserable sight which we have seen night after night in front of the fruit and vegetable stands. . . . It is a drove of poverty-stricken children, often girls, clad only in one or two ragged and dirty garments, down on their hands and knees in the gutters, greedily picking out of the mud and dirt and eating the bits of spoiled and decaying fruit which have been thrown away as worthless . . . judging by the famished looks and actions of the children we are sure there must be poverty and destitution in their wretched living places that only the sufferers know.[12]

Thus workers and their sympathizers, faced with the lightning changes in technology that led to job insecurity, the frequent wage reductions as the expansions abruptly stopped or shifted course, loss of personal contact with the management, and the effects of urban overcrowding, were convinced that European history was having a violent reprise on this side of the Atlantic. This labor unrest gave impetus to the trade union movement. Philadelphia, Taylor's hometown, was very much in the center of these changes, and its social and industrial life showed the strain. Thus the Knights of Labor met in Philadelphia in 1869, and in 1873 held their first district assembly in the same city.

It was in troubled times that Fred Taylor entered industry

as a lowly apprentice in a small factory in Philadelphia, then the second largest city in the country after New York, with an industrial force of approximately 140,000 in a total population of 647,000. Though less crowded than New York, and graced with a tradition of easy, elegant living, it was nevertheless a representative industrial city as far as the workers were concerned; yearly wages varied from a low of approximately $200 in the hosiery industry to a high of $550 in the locomotive works.[13]

When Taylor became an apprentice in 1874, it was already generally recognized that changed social conditions and the new technology were rapidly making apprenticeship obsolete. The original form of apprenticeship characteristic of the guilds, in which a young boy was bonded and indentured to a master for many years and in which the master served *in loco parentis,* had gradually declined with the decay of the guilds. However, in the first part of the nineteenth century, the persisting need for skilled workers had kept alive a modified form of apprenticeship, since the simplest test of proficiency was to exact from a job applicant proof that he had served a regular apprenticeship. The term "apprentice" was applied to students of law and medicine as well as to those learning trades; and until 1830, the University of Pennsylvania had apprentices in medicine regularly indentured.[14] As late as 1842, apprentices were a noticeable part of the Philadelphia social scene. In his *Annals of Philadelphia,* Watson, the disapproving chronicler, writes of them as follows:

But among all the changes to which we have ultimately arrived through the mutations of seventy years, the difference between the mode of dress among the apprentices of that remote period and the present mode among the same class, seem to be well worthy of notice. A modern apprentice must have his suit of broadcloth manufactured in the best looms of Europe, his hat of the finest fur and the latest fashion; his overcoat of the best and most approved patent stiffened stuff, with the exact tie in front, and his unmentionables brought up tight about him with the patent double roller gum-elastic suspenders; and nothing less than lepine gold watch with safety chain hung around his neck, will give him the finishing touch, and qualify his person for the administration of the gazing belles, equally well-dressed and ornamented to match him. Now, what a contrast does this afford to the dress of the apprentice seventy years since. Only figure to yourselves, readers, a young man eighteen years of age, of good proportions, handsome face, and blooming with beauty, dressed in a pair of deerskin breeches, coming hardly down to his knees, which before they could be allowed to come into the presence of ladies at a meeting on the Sabbath, were regularly blacked up on the preceding Saturday night at the dye kettle of Deacon Holman, in order to give them a clean and fresh appearance for Sunday . . . . What a contrast between the dress of an apprentice now, and a fellow sufferer seventy years since![15]

Watson, of course, could not foresee that within thirty years the swaggering boy in the broadcloth suit would be consigned to near oblivion.

In the 1870s, writers commenting on the state of the apprenticeship system gave many reasons for its decay. They attributed it to the growing social preference for clean hands and clean clothes and to a growing feeling among the workers that manual labor was not so respected as mental labor. Furthermore, they attributed the decline to the great opportunities offered by industrialization in greater immediate wages paid to unskilled laborers; this was a significant contrast with the three-to-five-year period that an apprentice had to spend earning virtually nothing while at the same time draining his family's finances. These critics lamented the increasing depersonalization of industry and the unwillingness of employers to accept responsibility for an apprentice's welfare—sickness or injury—when their need for skilled labor could be satisfied by the immigration from Europe. They blamed the trade unions in some crafts, for example, bricklaying, plastering, newspaper printing, for their hostility toward the institution of apprenticeship.

Whatever the reasons, in 1870, out of a work force of 127,590 men and women employed in Philadelphia's 8,000 manufacturing establishments, there were only about 3,500 boys working as apprentices—one apprentice to every two-and-a-half shops and to every twenty-six workmen. More revealing was the fact that out of fifty-four boys graduating in 1856 from Philadelphia Central High School, a school catering to the lower-middle class, thirty became clerks and salesmen, and only eleven, mechanics, while of thirty-eight graduating in 1867, only four became mechanics. Even in a school for orphans, Girard College, out of 221 former pupils, fewer than half were learning the mechanical trades.[16] Once inside the factory as an apprentice, a boy was more or less left to fend for himself. A survey conducted by the New Jersey Bureau of Statistics of Labor and Industries contained reports from a great number of trades in answer to the question: "Is there any system of teaching apprentices in the factory where you work? State the methods of teaching apprentices in your trade." The answers to the inquiry showed that there were at least several interpretations put upon the term apprentice. Some gave it the broad meaning "a learner of a trade"; others restricted it to learners bound for a term of years under written indentures. The general drift of the answers made it appear that though there were learners in every trade, they were not bound for a term of years under written indentures, nor were they systematically taught but were simply permitted to "pick up a trade" while working. The skilled workers answered as follows: "Very loose system; taken without indenture and discharged at their own pleasure or that of the employer with the trade only half learned." "They work at what they can do and gradually learn." "Pick it up the best way they can."[17] Apprenticeship was thus generally held to be exceedingly wasteful of the time of the learner and at best suited only for the lower classes—except in the case of sons of factory owners, who had to learn the business from the bottom up and to know a little of every trade before assuming the responsibilities of an owner-manager.

The owners of the small firm in which Fred started his work life as an apprentice were social acquaintances of his family, and Fred was thus necessarily in a different position from the other workers who had to work for their very livelihood.

... my father had some means, and owing to the fact that I worked during my first year for nothing, the second year for $1.50 a week, the third year for $1.50 a week, and the fourth year for $3.00 a week, I was given, perhaps, special opportunities to progress from one kind of work to another: that is, I told the owners of the establishment that I wanted an opportunity to learn fast rather than [earn] wages, and for that reason, I think, I had specially good opportunities to progress. I am merely saying that to explain why in four years I was able to get through with my apprenticeship as a pattern-maker and as a machinist. That is a very short time, as you will realize. I may add that I do not think I was a very high order of journeyman when I started in.[18]

We do not know of the workmen's feelings toward this "aristocrat" in their midst, but we do know that in his self-chosen exile from his preceding life style, Fred tried hard to identify with the workers. He imitated their dress and manners and always regretted that he could not learn to chew tobacco. More important, to the consternation of his Puritan family and friends, he learned to swear. Copley writes:

As was true of all his other activities, he steadily improved his swearing, made it less amateurish and more artistic; but the fact is that he never became able to do it quite like one to the manner born. The high-grade workmen with whom he came in contact appear invariably to have been first puzzled and then amused by it. They easily could feel the incongruity between this habit and his general character.[19]

Fred's swearing thus not only served his need for identification with the workers, but, in the very choice of time and place, it helped him to deal with his aggressive impulses toward the very family and friends whose life style he was repudiating.

... he would let loose a few good ones in the presence of the ultra respectable and the ultra staid. . . . He did not swear when most men would and he did swear when most men would not dream of it. . . . We may imagine that no feathered, nonwebfooted mother ever was more amazed and bewildered upon seeing her chicks take to water than was Emily Taylor when her offspring brought back from the shop a readiness to use words beginning with a big-big D. But that young imp, when reproved would only laugh and say: "Why mother, you don't understand the reason for it."[20]

By getting to know the workers and trying to be like them, the apprenticeship period helped in the necessary rejection of his father's "aristocratic" ways. In a lecture many years later at Harvard, Taylor talked about the workers thus:

Now, I assume that most of you gentlemen are not the sons of working men, and that you have not yourselves worked during any long period of time, at least, with working men, and on the same level with them. The fact is, that in all essential matters, they are just the same as you and I are. The working man and the college professor have fundamentally the same feelings, the same motives, the same ambitions, the same failings, the same virtues. And a moment's thought must convince any one of the truth of this fact, since the college professors of the present are universally the descendants of the working men of the past, while the descendants of the college professor are sure, in the course of time, to again return to the working classes. We are all of the same clay, and essentially of the same metal as well as physical fibre. . . . Any man who is intimately acquainted with the working classes of the United States must have profound respect for them. They are, in the main, sensible men. Not all of them, of course, but they are just as sensible as you and I are. There are some fools among them; so there are among us. They are, in many respects, misguided men. So are we. They require a great deal of information that they have not got. So do we. They are narrow, particularly narrow in their knowledge of men who are not workmen. So are we narrow, most of us particularly narrow in our knowledge of workmen. Those of us whose acquaintance with workmen consists chiefly in seeing them slouching along the street on their way back from work with dirty clothes, chewing tobacco, in many cases hardly looking up as they pass one by, stolid and indifferent-looking, almost inevitably come to the conclusion (not usually in words, but none the less definite) that these men are a different kind of animal from you and from me. On the other hand, the workman who sees in men of our class merely the outward signs of prosperity—good clothes, and the possession of carriages and automobiles, the careless holiday look, accompanied by short working hours—the workman who sees these outward signs is apt to conclude that men of our class are a different kind of animal from himself. The narrowness of the workman, then, in judging us is no greater than our narrowness in judging him.[21]

This staunch identification with the workers and the long hours of intense work activity were part of a vitally important therapeutic process. No wonder that in spite of his dislike for manual labor and the early restoration of his eyesight, Taylor, stubbornly and conscientiously, carried out the weary duties of his apprenticeship. In later years, he called it the most valuable part of his education:

My belief in the benefits to be derived from doing practical, everyday work . . . is not the result of a theory. It is founded upon close observation and study of young men who have had this experience and also a vivid remembrance of breakfasting each morning at five-thirty and starting to sweep the floor of a pattern-shop as an apprentice some thirty-two years ago, after having spent several years in preparing for Havard College. The contrast between the two occupations was great, but I look back upon the first six months of my apprenticeship as a patternmaker as, on the whole, the most valuable part of my education.[22]

And in another place:

The very best training I had was in the early years of my apprenticeship in the patternshop, when I was under a workman of extraordinary ability, coupled with a fine character. I then learned appreciation, respect, and admiration for the everyday working mechanic.[23]

The four years of apprenticeship, from 1874 to 1878, were also in a sense carefree years. As a member of the Young America Cricket Club he played tennis and cricket with his friends. He sang tenor in a choral society (his favorite song: "A Warrior Bold") and took an enthusiastic part in amateur theatricals in which, besides being well-known for his interpretation of the part of a broken-English-speaking German doctor, he was famous for the fidelity and true-to-life quality of his performance of feminine roles.[24] He had not yet articulated any plans for his future:

One day an old gentleman came to my exhibit (in the Philadelphia Exposition of 1876) and I saw at once by the questions which he asked that he was a fine mechanic. . . . he said:

"What is your idea for success in life?"

I said I didn't know, that I had no particular idea.

"Why," he said, "you must have something that you are working for."

I said, "Yes sir, I am working to get to be a machinist and earn $2.50 a day."[25]

These years were, however, critical in the development of Fred's personality. Below the surface calm, the work of the ego was permitted to go on. By its very monotony and its exhausting physical demands, his work life—indeed, its ritualization—became a part of his inner defenses. It gave him a breathing space, a change to find himself, and to "put himself together again." The apprenticeship period thus not only provided him a kind of haven in which to complete his necessary repudiations but allowed him to work in an area he regarded as a kind of social frontier and with men who were very different from any he had ever known, he also had a chance to carve out a niche of his own, independent of his father. In short, it gave him a chance at a new career, a prime element in a man's sense of identity. This career, of course, was to be that of a *reformer* and *prophet*.

This may seem surprising to those who think of Taylor

essentially as an engineer, albeit one with remarkable ingenuity, or as a manager who introduced many innovations into industrial management. Yet, as we shall see, the industrial world was only an arena for his true calling; and his work in industry was more a vocation in the sense of a summons (*Berufung*) than an avocation or profession (*Beruf*). The difficulty in accepting Taylor's ultimate self-image as a prophet lies primarily in the popular association of the word with religion and particularly in its supposed remoteness from the humdrum issues of factory life. In his last years, though, there even appeared a small religious element, reminiscent of Auguste Comte, as a kind of legitimization of his work, however secular. Thus his followers were not entirely joking when they referred to their "cult" as "the Almighty and his disciples."[26] When a friend argued that scientific management was the extension of old religious truths of love and service, Taylor is reported to have solemnly nodded his agreement.[27] The theme of the prophet was woven into the fabric of his personality; and his life, with its triumphs and its shattering disappointments, its brilliant illumination of a part of reality and its blindness to other parts, clearly reflected this theme which in his last years became dominant. In the apprenticeship period, however, there was no conscious awareness of it. In his last years, he looked back on his youth in the light of what he and his followers had become and integrated the apprenticeship period into his life history selectively: he ignored the dancing, the choral singing, the games with friends, the theatrical performances and concentrated only on the awakening. Thus:

Throughout my apprenticeship, of course, I had my eyes on the bad industrial conditions which prevailed at the time and gave a good deal of time and thought to some possible remedy for them.[28]

And in another place:

Not that I gained much knowledge during that time, nor did I ever become a very good pattern-maker; but the awakening as to the reality and seriousness of life was complete, and, I believe, of great value.[29]

In 1878, at the age of twenty-two, Frederick Taylor finished his apprenticeship as a patternmaker and machinist. In the same year, he joined the Midvale Steel Works as a common, unskilled laborer. The fact is curious, and the reason given by Taylor in his testimony at the hearings of the Special Committee of the House of Representatives to Investigate the Taylor and Other Systems of Shop Management in 1912 —namely, "I could not get work at my trade. Work at that time was very dull—it was toward the end of the long period of depression following the Panic of 1873"[30]—is not fully convincing. The owners of Midvale were friends of his father's. Fred always addressed William Sellers, one of the two owners, as "Uncle William" and was often teased by his co-workers about his social connections. His relations with the other owner, Clark, were even closer. Clark's son was Taylor's doubles partner in tennis and a very close friend who later married Taylor's sister. If he had really wanted to, then, with his Exeter education and his social connections, there would have been no difficulty in getting a white-collar job, at least as a clerk. This assumption is supported by the fact that soon after Taylor joined the firm he was asked to substitute as a clerk for a short time since the man holding that position had got mixed up in his accounts and the management, suspecting dishonesty, had discharged him. Taylor said of the experience, "I did the work all right, although it was distasteful to me, and after having trained another clerk in to do the work of the shop I asked permission of the foreman to work as a machinist."[31]

Working as a clerk at a white-collar job would have meant giving in to his past, compromising the still vulnerable choices of his identity struggle. And his strength as well as his weakness, as with any other "prophet," lay precisely in his inability to compromise, his "all or nothing" attitude.

In the year Taylor joined Midvale, there were perhaps four-hundred men employed there.[32] In a way, it was a microcosm of the industrial world of the period of transition between relatively small- and large-scale production, bigger than the typical factory before the start of industrial expansion and much smaller than the steelworks of the early twentieth century. The term "transitional" applied not only to the size of the labor force but also to the kind of technology and the management style. Midvale was thus to prove itself an ideal "laboratory" for Taylor's future work.

Midvale had been established at the close of the Civil War in 1867 by a group of Philadelphia capitalists as a general steel-manufacturing business under the name of Butcher's Steel Works. The steel industry in the United States was then in its infancy, and the technology of steel manufacture was yet undeveloped. The commercial development of the Bessemer process was perfected around 1858, while the development of the open-hearth process followed about ten years later. Butcher's Steel Works used the ancient crucible process, and the locomotive wheels made by this process proved costly as well as unreliable. The works incurred heavy losses; and the reorganization, under the name of Midvale Steel Company, was undertaken by two of its principal creditors, William Sellers, the head of a machine-tools manufacturing company, and a banker, E. W. Clark. They became owners of equal amounts of stock, and Sellers became the president of the reorganized company in 1873. Under his management progress was rapid. The introduction of the open-hearth process successfully enabled the company to manufacture locomotive wheels and steel axles for the Pennsylvania Railroad. In 1875, it received an order for gun forgings from the Navy, the first instance in American history that the United States government placed such an order with an American manufacturer. From that point on, Midvale's defense-oriented business steadily grew; and though its outward appearance was a bit dilapidated, it was one of the most technologically advanced companies in the steel industry.

The Works consisted of five or six run-down buildings: a small open-hearth furnace, a hammer and forge shop, a small rolling mill, a blacksmith shop, a machine shop, and a carpenter and pattern shop. Copley describes the buildings as "generally so dark that they continually called for artificial lighting, and this was furnished by kerosene torches that filled the place with a foul odor and shone with a lurid glare amid the smoke they created."[33]

In his autobiographical letter to Morris Cooke, Taylor wrote that he chose Midvale since it offered him a bigger arena for his mission of reforming existing industrial conditions.[34] We have already mentioned that in a later life stage the mission of prophet was to become the dominant theme of his life. As an aging great man, he was inclined to interpret the facts, the vague yearnings and the disquieting fantasies of his youth so as to be consistent with the prophet theme. More persuasive is the testimony of Harlow Person, one of Taylor's most distinguished associates, who wrote that Taylor went to Midvale because of the attraction of the powerful personality of William Sellers.[35] Indirectly, this is confirmed by Taylor's adulatory references to Sellers in his writings and in Copley's statement that ". . . above all persons in the industry, he [Sellers] had a powerful influence upon Frederick Taylor in Taylor's formative years."[36]

The theme pervading Taylor's "odyssey" of the early years in Midvale is "the search for a father." In the process of growing up, a boy's relationship to his father is first of all an individual one; that is, the boy reacts to a significant person called "father." In maturity, normally the person of the father is replaced by his role and reaction gives way to evaluation.[37] We have said, normally, for in many cases the boy, though now a man, continues to react. He cannot let go of his father, and it is a moot point whether the elements of reaction ever completely disappear. In the main, however, the "search for a father" does not mean the search for the father of one's lost childhood but for certain elements of the father image. As Parsons has pointed out, the father image can be analytically broken down into two main components, the *authority* that breaks up the boy's earlier dependency on his mother and the *model* for the boy's assumption of masculine roles.[38] These components are interdependent, and a breakdown is possible only for purposes of analysis. In this study, our stress is on the authority component of the father image. To a child, Father is synonymous with an external, omniscient wisdom, terrible in wrath, but also providing the guidance that is essential to the child's growing up. Affirmation by the father, next to mother's recognition, has been called one of the developmental elements in a man's sense of identity. It does not matter whether in the judgment of others the father is strict, cruel, or harsh; what he must be is tangible. Intangibly "good" fathers can be the worst.[39] Fred was looking for guidance, authority, and control of the kind that Franklin Taylor never provided. Fred was looking for a father whom he could at last obey, unquestioningly and without doubts. Franklin Taylor had been remote, kind but "intangible." Taylor's rejection of this remote father had become a "displaced" one; that is, he scorned all his father's qualities and the things his father loved: classical education, scholarly tastes, tact, good breeding, remoteness from practical affairs, and a fondness for abstract ideas.

Most of the things that are commonly regarded as the accomplishments of a young gentleman and a young lady he [Taylor] continued to view with contempt. Even such things as a young girl's "coming out" party became to him "ridiculous nonsense." He could not conceive that a young woman had finish just because she could gracefully receive her guests and gracefully dance and sing and play and chatter about Art. If she scorned the toil that fed her and enabled her to sleep warm, then, in his opinion, she, so far from having finished her education, had not even begun.[40]

Whereas his father had taken an interest in his son's classical education at Exeter—"You find Cicero easier than the Aeneid do you not. He has a fine style and my recollection is, that 'twas very easy reading."[41]—Fred could write in a school essay:

In practical life a knowledge of the classics is of about no benefit to any but professional men . . . when there are so many other studies, which are equally good training for the mind, and which would be of use to us in our business and our professions in after life I do not think that time is well spent in studying Latin and Greek.[42]

As his European diary records, his father had taken him to the many museums and art galleries of Europe and yet later on he could write:

The two years of school in France and Germany, and then a year and a half of travel in Italy, Switzerland, Norway, England, France, Germany, Austria, etc. (of all of which I disapprove for a young boy), then a return to the healthy out-of-door life of Germantown, than which I believe there is nothing finer in the world, in which sport is the leading idea, with education a long way back, second.[43]

His private "chamber of horrors"—professors, theologians, bankers, and Germans—seems thus also to be a collective portrait of his father.

Taylor's first superior at Midvale was one Charles Brinley, a man trained in metallurgical chemistry at Yale University.[44] After three years of postgraduate study, Brinley came to Midvale as a chemist where he set up one of the first chemical laboratories in the steel industry. A year after he came to Midvale, Brinley was placed in charge of the actual steelmaking and was very soon promoted to Superintendent of the Works. Brinley was a gentleman and a scholar who was more concerned with his scientific work and the problems of management-in-the-abstract than with men. He ignored Taylor, or as Copley puts it, "Brinley did not love this young man enough to be really harsh with him."[45]

Taylor's reaction to this scholarly aloofness was thus predictable:

Shortly after serving my apprenticeship, I worked in a shop under the superintendence of a college graduate. His natural carriage led him to hold his head rather high in the air, and he had an imperturbable rather wooden face, and looked at one with an expressionless eye. Every day he would walk through the shop, hardly saying anything to any of the workmen. In addition to this, he had the habit of using a silk handkerchief with perfume on it. This man was not only disliked, but cordially hated by all men. They could stand the silk handkerchief with perfume, but the corner of the handkerchief which he always left sticking out of the breast pocket of his coat was too much for them, and I must say I personally cordially shared their hatred. Years afterward, I discovered he was rather a kindly, nice sort of man.[46]

Brinley, then, was too much like Franklin Taylor in his aloofness, and as long as he was there at Midvale, Taylor "held himself in." It was only with the retirement of Brinley in 1882, when Taylor started working under the new Superintendent, Russel Davenport, that his astonishing burst of creativity, in management and engineering innovation, really began.

Taylor found his successive "fathers" in the persons of Russel Davenport and William Sellers. He talks of both these men and of their importance in his personal and professional development in a revealing lecture entitled "Success: A Lecture to Young Men Entering Business." In 1908, he had been asked by the College of Engineering of the University of Illinois to give a lecture to its students. The suggested topics were his research in the art of cutting metals or the production costs of manufacturing establishments.[47] Taylor was fifty-two years old at the time and on the threshold of public fame. Sellers had died four years earlier, Davenport in 1904, and his own father, then eighty-six, was approaching death. We can only speculate as to why at this particular time he rejected the suggested topics and instead chose to talk of what the two men had taught him. On the

frontispiece of the typescript there is a short couplet, missing in the printed version, that runs as follows:
"My bright-eyed daughter of the stars, what name?"
Gravely she answered, "I am called Success."
"Thy name, the lineage, whence thy beauty came?"
"Failure, my sire; my mother weariness."

The two men, in strictly controlling Taylor, taught him to control himself: they gave him "character."

Character is the ability to control yourself, body and mind; the ability to do those things which your common sense tells you you ought to do; the ability above all to do things which are disagreeable, which you do not like. It takes but little character to do difficult things if you like them. It takes a lot of character to do things which are tiresome, monotonous, and unpleasant.[48]

To succeed, a man had to learn unconditional obedience, which, expressed in Taylor's words, bordered on the ideal filial devotion in a strictly patriarchal family.

For success, then, let me give one simple piece of advice beyond all others. Every day, year in and year out, each man should ask himself, over and over again, two questions. First, "What is the name of the man I am now working for?" and having answered this definitely, then "What does this man want me to do, right now?" Not, "What ought I to do in the interest of the company that I am working for?" Not, "What are the duties of the position that I am filling?" Not, "What did I agree to do when I came here?" Not, "What should I do for my own best interest?" but plainly and simply, "What does this man want me to do?"[49]

Don't kick, certainly don't kick unless you are sure accomplishing your result. Your kick, in perhaps nine cases out of ten, will result merely in aggravating your employer, whether it is just or unjust, and your common sense should tell you that it is foolish to aggravate him unless some good is to come of it.[50]

Davenport was then the first man who exacted complete obedience from Taylor, an unquestioning obedience, which was later to become one of the primary features of Taylor's own scientific management and against which the workers' attacks were primarily directed.

Let me tell you how it was pounded into me. I was foreman of a machine shop more than half of the work in which was that of repairing and maintaining the machinery in a large steel works. Of course my chief interest and hope in life was that of doing some great thing for the benefit of the Works that I was in. My head was full of wonderful and great projects to simplify the processes, to design new machines, to revolutionize the methods of the whole establishment. It is needless to say that 90 out of 100 of these projects were impracticable, and that very few of them ever came to anything, but I was devoting every minute of my spare time, at home and on Sunday, and entirely too much time in the works to developing these wonderful and great projects. Now the Superintendent of the Works [Davenport] who had been a warm friend of mine for years, wanted me to keep all the machines going with the minimum loss of time, and kept telling me this over and over again. I, however, knew much better than he what was best for the interests of the works. I did not daily ask myself, "What does this man want me to do?" but I daily told myself just what I ought to be doing. He stood this as long as he could (which was a great deal longer than he ought to have stood it) and finally came into my office one day and swore like a pirate. This had never happened before and I, of course, at once made up my mind that I should get right out; wouldn't stand any such treatment. I, however, remembered my early advice, and waited forty-eight hours before doing anything. By that time I had very greatly cooled off, but for two or three weeks at regular intervals, my friend, the Superintendent, repeated this process of damning me up and down hill, until he finally beat it into my dumb head that I was there to serve him, and not to work in the interests of the company according to my own ideas, when these conflicted with his; and from that time forward I made quite rapid progress toward success.[51]

Another incident:

A workman came up to my house in the middle of the night to tell me that a valve had broken and shut down one of the largest departments in the works. I took the earliest train to every dealer who might possibly have that valve on hand, and also to establishments who were users of this kind of valve. About noon I returned to the works, feeling very well satisfied that I had left no stone unturned in my hunt for the valve. I started to explain to the Superintendent [Davenport] just how thoroughly I had done my work, when he turned on me.

"Do you mean to say that you haven't got that valve?"

"Yes, sir."

"Damn you, get out of this and *get that valve.*"

So I went to New York and got that valve. Not reasons, but results are wanted.[52]

Though nominally working under Davenport, Taylor soon came to report more and more to the president, Sellers, who influenced him deeply.

William Sellers was a Quaker who had been born in 1824, in Delaware County, Pennsylvania.[53] He was one of the most noted engineers in the country, his reputation resting primarily on his inventions and designs for machine tools. Besides being the president of Midvale, he ran his own machine-tools company, Williams Sellers and Company, and directed the Edgemoor Iron Company, which he had formed in 1868. He had an impressive physical presence: powerful build, bushy eyebrows, curving mustache, and an imperial beard. Extremely self-confident, he had the reputation among his employees of being able to "growl like a lion, kick like a steer, and bawl like a bull."[54] Copley tells a story about him which reflects his belief in himself. One of his employees, who had temporarily left him to go to another company, dropped into Philadelphia for a day and went to see his old boss.

"Now, how is this, Mr. Oertsen," said Mr. Sellers grimly, "that you have set up in opposition to us?"

"Oh," said Mr. Oertsen, "I am sure, Mr. Sellers, there is room in the world for us both."

"Well," Mr. Sellers boomed forth, as he attached his signature to a letter, "I always have noticed that there is plenty of room in this world for me."[55]

It was primarily Sellers Taylor had in mind when in a lecture he said of the old-style manager:

. . . the personality of the employer counted perhaps for more than any other element. It was not enough for a manager of men to be able, competent, and well trained. It was also necessary for him to secure and control his men through his attractive and masterful personality. Through all times and in all ages the great personal leaders of men have had rare gifts which command at the same time the admiration, the love, the respect, and the fear of those under him. Men with this rare combination of qualities are born, not made. The great captains of industry were usually physically large and powerful. They were big-hearted, kindly, humorous, lovable men, democratic, truly fond of their workmen, and yet courageous, brainy, and shrewd; with not the slightest vestige of anything soft or sentimental about them. Ready at any minute to damn up and down hill the man who needed it, or to lay violent hands on any workmen who defied them, and throw them over the fence. They were men who would not hesitate to joke with the apprentice boy one minute, and give him a spanking the next. Such men would be recognized in any age and in any country as real men, fit to be leaders of other men.[56]

To say the least, there was no sign of aloofness about Sellers, though the lessons in obedience were carried further:

William Sellers ranked undoubtedly in his time as the most noted engineer in this country. It was my good fortune to work under him for several years. During this time I was badly treated by one of the Superintendents who was over me. I stood it for a long time and then decided to go to Mr. Sellers about it. He listened and agreed with what I told him, and then turned to me, almost laughing, and said, "Do you know that all of this impresses me with the fact that you are still a very young man? Long before you reach my age you will have found that you have to eat a bushel of dirt, and you will go right ahead and eat your dirt until it seriously interferes with your digestion."[57]

Early in his direct dealing with Sellers there occurred an incident that Taylor became very fond of relating. Sellers gave him some drawings that he wished to see developed further. In a day or two, Taylor returned with an entirely new set of drawings of his own preparation.

"What are these?" asked Sellers as he started to look them over.

Enthusiastically Taylor informed him that he had become convinced that his (Sellers') ideas were impracticable and so he had worked up some of his own. In Sellers' office a fire was burning in the grate, and Sellers promptly threw the drawings into the fire.

"The next time," said Sellers, "perhaps you won't abandon any of my ideas as impracticable until you bring me the finished drawings and show me just where they are impracticable."[58]

What this ordeal of kind harshness meant to Taylor was that

. . . the most important idea should be that of serving the man over you his way, not yours; and that this lies, generally speaking, in giving him not only what he wants but also giving him a little extra present of some kind, in doing something for him which he has no right either to ask or to expect.[59]

Once Sellers had "proved" his right to be a father, Taylor strove hard to give him these extra presents.

In another establishment [Midvale] a young man [Taylor] . . . had worked up to be at the head of one of the departments. A drain which ran underneath this mill became clogged up. He sent his best foreman and a gang of men to clean it out. After they had tried to do it with jointed rods of all kinds, they failed, and reported to him that the only thing to do was to dig down, break open the drain, and clean out the obstruction. Now this drain was some twenty or thirty feet below the mill, and ran underneath the foundations, which made it extremely difficult to dig, and certainly involved the loss of several days in the operation of the mill. This young man made up his mind that the drain must be cleared, so he took off all of his clothes, put on overalls, tied shoes on to his elbows, shoes on to his knees, and leather pads on to his hips to keep from getting cut in the drain, and then crawled in through the black slime and muck of the drain. Time and again he had to turn his nose up into the arch of the drain to keep from drowning. After about 100 yards, however, he reached the obstruction, pulled it down, and when the water had partly subsided backed out the same way that he had come in. He was covered with slime perhaps half an inch thick, all over, which had to be scraped off with a scraper, and his skin was black for a week or two where the dirt had soaked in. He was, of course, very much laughed at, and finally the anecdote was told as a good joke at a meeting of the Board of Directors. The president of the company [Sellers] realized that this was just the kind of joke that his company appreciated. He realized that the company had been saved perhaps one or two thousand dollars in profits by the grit of this young man.[60]

Sellers', and to a lesser degree, Davenport's harshness toward Taylor was not punitive but rather of an affirmative kind; one that took cognizance of Taylor's person, that supported and guided him in the astonishing burst of innovation that followed the retirement of Taylor's first boss, Brinley, in 1882. Sellers' role in Taylor's early work cannot be overestimated. It was as if Taylor had at last been permitted to be a man and do a "man's work." It must be remembered that to most of the other executives and to the workers "crazy" Taylor with his "monkey-mind" was a figure of fun. He was so often called a crank by one of the executives that he protested violently in language not customarily used with a nominal superior. Copley writes:

So it became the fashion to laugh at the young man . . . to dismiss many of his actions as those of a crank. His speech truly was extraordinary. His words often came from him so fast that they tumbled all over one another. Sometimes his speech rose to a violence that seemed to classify him as supernormal, if not abnormal.[61]

Carl Barth, one of Taylor's closest collaborators, who began his employment in the drafting room of Sellers' plant in 1881, reported that whenever Taylor appeared at the plant nearly everyone "took on a smile."[62]

It is reported that several years after Taylor left Midvale, he happened to meet Sellers' successor, Harrah, in the lobby of a Philadelphia hotel and the following incident occurred:

"Hello, Taylor, what are you doing now?"

Taylor replied that he was systematizing the Cramp Shipyards and then politely enquired as to how things were going with his former chief.

"Oh," said Mr. Harrah, "I am doing fine. I am making a lot of money. And do you know what I am going to do when I have made a few more millions? I am going to build the finest insane asylum this world has ever known, and you, Taylor, are going to have there an entire floor."[63]

But as long as the supportive "father," in this case, Sellers, was behind him—and this pattern was to be repeated again —the mockery and the derision only spurred him on. Sellers gave him the permission to experiment in metal-cutting. Everyone at Midvale was actively opposed to his experiments and, in Copley's words, ". . . it is extremely unlikely that there was then in industry another chief executive who would have given young Taylor any encouragement at all."[64]

As Taylor said:

Mr. Sellers, in spite of the protests which were made against the continuation of the work, allowed the experiments to proceed; even, at first, at a very considerable inconvenience and loss to the shop. The extent of this inconvenience will be appreciated when it is understood that we were using a 66-inch diameter vertical boring mill, belt driven by the usual cone pulleys, and that in order to regulate the exact cutting speed of the tool, it was necessary to slow down the speed of the engine that drove all the shafting in the shop; a special adjustable engine governor having been bought for this purpose. For over two years the whole shop was inconvenienced in this way, by having the speed of its main line of shafting greatly varied, not only from day to day, but from hour to hour.[65]

The same opposition prevailed in the case of time-study, as evidenced by one of his friends at Midvale.

I can well remember when, at the Midvale Steel Works, he began what seemed to us all at the time a hopeless and useless undertaking, the ascertaining exactly how long it took a workman to do a given piece of work. Imagine a young cadet of industry, a student just out of the technical school, with a stop-watch and a hugh diagram before him, stationed by Taylor opposite a workman to note minute by minute, aye, almost second by second, each and every movement. Now he takes up a tool; click goes the stop-watch, and down on the prepared diagram goes the number of seconds that are required for the movement; and so on, day after day, month after month, until stacks of these diagrams of the time required for the workman to do the simplest act were collected. No wonder many thought the whole work fanciful and its cost of thousands of dollars thrown away.[66]

There is considerable evidence that Sellers was barely aware of many of Taylor's experiments. In fact, he was one of the very few people at Midvale who did not even know of the time-study when it first began.[67] But as we have stressed above, what Taylor needed, and what Sellers provided in his gruff way, was a personal affirmation. "Now young man," he said, "I know that you are a fool. But I am going to let you go right ahead and spend that money to prove that you are a fool."[68]

No wonder that at the time of one of his greatest disappointments, the dismissal from Bethlehem in 1901, he went back to continue his work at William Sellers and Company under his old superior, "Uncle William."

It has been argued that the polarity of controlling and being controlled is a significant issue in the work life of an adult.[1] We have already described Taylor's years at Midvale in terms of his relationship to those in authority, his complete submission to Davenport and Sellers. Here we shall look at the other pole—Taylor's attempts at controlling, or rather, overcontrolling, which led to his fight with the workers in the machine shop almost immediately after his coming to Midvale. After his short stint as a clerk in the accounts department, Taylor had asked to be relieved and was given permission to work as a machinist on a lathe. He did this work for two months in apparent harmony with his fellow workers. If, because of their different worlds, there was no camaraderie between him and the other workers, there was at least no friction as long as he was one of them. However, this did not last long, for

Shortly after this they wanted a gang boss to take charge of the lathes they appointed me to this position.

Now, the machine shop of the Midvale Steel Works was a piecework shop. All the work practically was done on piecework, and it ran night and day—five nights in the week and six days. Two sets of men came on, one to run the machines at night and the other to run them in daytime.

We who were the workmen of that shop had the quantity output carefully agreed upon for everything that was turned out in the shop. We limited the output to about, I should think, one-third of what we could very well have done. We felt justified in doing this, owing to the piecework system—that is, owing to the necessity for soldiering under the piecework system—which I pointed out yesterday.

As soon as I became gang boss the men who were working under me and who, of course, knew that I was onto the whole game of soldiering or deliberately restricting output, came to me at once and said, "Now, Fred, you are not going to be a damn piecework hog, are you?"

I said, "If you fellows mean you are afraid I am going to try to get a larger output from these lathes," I said, "Yes; I do propose to get more work out."

I said, "You must remember I have been square with you

fellows up to now and worked with you. I have not broken a single rate; I have been on your side of the fence. But now I have accepted a job under the management of this company and I am on the other side of the fence, and I will tell you perfectly frankly that I am going to try to get a bigger output from these lathes."

They answered, "Then, you are going to be a damned hog."

I said, "Well, if you fellows put it that way, all right."

They said, "We warn you, Fred, if you try to bust any of these rates we will have you over the fence in six weeks."

I said, "That is all right; I will tell you fellows again frankly that I propose to try to get a bigger output off these machines."

Now, that was the beginning of a piecework fight which lasted nearly three years, as I remember it—two or three years—in which I was doing everything in my power to increase the output of the shop while the men were absolutely determined that the output should not be increased. Anyone who has been through such a fight knows and dreads the meanness of it and the bitterness of it. I believe that if I had been an older man—a man of more experience —I should have hardly gone into such a fight as this—deliberately attempting to force the men to do something they did not propose to do.

We fought on the management's side with all the usual methods, and the workmen fought on their side with all of their usual methods. I began by going to the management and telling them perfectly plainly, even before I accepted the gang boss-ship, what would happen. I said, "Now, these men will show you, and show you conclusively, that in the first place, I know nothing about my business; and that, in second place, I am a liar, and you are being fooled, and they will bring any amount of evidence to prove these facts beyond a shadow of doubt." I said to management, "The only thing I ask of you, and I must have your firm promise, is that when I say a thing is so you will take my word against the word of any twenty men or any fifty men in the shop." I said, "If you won't do that, I won't lift my finger toward increasing the output of this shop." They agreed to it and stuck to it, although many times they were on the verge of believing I was both incompetent and untruthful.

Now, I think it perhaps desirable to show the way in which that fight was conducted.

I began, of course, by directing some one man to do more work than he had done before, and then I got on the lathe myself and showed him that it could be done. In spite of this, he went ahead and turned out exactly the same old output and refused to adopt better methods or to work quicker until finally I laid him off and got another man in his place. This new man—I could not blame him in the least under the circumstances—turned right around and joined the other fellows and refused to do any more work than the rest. After trying this policy for a while and failing to get any results, I said distinctly to the fellows,

"Now, I am a mechanic; I am a machinist. I do not want to take the next step, because it will be contrary to what you and I look upon as our interest as machinists, but I will take it if you fellows won't compromise with me and get more work off of these lathes, but I warn you if I have to take this step it will be a durned mean one." I took it.

I hunted up some especially intelligent laborers who were competent men, but who had not had the opportunity of learning a trade, and I deliberately taught these men how to run a lathe and how to work right and fast. Every one of these laborers promised me, "Now, if you will teach me the machinist's trade, when I learn to run a lathe I will do a fair day's work," and every solitary man, when I had taught them their trade, one after another turned right around and joined the rest of the fellows and refused to work one bit faster.

That looked as if I were up against a stone wall, and for a time I was up against a stone wall. I did not blame even these laborers in my heart, my sympathy was with them all of the time, but I am telling you the facts as they then existed in the machine shops of this country, and in truth, as they still exist.

When I had trained enough of these laborers so that they could run the lathes, I went to them and said, "Now you men to whom I have taught a trade are in a totally different position from the machinists who were running these lathes before you came here. Every one of you agreed to do a certain thing for me if I taught you a trade, and now not one of you will keep his word. I did not break my word with you, but everyone of you has broken his word with me. Now, I have not any mercy on you; I have not the slightest hesitation in treating you entirely differently." I said, "I know that very heavy social pressure has been put upon you outside the works to keep you from carrying out your agreement with me, and it is very difficult for you to stand out against this pressure, but you ought not to have made your bargain with me if you did not intend to keep your end of it. Now, I am going to cut your rate in two to-morrow and you are going to work for half price from now on. But all you will have to do is to turn out a fair day's work and you can earn better wages than you have been earning."

These men, of course, went to the management, and protested that I was a tyrant, and a nigger driver, and for a long time they stood right by the rest of the men in the shop and refused to increase their output a particle. Finally, they all of a sudden gave in and did a fair day's work.

I want to call your attention, gentlemen, to the bitterness that was stirred up in this fight before the men finally gave in, to the meanness of it, and the contemptible conditions that exist under the old piecework system, and to show you what it leads to. In this contest, after my first fighting blood which was stirred up through strenuous opposition had subsided, I did not have any bitterness against any particular man or men. My anger and hard feelings were stirred up against the system; not against the men. Practically all those men were my friends; and many of them are still my friends. As soon as I began to be successful in forcing the men to do a fair day's work, they played what is usually the winning card. I knew that it was coming. I had predicted to the owners of the company what would happen when we began to win, and had warned them that they must stand by me; so that I had the backing of the company in taking effective steps to checkmate the final move of the men. Every time I broke a rate or forced one of the new men whom I had trained to work at a reasonable and proper speed, some one of the machinists would deliberately break some part of his machine as an object lesson to demonstrate to the management that a fool foreman was driving the men to overload their machines until they broke. Almost every day ingenious accidents were planned, and these happened to machines in different parts of the shop, and were, of course, always laid to the fool foreman who was driving the men and the machines beyond their proper limit.

Fortunately, I had told the management in advance that this would happen, so they backed me up fully. When they began breaking their machines, I said to the men, "All right; from this time on, any accident that happens in this shop, every time you break any part of a machine you will have to pay part of the cost of repairing it or else quit. I don't care if the roof falls in and breaks your machine, you will pay all the same." Every time a man broke anything, I fined him and then turned the money over to the mutual benefit association, so that in the end it came back to the men. But I fined them, right or wrong. They could always show every time an accident happened that it was not their fault and that it was an impossible thing for them not to break their machine under the circumstances. Finally, when they found that these tactics did not produce the desired effect on the management, they got sick of being fined, their opposition broke down, and they promised to do a fair day's work.

After that we were good friends, but it took three years of hard fighting to bring this about.[2]

The fight indeed was a bitter one and was later used by Taylor's opponents as an example of Taylor's cruelty and hostility toward the workers. That Taylor's methods were arbitrary and authoritarian in the extreme there can be little doubt. In one case, he began by fining a man two dollars, and then as the machine parts continued to break, he doubled the fine until reached the sum of sixty-four dollars,[3] which in those days represented more than two months' wages to a worker. Another man was fined for having a scratch on his machine, and when he protested that he was not responsible for the scratch, he was told that he was fined for not reporting it. The fines were imposed left and right, not only for damage to the machines, tools, or the work, but also for the violation of any rules, such as reporting late or leaving without permission.[4] No wonder that some of the workers threatened him with physical violence and in one case, actually threatened to shoot him.

His alarmed friends and relatives advised him to abandon his custom of walking home after work along the deserted railroad tracks. "They can shoot and be damned," is his reported answer and he let it be known in the Works that if he was ever attacked he would not stick to any of the rules of fighting but it would be "bite, gouge, and brickbats."[5]

In spite of this evidence, Taylor, in his testimony at the congressional hearings of 1912, maintained that his relationship with the workers was one of mutual friendliness and that any strains existed only inside the Works and were forgotten by him, and presumably by the workers, immediately outside working hours.

. . . those men were my personal friends, but when we went through the gate of that place we were enemies—we were bitter enemies. I was trying to drive them and they were not going to be driven.[6]

And again, in detail:

Now that may sound like an anomaly, but I am telling you the fact. My sympathies were with the workmen, and my duty lay to the people by whom I was employed. My sympathies were so great that when, as I have told you before, they came to me for personal advice as a friend and asked me in a serious, sober way, "Fred, if you were in my place, would you do what you are asking me to do, turn out a bigger output?" My answer was, as I have said in the record before, "if I were in your place, I would do just what you are doing; I would fight against this as hard as any of you are; only," I said "I would not make a fool of myself: when the time comes that you see I have succeeded, or the men on our side have succeeded, in forcing or compelling you to do a larger day's work, I would not then make a fool of myself. When that time comes, I would work up to proper speed." I told them that over and over again. Our official relations were of the most strained and most disagreeable and most contemptible nature, but my personal relations with most of those men throughout the fight were agreeable.[7]

It is difficult, to say the least, to believe in Taylor's account of his personal relations with the workers as a statement of objective truth. According to Taylor's own testimony, after the depression of 1873, jobs were scarce, and the dismissal of many workers and the hardships caused them could scarcely have been conducive to good personal relations. Add to this the huge fines, the threats of physical violence, and even of shooting, and Taylor's version of his relations with the workers sounds like hypocrisy, a charge which many labor leaders later made against him.

Taylor, however, sincerely believed that his relations with the workers were on the whole friendly, in spite of the existing enmity during the working hours. If the evidence seems to belie this assertion, one can easily believe that for Taylor it had a psychic reality, and thus a different kind of truth; the "anomaly" he talks about was an expression of his own ambivalence.

Ever since Freud's early papers on the obsessive-compulsive character, mounting clinical evidence has established the fact that seeming contradictions, such as between love and hate, passivity and activity, masculinity and femininity, can exist simultaneously and are characteristic of the obsessional personality.[8] It is of course true that these are present in everyone as the ambivalence and bisexuality inherent in human nature; however, typically as soon as these opposing tendencies rise to consciousness, they are taken care of by fusion and synthesis. In the case of an individual who becomes obsessional, this fusion seems to fail.[9] The normal ambivalence in such an individual is heightened, thus increasing inner conflict. For an obsessional, hostility and aggression against the environment run parallel with the inner conflict of his own ambivalent strivings. As we have noted, in his apprenticeship days, Taylor wanted to identify with the workers, trying to chew tobacco and cursing with them, and had found among them and in the dirty surroundings of the factory a kind of casual intimacy which he had not known in the spotlessly clean and carefully regimented household of Emily Taylor. Now, merely being on the management side of the fence did not change his ambivalence toward authority although in this case *he* was the one who was exercising it. Even as he tried more and more harshly to control the workers, he empathized and also suffered with them. In trying to control them he was also attempting to control his own rebellious strivings which had been projected onto the workers. This open conflict, mirroring his own inner conflict, was bound to be accompanied by increasing anxiety:

I was a young man in years, but I give you my word I was a great deal older than I am now with worry, meanness, and contemptibleness of the whole damn thing. It is a horrid life for any man to live, not to be able to look any work-man in the face all day long without seeing hostility there and feeling that every man around one is his virtual enemy. These men were a nice lot of fellows and many of them were my friends outside of the Works. This life was a miserable one and I made up my mind either to get out of the business entirely and go into some other line of work, or to find some remedy for this unbearable condition.[10]

Thus, in late 1881, three years after he had come to Midvale, Taylor reached a crossroads, both in his personal development and in his professional career. During these three years, his immediate superior had been the aloof "gentleman," Brinley. Deprived of the fatherly approval and support that he desperately needed from those in authority and embroiled in an even more bitter conflict with the workers with whom a part of him still identified, Taylor's inner struggle between the dynamic polarities to control and to be controlled was causing him increasing anxiety. His way of dealing with this conflict during these three years was in the classic obsessive-compulsive style—in ceaseless activity. David Shapiro has characterised this style as follows:

The most conspicuous fact about the activity of the obsessive-compulsive is its sheer quantity and, along with this, its intensity and concentration. These people may be enormously productive in socially recognized ways, or they may not. However that may be, they are typically, intensely, and more or less continuously active at some kind of work. . . . The activity—one could just as well say life—of these people is characterized by more or less continuous experience of tense deliberateness, a sense of effort, and of trying.[11]

In these first years, Taylor worked in the shops of Midvale from 6:30 in the morning to 5:10 in the evening and then walked the two miles back to his home. He often volunteered to work on Sundays as well as overtime on weekdays. In his disguised autobiographical lecture he tells us,

In an egineering establishment [Midvale] there were ten or fifteen young college men who were trying to work up into good positions. Among them was one man [Taylor] of no special ability. He appears to have been endowed, however, with fully the ordinary amount of common-sense. At any rate, he saw an opportunity for advancement which the other young men failed to see.

Most of the departments of the works ran night and day, so that every Saturday night and Sunday urgent repairs were required to keep the place running. Naturally, the work of making these repairs was in no way sought for by these young college fellows. They all had something much more interesting to do on Sunday—either choir practice or lawn tennis or social engagements of some kind. So that the superintendent in charge of repairs had a hard time to get the men he wanted to work hard, and chiefly on Sunday.

One of these young college men [Taylor], however, went to the repair Superintendent, and told him that he didn't mind Sunday work at all—in fact, he rather liked it. He said he had served his apprenticeship as a machinist, and didn't mind being called upon at any time. This was such a new experience to the repair Superintendent that he sent for him to come in on the following Sunday. He did so well that he kept him at work practically every Sunday throughout the year, and also quite frequently all of Saturday night, and, contrary to what usually happened, he never had any kicks or complaints from this young man.

All of this man's friends, however, laughed at him and remonstrated with him for being so foolish as to take much more than his share of Sunday work. This was particularly true of the rest of the college fellows. His parents, his social friends, also told him that he was nothing but a fool to work in this way.[12]

This was not all. After work he studied at home, for he had found himself "very much short of scientific education, and began by taking a home-study course in mathematics and physics, which was given by the scientific professors at Harvard University." He continues," After getting all that I could by correspondence in this way, I then went to the Professors at Stevens Institute and asked them for proper textbooks, etc., and this started my home course at Stevens."[13]

After walking home from work and eating dinner he would set his alarm clock for 2 A.M. when he would rise, bathe, and dress in his working clothes to study until 5 A.M. He would then lie down to get half an hour's sleep before eating breakfast and catching the 6 o'clock train at the Reading railway station, near his Ross Street home, which would bring him to work.[14] This regimen must have lasted only for a very short time, for his study habits were soon to become "curiouser and curiouser." One of his best friends wrote:

Soon after entering Midvale, where the hours were long and his duties strenuous, his eyesight improved and he determined to take a course for home study at the Stevens Institute of Technology. This meant hard work day and night for four years, but he never faltered, and many times after burning the midnight oil over his studies, I have known him to dispel the nervous tension and put himself in trim for much-needed sleep during the few hours that remained before he was due again at Midvale, by running through the streets of Germantown for half an hour. At first this unusual activity in the early morn aroused the suspicion of the police, but they soon found that there was no cause for alarm in Taylor and allowed him to run along undisturbed . . . .

During these strenuous times, I doubt if he ever had more than four or five hours sleep out of the twenty-four, but no doubt his sleep was just as intense and effective as everything else that he did.[15]

Ceaseless activity, as we have mentioned earlier, is one way of dealing with anxiety. In Taylor this not only extended into the areas of work and study but also manifested itself in his leisure-time activities (what little leisure there was). These activities, which for most people are playful and fun, were in Taylor's case characterized by the same effortfulness and tense deliberateness. His "working at games" in childhood was during this period in Midvale applied to tennis, at which he soon became an expert. He thought and deliberated not only about each stroke but also about the tennis equipment, taking out patents for a new kind of tennis net, new net supports, and a tennis racquet that was bent in the middle.

All this intense activity, however, was not sufficient to allay mounting anxiety. The battle for control between Taylor and the workers took place in the sphere of work; in those three years Taylor's battle tactics had been what he was later to characterize as the older style of management, namely: "First: Holding a plum for them to climb after; and Second: Cracking the whip over them with an occasional touch of the lash."[16] It should be emphasized here that although the battle focused on the problem of work—namely, increased output—the real issue was one of *control*. A proper day's work, a "fair day's work," Taylor felt, would automatically organize and control the entire behavior of the workers outside as well as inside the factory: The moral effect of this habit of doing things according to law and method is great. It develops men of principle in other directions. When men spend the greater part of their active working hours in regulating their every movement in accordance with clear-cut formulated laws, they form habits which inevitably affect and in many cases control them in their family life, and in all of their acts outside the working hours. With almost certainty they begin to guide the rest of their lives according to principles and laws, and to try to insist upon those around them doing the same. Thus the whole family feels the good effects of the good habits that have been forced upon the workman in his daily work. . . .[17]

The difficulty now was that although in the three-year fight Taylor had partly succeeded in his effort to control the workers, this success had been a personally painful one. His ambivalence toward authority and his partial identification with the workers also made *him* feel the touch of the "lash" which he applied against the workmen, and this to him was a "horrid life" and an "unbearable condition." Quite easily Taylor could have drifted further along this road, driving the workers and himself with an ever-increasing frenzy, ultimately losing touch with a part of reality. The "hostility in every face" would have meant certain threat and feelings of persecution would have increased, leading to renewed efforts at exercising a kind of omnipotent control. That Taylor did not drift into such paranoid oblivion we must attribute in large part to the steady affirmation and authoritative support provided by Sellers, which served to strengthen his ego in this inner conflict. For once such a conflict has been precipitated, the outcome depends not only on the strengths that have accrued to the ego during all previous development but also on the continuing affirmation and confirmation of persons who have become significant in one's life.

The "aloof" Brinley had retired in 1881, and Taylor had come to work under the new superintendent, Russel Davenport, though he was now dealing more and more directly with Sellers. As described in an earlier chapter, these two men, and especially Sellers, helped Taylor in a way that can only be called therapeutic. Their support enabled him to reexamine his fight with the workers (without giving up the goal of controlling them) from a more rational standpoint, that is, by relying on logical mental processes instead of the magical wish for "omnipotent control."[18]

When I got to be a foreman of the shop and had finally

won out and we had an agreement among the men that there would be so much work done—not a full day's work, but a pretty good day's work—we all came to an understanding, and had no further fighting. Then I tried to analyze it, and said: "The main trouble with this thing is that you have been quarrelling because there have been no proper standards for a day's work. You do not know what a proper day's work is. Those fellows know the times more than you do, but personally, we do not know anything about what a day's work is. We make a bluff at it and the other side makes a guess at it and then we fight. The great thing is that we do not know what is a proper day's work."[19]

Realizing this deficiency on my part, I asked permission from Mr. William Sellers, the president of Midvale Steel Company, to make a series of careful scientific experiments to find out how quickly various kinds of work that went into the shop ought to be done.

Now, those experiments were started along a variety of lines. One of the types of investigation which was started at that time was that which has come to be generally known as "motion study" or "time study". A young man was given a stop-watch and ruled and printed blanks. . . . This man for two years and a half, I think, spent his entire time in analyzing the motions of the workmen in the machine shop. . . . Before starting to describe these experiments, however, I want to make it clear to you that these scientific experiments, namely, accurate motion and time study of men and a study of the art of cutting metals, which were undertaken to give the foreman of the machine shop of the Midvale Steel Works knowledge which was greatly needed by him, in order to prevent soldiering and the strife that goes with it, marked the first steps which were taken in the evolution of what is called scientific management. These steps were taken in an earnest endeavour to correct what I look upon as one of the crying evils of the older systems of management. And I think that I may say that every subsequent step which was taken and which has resulted in the development of scientific management was in the same way taken, not as the result of some preconceived theory by any one man or any number of men, but in an equally earnest endeavor to correct some of the perfectly evident and serious errors of the older type of management. . . . Personally, I am profoundly suspicious of any new theory, my own as well as any other man's theory, and until a theory has been proved to be correct from practical experience, it is safe to say that in nine cases out of ten it is wrong.[20]

The steps which Taylor took, partly as a gift, to show his gratitude to Sellers, an old-style manager, were to supersede the old-style managers.

One can also look at Taylor's attempts to control the pace and the method of work from the viewpoint of the workers. Here one must attempt to recapture the world image of the workers of this period. Most of the workers in Philadelphia's factories were first-generation immigrants from Germany and Ireland. Whereas today the primary association of the word "worker" is with a factory, this association did not yet exist in the middle of the nineteenth century. For most immigrants, factory work was an experience radically different from anything they were familiar with. For them "worker" meant artisan or craftsman, a familiar and respected figure in the traditional social order of the old country. For almost five hundred years, roughly from 1300 to 1800, the artisans and their guilds had held a position of high regard in European society. Thus, for a long time, they had been shaping the world image of a worker as a producer of goods. The prime element in this world image was that of work as a *total* experience. Though the division of work had started with the rise of the guilds, it was still a limited affair. A craftsman working with glass not only blew the glass but prepared the melting, cooling, and heating ovens, burned the special wood to get the ash which he himself mixed with sand. The craftsman had almost complete independence in the planning and carrying out of all operations, which were left to his individual judgment and skill. The high esteem for the European craftsman is further evidenced by the fact that the difference between the artisan and the artist (even linguistically) was not considered a great one.

The artisan was not an industrial worker but an industrial artist. For though one distinguished between art, which served the beautiful, and craft, which served the useful, there was general agreement with the Latin poet Horace that the real master is the one who combines the beautiful with the useful. Thus, a painter such as Dürer did not think of himself only as an artist but equally as a technician and craftsman. Similarly, in Italy, Brunelleschi and Donatello had walked through the streets dressed in the traditional garb and the wooden shoes of master craftsmen.[21] One has only to remember the smithy of Carl IX, the lathe of Louis XVI in the Louvre, and the watches made by Carl V in St. Juste to grasp the importance of and the respect paid to work as a craft.

For workers brought up with such a world image, Taylor's attempts at absolute regimentation and his methods of scientific management must have threatened their deepest beliefs, no less important for being quite unconscious. Thus, if they resisted and fought back harder than workers might today, it was because the threat was somehow perceived to be infinitely great, to run against their "deepest grain."

One could argue, with some justification, though without full proof, that this world image of work—as an area of psychological autonomy and self-fulfillment, of personal artistry, subjective, even idiosyncratic—that this world image, though less obvious today, persists in the deeper layers of our unconscious, and that the workers' fight in many countries against "rationalization" of work is at least partly a response to the threat to this world image. This, of course, raises many questions—How important is such a world image in an individual personality? How long does it take in a changing historical situation for such world images to change? Do they ever completely disappear or are their echoes left?—critical questions but perhaps of only peripheral concern to us here.

Starting sometime late in 1882, Taylor himself worked at

the time study in Midvale until 1883, when Emlen Miller was employed to devote his full time to it. The use of the stopwatch in the factory was nothing new, for work had been timed before. Adam Smith in his *Wealth of Nations* (1776) had listed the operations involved in the manufacture of pins, and it was conceivable and quite possible to time these operations to see how long each one actually took. This kind of work timing had been done in France in the eighteenth century, and Charles Babbage's *Economy of Machinery and Manufacture* contained statistical tables showing the average time taken by the operatives in the manufacture of pins.[22] This, however, was not time study. As Taylor said:

This table involves no study whatever of the movements of a man, nor of the time in which his movements *should* have been made. Mere statistics as to the time which a man takes to do a given piece of work do not constitute "time study." "Time study," as its name implies, involves a careful study of the time in which work ought to be done.[23]

Time study, then, enters into the realm of management control. Taylor has described the nature of the study in two parts—analytic and constructive—as follows:

1. Divide the work of a man performing any job into simple elementary movements.
2. Pick out all useless movements and discard them.
3. Study, one after another, just how each of several skilled workmen makes each elementary movement, and with the aid of a stopwatch select the quickest and best method of making each elementary movement known in the trade.
4. Describe, record, and index each elementary movement, with its proper time so that it can be quickly found.
5. Study and record the percentage which must be added to the actual working time of a good workman to cover unavoidable delays, interruptions, and minor accidents, etc.
6. Study and record the percentage which must be added to cover the newness of a good workman to a job, the first few times that he does it. (This percentage is quite large in jobs made up of a large number of different elements comprising a long sequence infrequently repeated. This factor grows smaller, however, as the work consists of a smaller

number of different elements in a sequence that is more frequently repeated.)

7. Study and record the percentage of time that must be allowed for rest, and the intervals at which rest must be taken, in order to offset physical fatigue.

The constructive work of time study is as follows:

8. Add together into various groups such combinations of elementary movements as are frequently used in the same sequence in the trade, and record and index these groups so that they can be readily found.

9. From these several records, it is comparatively easy to select the proper series of motions which should be used by a workman in making any particular article, and by summing the times of these movements, and adding proper percentage allowances, to find the proper time for doing almost any class of work.

10. The analysis of a piece of work into its elements almost always reveals the fact that many of the conditions surrounding and accompanying the work are defective; for instance, that improper tools are used, and that the machines used in connection with it need perfecting, that the sanitary conditions are bad, etc. And knowledge so obtained leads frequently to constructive work of a high order, to the standardization of tools and conditions, to the invention of superior methods and machines.[24]

We have treated the time study in some detail because of its central position in scientific management. Besides giving birth to a wholly new profession, industrial engineering, time and motion study was generally the first step in the introduction of scientific management into a factory. As anyone who has worked in the average factory of a developing country knows, "modernization" is often synonymous with Taylor's work and is heralded by the employment of the time-study man. It has been recently questioned whether one can, if fact, add "bits of motion" and claim that the total represents the most efficient motion; or whether in a unified motion, as in a Gestalt, the whole is not greater than the sum of the parts. This point is emphasized by James Gillespie, a leading British industrial engineer:

Motion study has become micromotionism and with its

motion cameras, therbligs, micromotion clocks . . . and its useless time charts, it has become a complex unwieldy technique. Worse still, with its . . . publication of principles such as that of minimum movement, it has divorced itself from practical, humanitarian knowledge.[25]

Daniel Bell adds that "practical, humanitarian" knowledge is the finding that a man's characteristic or "natural rhythms" in, for example, the use of his hands may ultimately be more efficient than the mechanistic concept of *the* one best way.[26] As Bell points out further, in American industry there are a dozen performance rating systems, volumes of "standard data" on specific jobs, "flow charts," and so on. By consulting a thick reference guide, *The Manual of Standard Time Data for Office,* an efficiency expert can, for example, determine whether a billing clerk is working at an expected speed. Each of his motions is filmed and then analyzed and timed against an electric clock constantly in the camera view, and thus each of his movements can be expressed in decimal fractions of an hour. There is a constant search by industrial engineers to find irreducible "atoms" of motion which can then be recombined in infinite variations. Thus, such an attempt is made in the creation of Methods-Time-Measurement (M-T-M) with its concise catalog of defined work motions (reach, move, turn, grasp, and so forth) with a scale of predetermined time values for each motion so that a standard time can be established for each job in the industry.[27]

Here it is not our intention either to describe the development of the time study or to go into its merits and demerits in detail. Our object is to try to see it in relation to the personality of its inventor, Frederick Taylor, to understand more clearly both the developmental aspects and the style of that relationship. After Taylor "found himself" at Midvale, time study was the first of a spate of innovations that followed. In its technique—the breaking down of work operations into their smallest movements and the obsession with time—we are able to see the way in which Taylor's indelible and idiosyncratic personal style—"compulsive" yet innovative—permeated scientific management, in an unconscious effort, or so it seems, to turn Midvale into a productive version of Emily Taylor's household, "a thing ruled, regular." We have already suggested that the object of the time study was to *depersonalize* control so that the hostility of the workers would no longer constitute a personal attack on Taylor but be directed against invincible science and scientific method. Thus, at every opportunity, Taylor stressed the scientific nature of the time study—even in the times which had to be added to a job to compensate for unavoidable delays and unpredictable breakdowns. The following exchange in the Hearings of the Special House Committee highlights this fact:

The Chairman:
By what scientific formula or mathematical calculation did you arrive at an addition of 20 to 27 per cent to the time which you have determined by that stop watch?

Mr. Taylor:
We have done that through a very careful study—and this study has been repeated over and over again—of workmen well suited to their jobs. They were told, "Now, men, we want to arrive at a proper allowance for unavoidable accidents and delays, and I want you to cooperate with me" . . . .

The Chairman:
Is not that 20 to 27 per cent arbitrarily arrived at by the judgment of a person watching the operation, of the time that should be added?

Mr. Taylor:
No, sir; not the arbitrary judgment of anyone. An arbitrary judgment would be something that a man guessed at. But this is a scientific investigation, a careful thorough scientific investigation of the facts. It is based on the fact that in perhaps as many as 20 cases, with different men on this general type of work, this figure has been proved to be correct. This is not founded on any one judgment; it is based on facts.[28]

But Taylor saw that it was not enough to determine merely the amount of work that ought to be done. The second problem was to secure the cooperation of the workers in producing the output determined by the time study as a "fair day's work." He was now faced with the problem of work motivation.

In the last chapter, we attempted to understand the dynamics of Taylor's conflict with the workers in Midvale and outlined the main elements of a system which was aimed at the resolution of this conflict. It is perhaps unnecessary to add that these obscure events in an otherwise undistinguished American factory were fated to be of profound significance for the work life of industrial workers throughout the world. The question that needs to be examined in greater detail relates to the validity of Taylor's solution in the general problem of human work; to what extent are the axioms of "scientific management" consistent with and how far do they violate the essential, or even, the *existential* "meaning" work has for an individual.

On being asked the criteria for "healthy personality," Freud is reported to have given a terse answer—"lieben und arbeiten" (love and work).[1] Disregarding the merits of the controversy surrounding the first part of his answer, the preeminent position of work in the life of an individual is rarely disputed in most of the world's cultures, or at least (in Spenglerian terms) in the "high cultures." In the industrial world as well as in countries aspiring to industrialization, the lives of men are work conscious and work oriented. This primacy of work in an individual's life is so taken for granted that at first glance it comes as something of a shock to learn that this phenomenon is of comparatively recent origin.

For the Greeks (one always starts with the Greeks), the ideal, the good, and by implication, the happy man was one who could avoid working. Work was a curse without any redeeming features. Their name for it—ponos—has the same root as the Latin *poena,* sorrow.[2] To the poets and the philosophers, from Homer to Xenophon to Plato, work was the revenge of gods who hated mankind. In that they held work to have a brutalizing effect on the mind, most of them despised not only the slaves who performed menial tasks but also the free artisans and craftsmen. The only form of

THE PROBLEM OF WORK 5

work that was grudgingly accepted as not unworthy of a citizen was agriculture, which brought livelihood, and especially independence—the Greek ideal.

As in many other spheres, the Roman adopted the Greek attitudes toward work. If an individual, that is, the citizen, was compelled to have an occupation, there were worthy occupations that came under the heading *utilitas,* and unworthy ones, *necessitas.* Cicero decreed that only two occupations were worthy of a free man, agriculture and big business, especially when either led to rural retirement as a country gentleman.³ To these, others added medicine and architecture and, of course, politics. All other occupations were the very doubtful privilege of the slaves.

Although the religions gave work more spiritual dignity, it was still viewed negatively. To the Hebrews, work was an expiation through which men atoned for the sins of their ancestors, while early Christianity recommended work not because of any intrinsic value but because it was painful and humiliating, a scourge for the pride of the flesh.

The modern view of work in Western culture—work as the basis of life—is generally thought to have originated with the Reformation and particularly with Luther, for whom work was a way of serving God. Philosophical elaborations of this view were provided by Locke, who saw in work the source of all possessions, and Adam Smith, who viewed work as the source of all wealth, and culminated in Marx, to whom work was not only the source of all productivity but the expression of man's humanity. Bergson not only agreed with Marx but went further in supplying work with a mystical dimension. To him, the development of man's work technology was the continuation of the *élan vital* that created the universe. Both to Marx and to Bergson, a man is truly *homo sapien* only when he is *homo faber.*

In Puritanism and especially in Calvinism, an intrinsic merit is attributed to work—work for the sake of work,

work as an end and purpose in itself. Although the Catholic conception of work did not go so far, the orthodox movement of Christian Socialism regards work as the foundation of all human progress, as a duty imposed by divine and human laws. This high value placed on work in an individual life is not limited to the West; witness the high status of Karmayoga ("Yoga of work") in the Indian philosophies of self-realization, in which work alone, disinterested work, without expectation of reward or fear of punishment, is held to be man's supreme duty. Such work is not only the highest form of human but also of Divine activity. As Krishna says in the *Bhagvad Gita*, "If I did not work, the worlds would be destroyed." Once again, work thus becomes the supreme human activity. Or, as Goethe expresses it in *Faust*, neither possession, nor power, nor sensuous satisfaction can fulfill man's desire for meaning in his life; he remains in all this separate from the whole, hence unhappy: only in being productively active can man make sense of his life.

In light of these earlier views of work and the fact that work is so often associated with burden, fatigue, monotony, as in Marx's "alienated" and Durkheim's "abnormal" work, one is led to ask whether the modern view of work is something more than the excessive outpouring of academic and literary minds. If work were everything it is said to be, why should we be preoccupied still with the issues of satisfaction and motivation in working? If work is the *sine qua non* of human happiness, why conjure up complex theories of work incentives? The answer is perhaps that even more than "love," the concept of work is not a very clear one and conceals beneath its surface many other, more troublesome issues.

What then is work? Negatively it can be defined as that which is not play, though the dynamics of both can be reduced to a simple three-step model: tension—action—discharge of tension.[4] It is obvious that work differs from play in adult life; in a child's case the difference is not so clear. Whereas for an adult, play is a vacation from social and economic reality, for a child, play is a form of dealing with experience by creating model situations and of mastering reality by experiment and planning.[5] What differentiates work from play in an adult is that it is a purposeful activity that produces commodities. Both the concepts "purposeful activity" and "production of commodities" are important. And yet, production of commodities can be accidental, while play, for example, a round of golf, can also be purposeful. This definition of work, then, though necessary, is not in itself sufficient. What we are interested to understand is the relationship of work to the individual. We want to know why one works, not only in the sense of why one works at all, but also: "Why does one work as one does?" In a sense, our attempt here is to interpret Camus's statement, "Without work all life goes rotten. But when work is soulless, life stifles and dies."[6]

At all times, from birth to death, a person lives in three systems: the system of the body (somatic aspect), the system of the ego (ego aspect), and the system of the polis (social aspect). Thus, throughout his life a man is simultaneously an organism, an ego, and a member of a social group. A disturbance in one system then always affects the other two systems. This fundamental structure we may take as the starting point for a systematic theory of work motivation. The drives, needs, and wants catalogued in various theories of motivation may, on closer examination, be seen as expressions of one or the other of these three aspects of man. Work motivation has thus the following three aspects:

1. The *labor* aspect to satisfy bodily needs (somatic).
2. The *career* aspect to satisfy ego needs (ego).
3. The *association* aspect to satisfy the social needs (social).

Let us consider each of these briefly.

1. THE LABOR ASPECT OF WORK—THE SOMATIC ASPECT

Hannah Arendt has made an important distinction between

"labor" and "work."[7] Etymologically, this distinction has always existed in the Indo-European group of languages, even though in different historical periods the words have often been used synonymously. Thus, in Latin, there is a difference between *laborare* and *facere*, in French between *travailler* and *ouvrer*, and in German between *arbeiten* and *werk*. The term "labor," then, would be limited to the purposeful activity necessary to satisfy one's own, and perhaps by extension, also one's family's primary bodily needs; work may be "productive," however, above and beyond the satisfaction of these needs. Work as drudgery, as a fatiguing necessity, is then related to its labor aspect. It is this aspect that has generally been held to be debasing and demeaning to the individual. It is this aspect Marx has in mind when he speaks of the "alienation of labor." In his view, capitalism would exaggerate the labor aspect of work:

What constitutes the alienation of labor? First, that the work is external to the worker, that it is not part of his nature; and that, consequently, he does not fulfill himself in his work but denies himself, has a feeling of misery rather than well being, does not develop freely his mental and physical energies but is physically exhausted and mentally debased. The worker therefore feels himself at home only during his leisure time; whereas at work he feels homeless. His work is not voluntary but imposed, forced labor. It is not the satisfaction of a need, but only a means for satisfying other needs.[8]

Marx thus condemned a situation in which the human being was becoming an *animal laborans,* for animals ". . . produce only under the compulsion of direct physical need, while man produces when he is free from physical need and only truly produces in freedom from such need."[9]

Thus, the condemnation of work and its drudgery in other historical epochs and cultures as well as by Marx is limited only to its labor aspect. It was the labor aspect that was the necessary evil mankind had to accept until the day, as Aristotle wrote, ironically, "when the shuttles fly back and forth of themselves, and the plectrum, untouched by human hands, makes the strings of the lyre resound."[10] In Marx's communist society, it was the labor aspect that was to be reduced to a minimum or even eliminated so that each day a man could work at as many different occupations as he cared to. This was the ultimate freedom promised in the future communism.

In the modern era, however, some men have placed the highest value on precisely this aspect of work; and these men have generally been the opponents of large-scale industrialization and mass industry. Tolstoy equated labor ("bread labor") with the highest form of practicing religion, and Gandhi shared his view that a man should produce only for himself and for his family's elementary needs:

Nine-tenths of humanity lives by tilling the soil. How much happier and more peaceful would the world become if the remaining tenth followed the example of the overwhelming majority at least to the extent of laboring for their food.[11]

From the labor, or the somatic, aspects of work, the answer to the question "Why does one work at all" would be, "One works because one must live"—an answer that is sanctioned by moral commandments. "He who does not work shall not eat." "In the sweat of thy brow shalt thou earn thy bread."

2. THE CAREER ASPECT OF WORK—THE EGO ASPECT

"I don't like work—no man does—but I like what is in the work—the chance to find yourself. Your own reality—for yourself, not for others—what no other man can ever know."[12] So Conrad wrote in *Heart of Darkness*.

By career, we mean here work activity through life as it relates to an individual's chosen occupation. Because of the predominantly clinical orientation of early psychoanalysis, work was studied mainly in relation to conflict situations in individual lives. Thus, the contributions to the problem of work in its career aspect fell mainly into three categories:[13] first, the relationship of career choice to a particularly important infantile conflict or impulse, as in the case of a builder of dams and bridges who as a child had difficulties establishing bladder control; second, the relationship of a

80

particular career to the existence of more or less conscious needs, as in the case of an actor whose narcissistic or exhibitionistic needs are satisfied by his profession; and third, the interpretation of a career as a component of an individual's defensive structure against disturbing impulses, thoughts, and feelings, as in the case of a social worker who has strong aggressive impulses that he wards off in the reaction-formation.

With the gradual development of ego psychology, however, it was realized that such explanations are only partial and that certain satisfactions derived from work are also indispensable and independent needs of the *ego*, the organizing principle of the individual personality.

Ives Hendrick first expressed this explicitly by postulating a "work principle," which stated that pleasure derives from the efficient use of the central nervous system in the performance of certain well-integrated ego functions that enable the individual to control or alter his environment.[14] It is a debatable point whether the ultimate motive for work lies in the gaining of this pleasure or whether it lies in the need for individual self-preservation, not in the sense of a direct instinctual urge but as mediated by intelligence and reinforced by conscience.[15] It is, however, generally accepted that work is one of the most highly integrated ego activities, the performance of which reduces tension.

Robert White has developed this further. In his view, work proceeds from an "effectance motivation."[16] An individual "wishes" or has the "need" to exert an influence upon his surroundings. Competence, the primary aim of the "effectance motivation," is defined by White as "an organism's capacity to interact effectively with its environment."[17] Effectance motivation aims at a feeling of efficacy; learning comes merely as its consequence. In a sense, it is the psychological counterpart of Luther's view that each kind of work is as good as another. As White describes it, "the feeling of efficacy is a biological endowment as basic as the satisfaction that accompanies feeding or sexual gratification, though not nearly as intense."[18] His evidence is based on studies of child behavior, particularly Piaget's, and the recent studies in animal behavior which show that the exploratory and playful activities of animals seem to be independent of the goal of these activities. White does not limit his concept of competence to dealings with the physical environment but extends it to what he calls social competence:

The feeling of being able to have some effect on people, to get them to listen, provide some of the things we want, receive some of the love and help we want to give—this feeling of social competence is a substantial foundation of self-respect and security.[19]

White's concept of social competence, if valid, would thus seem to form a bridge from the ego aspect of work to the findings of the "human relations" school to be discussed.

In the "time-table" of human development, work, according to Erikson, becomes the predominant motif in the fourth stage of a child's life, which corresponds to the latency period in Freud's writings.[20] Even in a child of two or three, of course, one sees the importance of prototypal ego satisfactions, such as in the mastery of standing, walking, vocalizing, and the like, but as the child approaches six, fantasy and play no longer satisfy all his needs. As Erikson puts it:

The ego's tendency to turn passivity into activity acquires a new field which is superior to the turning of passive to active in infantile play, since now the inner need of activity, practice and work completion is ready to meet the corresponding demands and opportunities in social reality.[21]

Work now enters a child's life as the field for identification with his parents as workers and tradition bearers rather than as sexual and familial beings. Work in this stage not only helps the child to transcend—or escape from—infantile sexual conflict, it also sets a positive developmental task for the individual ego. It is the beginning of a child's "technological ethos":

A sense of competence . . . characterises what eventually becomes workmanship. Ever since his "expulsion from paradise," of course, man has become inclined to protest work as drudgery or slavery, and to consider most fortunate those who seemingly can choose to work or not. The fact, however, is that man must learn to work, as soon as his capacities are ready to be "put to work," so that his ego's power may not atrophy.[22]

The common theme running through all these formulations of work motivation is the idea that effectiveness in work activity is necessary for healthy development and vital personality. Psychoanalytic practice and research show that an impairment in man's ability to work, whether due to internal conflicts or external circumstances, may have drastic effects on his healthy "con-"functioning.[23] Freud's "formula" of love and work has stood the test of new evidence.

3. THE ASSOCIATION ASPECT OF WORK—THE SOCIAL ASPECT

The French sociologist, Emile Durkheim, Taylor's contemporary, was one of the first to note the importance of the association aspect of work. In Durkheim's view, a "normal" division of labor was essentially a source of solidarity for an individual within a group. In such a "normal" division of labor the worker did not lose sight of his co-workers as he acted upon them and reacted to them.[24] Any form of work activity that failed to effect this "solidarity" was "abnormal."

Later research, particularly that of Elton Mayo and his followers, the so-called "human relations" school, confirmed that this association aspect was not only a postulated "normal" but an essential need in an individual's work activity. Mayo concluded that in work motivation the desire to stand well with one's fellows—the so-called human instinct of association—easily outweighed merely individual interests.[25] Whatever the merits of the dispute about the relative importance of individual needs, there is little doubt that issues of belonging, respect, and acceptance as a member of a group are critical to individual self-esteem and identity development and thus form a subtle but clear aspect of an individual's work motivation. It is these social satisfactions of work which we have termed its association aspect.

The very abbreviated form of the three-dimensional model of work motivation which has been presented here may be compared with another model, Abraham Maslow's "need categories."[26] Maslow postulates a need hierarchy, "higher" needs becoming dominant once "lower" needs are relatively satisfied. His categories are: physiological, safety, social, ego, and self-fulfillment needs. The physiological, ego, and social needs would correspond to our somatic, ego, and social aspects. The safety need we would interpret as a part—the "negative" aspect—of the three primary dimensions, arising in response to a threat to any one of the three primary aspects. The self-fulfillment need would appear to be an intense form of the ego aspect; in a sense, it is the ideal form (in Plato's sense) of the ego aspect—Conrad's "finding one's self."

Excepting perhaps the very basic forms of the somatic aspect, the question of hierarchical ordering is problematical. The relative importance of the three aspects of work motivation, their "mix" in the work activity of an individual, varies with his culture and its interplay with his work culture; it varies with the development of his personality and with his life stage; it varies with an individual's particular historical time. One is, of course, aware that the introduction of this element of relativity into work motivation makes the task of personnel management even more difficult than it already is. The inescapable conclusion is that any action aimed at increasing internal or external rewards can be effective only if it can successfully "locate" the individual in all three dimensions of work motivation. On the other hand, however, it is as much of a truism to say that each man is different as that all men are the same; the social definition of an occupation, the membership of a particular group, can be a rough guide to actions and programs for increasing work effectiveness.

Thus far we have been speaking of normal work activity. The problem of work motivation is, however, complicated by the fact that work often becomes the arena in which individuals act out neurotic conflicts. Work blocks or work inhibitions, for example, prevent some from performing effectively. More relevant to our study is the tyranny in a personality of an especially strong super-ego which may lead to a compulsive need to work, in which a day free from work provokes an anxiety that can be relieved only by working.

We have mentioned this compulsive element in Taylor's work activity. Taylor could never stop working long enough to relax. Leisure being anathema to him, he even worked at his play. He could not bear to see an idle machine or an idle man, or, as Daniel Bell puts it, "He himself never loafed and he'd be damned if anyone else would."[27] For Taylor, work not only had an intrinsic value but also a magical healing power. He wrote to a friend:

I most heartily agree with your views regarding the curative effects of hard work. I look upon it as the greatest blessing we have and almost every day of my life thank my stars that in spite of Lou's [his wife] illness, I have enough work to occupy all my spare time.[28]

We must ask to what extent this relationship to work was intensely personal—psychological—and to what extent it was cultural. In the Puritan ideology, the virtuous man was strong willed, active, austere, and hardworking. Idleness, luxury, prodigality, everything that softens the soul, was shunned as a deadly sin. Dislike of work was considered a sign that election to God's kingdom was doubtful. Work alone sufficed and pleased both God and man, *but* work could not be casual. Intermittent, occasional work would not do. Work had to be methodical, disciplined, rational, uniform, and hence specialized. It was one's duty to extract the greatest possible gain from one's work. Success was the certain indicator that the chosen profession was pleasing to God. It would thus be easy to explain Taylor's relationship to work as a reflection of the dominant Puritan ideology— and it would be equally superficial to do so. Ideology is transmitted to an individual through the social groups of which he is a member—family, class, and so on. That the large number of immigrants—German Protestants and Catholics and Irish Catholics—who worked in Philadelphia's factories shared this work ideology is doubtful. But we do know that Philadelphia's upper class—and Taylor's father —shared, at most, only certain elements of this ideology. We have already seen that though work was favored, intermittent, occasional, and casual work was the norm for a gentleman and that to extract the greatest possible gain from one's work was positively ungentlemanly, beneath the dignity of a "Proper Philadelphian." To strive for professional success lowered one's caste. Some of the workers serving under Taylor seemed to have dimly perceived this anomaly:

Another thing which impressed us was his love for work, regardless of the fact that he was not obliged to work, if we properly understood his financial condition, and this work was of the most strenuous kind. Even in recreation, or anything he went into, he went into it in a most strenuous way.[29]

Taylor's work habits thus seem to have been more a reflection of a personal drivenness than the expression of a cultural norm. His work was, however, also a source of ego gratification; its challenge, its demanding nature, and the immense pleasure he took in the solution of problems that arose during its course provided his work with the all-important ego dimension.[30] Henry Gantt employs a poem by Kipling in making the same point:

The fact that for several years he continually worked at problems that brought him no financial return is evidence that he had reached the stage when

"We shall work for an age at a sitting
And never be tired at all;
And no one shall work for money,
And no one shall work for fame;
But each for the joy of working
And only the Master shall praise,
And only the Master shall blame."[31]

It is only in the light of Taylor's conscious and unconscious attitudes toward work that one can understand his analysis of the restriction of output by the workers, first stated in a paper entitled, "Shop Management," which was read before the American Society of Mechanical Engineers in June 1903. In this paper, Taylor maintained that the workers restricted their output due to laziness, or as he called it, "soldiering."

"Soldiering" or, as it has also been variously called, "stalling," "quota restriction," "goldbricking" in the United States, *"bremsen"* (braking) in Germany, "hanging it out" or "Ca'canny" in English or Scottish, seems to have been a fact of most factory life ever since the industrial revolution. We shall here define it as the willful refusal by the workers to do more than what they believe should be turned out even when they are capable of it, which is at the same time certainly less than what their employers believe they can or should do. Everyone with an experience of factory life knows that "soldiering" is a widespread phenomenon of varying intensity, and apparently independent of economic systems and cultures. The following conversations in a perceptive paper[32] by Donald Roy could have (allowing for differences in language and monetary units) taken place in any machine shop in the world. In fact, they have a striking similarity to the arguments of the workers in Midvale, seventy years earlier. Here is an old worker initiating a new one:

"Don't you know," cried Starkey angrily, "that $1.25 an hour is the most we can make, even when we can make more! And most of the time we can't make that! Have you ever worked in piecework before?"

"No."

"I can see that! Well, what do you suppose would happen if I turned in $1.25 an hour on these pump bodies?"

"Turned in? You mean if you actually did the work?"

"I mean if I actually did the work and turned it in!"

"They'd have to pay you, wouldn't they? Isn't that the agreement?"

"Yes! They'd pay me—once! Don't you know that if I turned in $1.50 an hour on these pump bodies tonight, the whole goddamned Methods Department would be down here to-morrow? And they'd retime this job so quick it would make your head swim! And when they retimed it, they'd cut the price in half! And I'd be working for 85 cents an hour instead of $1.25!"

The comment of another worker on the job of a fellow worker:

"That's gravy! I worked on those, and I could turn out nine an hour. I timed myself at six minutes."

I was surprised. "And I got ten hours," said Ed. "I used to make out in four hours and fool around the rest of the night."

An entry in the writer-worker's diary:

Ed claimed that he could make over $3 an hour on the two machines he was running, but he could turn in only $1.60 an hour or, occasionally, $1.45 or $1.50 for the two machines together. Ed said that he always makes out for ten hours by eleven o'clock, that he has nothing to do from 11:00 to 3:00, and has even left early, getting someone to punch his time card for him.

"That's the advantage of working nights," said Ed. "You can make out in a hurry and sit around, and nobody says anything. But you can't get away with it on day shift with all the big shots around. Jack has to take it easy on these housings to make them last eight hours, and that must be tough."

The writer who had been subject to warnings, predictions, and pressures from his fellow workers could now record:

By August I was more sophisticated in the art of loafing, and complaints of being "stymied" were not recorded. . . . I reached my peak in quota restriction in June 27, with but three and a half hours of productive work out of eight.

Writing in 1908, the German sociologist Max Weber observed that a factory may restrict output due to social as well as economic circumstances—namely, in those industries in which the workers themselves exercise an influence on the amount of work turned out.[33] He goes on to say:

The fact that the attitude (Gesinnung) of the work force and particularly its relationship to the employer, influences the output of work has been reported in no uncertain terms though without exact proof. The complaints on the "braking" done by the workers are quite old, but in the last few years they have undoubtedly increased and are, it seems, exactly parallel to (1) the increasing rationalization of the wage systems and (2) the increasingly better organization of the employers and the consequent lessening of the chances of a [successful] strike. However, if the complaints of the employers blame the spread of "braking" on trade-unions, then this view, at least as of today, seems to be a much too superficial one. "Braking," not only the unintentional and intermittent, but the conscious and the intentional, will occur even in the absence of union organizations wherever the workforce or even some considerable fraction of it, feels some measure of solidarity. Though it can be the expression of more or less consciously realized general dissatisfaction (Misstimmung) amongst the workers, it is mainly the way in which the work force, consciously and stubbornly, wages a struggle against the employer on the price of its work. It can have as its object the raising of piece rates, or, when the piece rates remain constant, in the maintenance of the traditional tempo of work. Whenever "braking" is a part of the wage policy (Akkordpolitik) of the workers, it represents the unavoidable reaction to the wage policy of the employer the results of which the workers continually feel on their own bodies.[34]

Although Weber notes "general dissatisfaction" as one of the causes of "braking," his analysis centers on the differing economic interests of the employer and the workers. Although he mentions the associational aspect of work (necessary group solidarity), his analysis of the causes of "braking" focuses on what we have called the labor aspect. According to Weber, "braking" becomes unavoidable whenever the management wants to change the wage rates or methods of work in any way that the workers hold disadvantageous to them. It is often preferred to the strike since

in contrast to the strike it neither needs the apparatus of a formal organization nor the provision of strike funds and does not put the workers completely "out of bread" (gänzlich aus dem Brot), the workers only temporarily restricting their earnings. In comparison to the strike, the workers' tactical situation is also better insofar as the opponent is not always in a position to prove how and how much the individual workman has been "braking." A formal dismissal of an otherwise not uncapable worker on the unproven grounds of "braking" gives the employer a bad reputation wherever the workers are not completely powerless.[35]

In Weber's view, "braking" took place in eras of economic upswing, and especially whenever a factory attempted to introduce a change in the line of products. He predicted that with the increasing organization of employers, "braking" would come to be more and more preferable to the strike. From Weber's analysis it follows that the strike is not the sole or even a fully reliable indicator of industrial conflict. Rather, a strike would appear to indicate merely the degree of formal organization among employers and workers. A reliable account of industrial conflict in a factory, industry, or a country would have to assess the amount and intensity of "braking," a task whose difficulties are apparent.

In contrast to Weber, Mayo argues that it was not the economic conflict with the employer that led to output restriction but the breakdown of the social cohesion of groups after the industrial revolution—a breakdown precipitated by the rapidity of technological change and by the lag in men's adjustment to it. The workers were unable to develop what he has called the "nonlogical" social code that is typical of social adjustment:

The non-logical response, that, namely, which is in strict conformity with a social code, makes for social order and discipline, *for effective collaboration in a restricted range of activity,* and for happiness and a sense of security in the individual.[36]

This nonlogical response was destroyed since

In the United States changes finally came with such rapidity that any attempt to save the non-logic of collaboration became futile. It was as if we were to drill a regiment with a new set of commands and a new drill book every day. The result was not discipline and collaboration but disorder and resistance. The rapid pace of industrial development, uninformed by human research or knowledge, dispersed the last possibilities of collaborate and social effort and imposed upon the workers a low level of human organization from which social participation and social function were excluded. This low level organization, like trade unionism, also represents a conservative and reactionary attempt to conserve human values; its chief symptom is "stalling," a procedure apparently resented as much by the workers themselves as by the management. Since this seems to be as characteristic of Russia as of the United States, it is probable that the human problems involved are fundamental and contain no "political" element. Again it may be said that the question is not who is to control. . . .[37]

In Mayo's view, the restriction of output by the workers is thus not a response to the employer's attempt to change the price of work or work conditions; rather, it occurs because it is "functional" to the solidarity and emotional security of the group in the face of threatening changes. The employer is only indirectly involved, as the (perhaps) uncomprehending introducer of these changes. To combat "stalling," the employer would have to analyze and understand the process in terms of logical reasoning, the nonlogic of social codes in action, and the irrational elements involved. "If we had an elite capable of such analysis, very many of our difficulties would dwindle to a vanishing point."[38] Mayo's analysis thus falls exclusively into what we have called the associational aspect of work.

Before analyzing the phenomenon of output restriction from the third, the *ego* aspect of our model, it may be instructive to assess the relevance of traditional psychoanalytic formulations to the problem. Freud's work on group psychology comes immediately to mind. Without going into the ontogeny ("father-sons") or his speculations on the phylogeny ("the primal horde") of groups, let us briefly review Freud's views on group formation and group solidarity.

In his observations on the army as a group, Freud noted that the soldier takes his commander as his ideal, as the one "who-he-wants-to-be" (ego ideal), while he himself identifies with his fellow soldiers and derives from this community the obligation of mutual service and help.[39] The members of the group, originally rivals for the love of their leader, settle for equal shares of his love. They have thus succeeded in identifying with one another by means of a love for the same person. Group solidarity thus derives from what was originally envy, and the social feeling or "group spirit" of the members is based upon the reversal of an original mutual hostility into a positive bond of identification. The ideal, now incarnate in the leader, imposes restrictions, prohibitions, and limitations on the individual. In the subordinate individual there arises the conflict between attempts at complete domination of the leader and absolute submission to him, both of which are unconsciously designed to take sole possession of him. Freud suggested that this separation of the ego ideal from the ego in an individual cannot be borne long without temporary and periodic suspensions of the ideal which, in turn, may result in periodic ego rebellions, either "spontaneous" or "incited" by a perceived ill treatment from the ideal.

In a work group then, in the first case, output restriction would tend to be periodic and almost inevitable. In the second, it would be accompanied by dissatisfaction and guilt because of the conflict between ego and ego ideal in the individual worker. Freud compared this tension to psychogenic melancholia; and Mayo probably had this manifestation in mind when he wrote that "stalling" may be resented not only by the managers but also by the workers. Such an analysis is, however, too generalized and assumes certain fundamental analogies between an army and a modern factory which are untenable. In the case of a modern factory, the existence at all of such an ego ideal—in this pure form—is not self-evident. If it exists, where is it located? Further, although the kinds of transferences and resistances Freud describes are, of course, possible in certain groups at certain levels of factory organization, in the main, Freud's model is more descriptive of the charismatic than the bureaucratic phenomenon.

The restriction of output can perhaps be explained more coherently with reference to the ego aspect of our model. As part of the worker's effectance motivation—effective interaction with his environment—restriction of output may be the expression of his fight to maintain or control this environment. Restriction of output is thus still a possibility even if the changes made by the management aim to improve this environment without any economic loss to the worker.

There is no single explanation for the restriction of work output; an analysis may be based on any one of the somatic, ego, or social aspects of work. In a concrete case, the problem becomes one of taking all three aspects into account and giving each one its proper weight. For the worker, faced with radical change, it is the highly subjective "mix" of these three aspects—the conscious and unconscious sense of relative "advantages" and "disadvantages"—which would govern "soldiering" activity.

As mentioned earlier, Frederick Taylor stated the *raison d'être* of scientific management to be the development of a just system to deal with "soldiering." His analysis of the problem, based on his own working experience and stated in his own colorful language, is, in some aspects, strikingly similar to Weber's. Thus:

This loafing or soldiering proceeds from two causes. First, from the natural instinct and tendency of men to take it easy, which may be called natural soldiering. Second, from more intricate second thought and reasoning caused by their relations with other men, which may be called systematic soldiering. There is no question that the tendency of the average man (in all walks of life) is toward working at a slow, easy gait, and that it is only after a good deal of thought and observation on his part or as a result of example, conscience, or external pressure that he takes a more rapid pace. There are, of course, men of unusual energy, vitality, and ambition who naturally choose the fastest gait, who set their own standards, and who work hard, even though it may be against their best interests. But these few uncommon men only serve by forming a contrast to emphasize the tendency of the average.

This common tendency to "take it easy" is greatly increased by bringing a number of men together on similar work and at uniform standard rate of pay by the day.

Under this plan the better men gradually but surely slow down their gait to that of the poorest and the least efficient. When a naturally energetic man works for a few days beside a lazy one, the logic of the situation is unanswerable.

"Why should I work hard when that lazy fellow gets the same pay that I do and does only half as much work?"

A careful time study of men working under these conditions will disclose facts which are ludicrous as well as pitiable.

To illustrate: The writer has timed a naturally energetic workman who, while going and coming from work, would walk at a speed of from three to four miles per hour, and not infrequently trot home after a day's work. On arriving at his work he would immediately slow down to speed of about one mile an hour. When, for example, wheeling a loaded wheelbarrow, he would go at a good fast pace even uphill in order to be as short a time as possible under load, and immediately on the return walk slow down to a mile an hour, improving every opportunity for delay short of actually sitting down. In order to be sure not to do more than his lazy neighbor, he would actually tire himself in his effort to go slow.

These men were working under a foreman of good reputation and highly thought of by his employer, who, when his attention was called to this state of things, answered: "Well, I can keep them from sitting down, but the devil can't make them get a move on while they are at work."

The natural laziness of men is serious, but by far the greatest evil from which both workmen and employers are suffering is the systematic soldiering which is almost universal under all the ordinary schemes of management and which results from careful study on the part of the workmen of what will promote their best interests.

The writer was much interested recently in hearing one small but experienced golf caddy boy of twelve explaining to a green caddy, who had shown special energy and interest, the necessity of going slow and lagging behind his man when he came up to the ball, showing him that since they were paid by the hour, the faster they went the less money they got, and finally telling him that if he went too fast the other boys would give him a licking.

This represents a type of systematic soldiering which is not, however, very serious, since it is done with the knowledge of the employer, who can quite easily break it up if he wishes.

The greater part of the systematic solidering, however, is done by the men with the deliberate object of keeping their employers ignorant of how fast work can be done. So universal is soldiering for this purpose that hardly a competent workman can be found in a large establishment, whether he works by the day or on piece work, contract work, or under any of the ordinary systems, who does not devote a considerable part of his time to studying just how slow he can work and still convince his employer that he is going at a good pace.

The causes for this are, briefly, that practically all employers determine upon a maximum sum which they feel it is right for each of their classes of employees to earn per day, whether their men work by day or by piece.

Each workman soon finds out about what this figure is for his particular case, and he also realizes that when his employer is convinced that a man is capable of doing more work than he has done, he will find sooner or later some way of compelling him to do it with little or no increase of pay.

Employers derive their knowledge of how much of a given class of work can be done in a day from either their own experience, which has frequently grown hazy with age, from casual and unsystematic observation of their men, or at best from records which are kept, showing the quickest time in which each job has been done. In many cases the employer will feel almost certain that a given job can be done faster than it has been, but he rarely cares to take the drastic measures necessary to force men to do it in the quickest time, unless he has an actual record proving conclusively how fast the work can be done.

It evidently becomes for each man's interest, then, to see that no job is done faster than it has been in the past. The younger and less experienced men are taught this by their elders, and all possible persuasion and social pressure is brought to bear upon the greedy and selfish men to keep them from making new records which result in temporarily increasing their wages, while all those who come after them are made to work harder for the same old pay.

Under the best day work of the ordinary type, when accurate records are kept of the amount of work done by each man and of his efficiency, and when each man's wages are raised as he improves, and those who fail to rise to a certain standard are discharged and a fresh supply of carefully selected men are given work in their places, both natural and systematic soldiering can be largely broken up. This can only be done, however, when the men are thoroughly convinced that there is no intention of establishing piece work even in the remote future, and it is next to impossible to make men believe this when the work is of such a nature that they believe piece work to be practicable. In most cases their fear of making a record which will be used as a basis for piece work will cause them to soldier as much as they dare.

It is, however, under piece work that the art of systematic soldiering is thoroughly developed; after a workman has had the price per piece of the work he is doing lowered two or three times as a result of his having worked harder and increased his output, he is likely entirely to lose sight of his employer's side of the case and become imbued with a grim determination to have no more cuts if soldiering can prevent it. Unfortunately for the character of the workman, soldiering involves a deliberate attempt to mislead and deceive his employer, and thus upright and straight-forward workmen are compelled to become more or less hypocritical. The employer is soon looked upon as an antagonist, if not an enemy, and the mutual confidence which should exist between a leader and his men, the enthusiasm, the feeling that they are all working for the same end and will share in the results is entirely lacking.

The feeling of antagonism under the ordinary piece-work system becomes in many cases so marked on the part of the men that any proposition made by their employers, however reasonable, is looked upon with suspicion, and soldiering becomes such a fixed habit that men will frequently take pains to restrict the product of machines which they are running when even a large increase in output would involve no more work on their part.[40]

This description of soldiering, apart from the analysis of its cause, shows a remarkable insight into the prevailing practices not only of the 1880s but also of the present time, as a comparison with the earlier reported workers' conversations would conclusively show.

Taylor's emphasis on the exclusively economic aspect of the problem and on the primacy of economic man was to have considerable influence on the course of industrial management, for he alone among the first writers on the subject held as his main interest the provision of guidance and suggestions to managers as to how to combat this "systematic soldiering." His emphasis on the economic man is not only in the classic tradition of Adam Smith and Ricardo but is shared, at least to a certain degree, by many sociologists today. Thus Roy writes:

Now the operators in my shop made noises like economic men. Their talk indicated that they were canny calculators and that the dollar sign fluttered at the masthead of every machine. Their actions were not always consistent with their words; and such inconsistency calls for further probing. But it could be precisely because they were alert to their economic interests—that the operators did not exceed their quotas. It might be inferred from their talk that they did not turn in excess earnings because they felt that to do so would result in piecework price cuts; hence the consequences would be either reduced earnings from the same amount of effort expended or increased effort to maintain the take-home level.[41]

Similarly, the German sociologist Helmut Schelsky reports that the answer of a majority of the German workers to the question, "Why does one work?" was "to live" or "to earn money."[42]

Taylor's cure for soldiering was the application of the "task and bonus idea." The task idea was that management would plan the work of every workman at least one day in advance, each worker then receiving complete written instructions describing in detail the task he is to accomplish, the time required (determined by the time study), and the means to be used.[43] Taylor goes on to say:

There is absolutely nothing new in the task idea. Each one of us will remember that in his own case this idea was applied with good results in his schoolboy days. No efficient teacher would think of giving a class of students an indefinite task to learn. Each day a definite, clear-cut task is set by the teacher before each scholar, stating that he must learn just so much of the subject; and it is only by this means that proper, systematic progress can be made by the students. . . . All of us are grown-up children and it is equally true that the average workman will work with the greatest satisfaction, both to himself and to his employer, when he is given each day a definite task which he is to perform in a given time, and which constitutes a proper day's work for a good workman. This furnishes the workman with a clear-cut standard, by which he can throughout the day measure his own progress, and the accomplishment of which affords him the greatest satisfaction.[44]

In Taylor's view, the ego needs of work could be fulfilled— at least for the average workman—in the *completion* of the work rather than in the *challenge* it afforded. If the ego needs still remained unfulfilled, then this was the price of progress:

Now when through all of this teaching and this minute instruction the work is apparently made so smooth and easy for the workman, the first impression is that this all makes him a mere automaton, a wooden man. As the workmen frequently say when they first come under the system, "Why, I am not allowed to think or move without someone interfering or doing it for me!" The same criticism and objection, however, can be raised against all other modern subdivision of labor.[45]

In the recollections of men who first worked under scientific management there is a note of hidden pathos when they talk of what this change meant.

. . . he [Taylor] would always say that he had others to think, and we were supposed to do the work. I remember he said to me, many times, I have you for your strength and mechanical ability, and we have other men paid for thinking, and I think he used to try to carry this out pretty well. But I would never admit to him that I was not allowed to think. We used to have some pretty hot arguments just over this point.[46]

Similarly, Taylor downgraded the associational needs of work activity, holding them to be inimical to the ideal of efficiency.

As another illustration of the value of a scientific study of the motives which influence workmen in their daily work, the loss of ambition and initiative will be cited, which takes place in workmen when they are herded into gangs instead of being treated as separate individuals. A careful analysis had demonstrated the fact that when workmen are herded toegther in gangs, each man in the gang becomes far less efficient than when his personal ambition is stimulated, that when men work in gangs their individual efficiency falls almost invariably down to or below the level of the worst men in the gang; and that they are all pulled down instead of being elevated by being herded together. For this reason a general order had been issued in the Bethlehem Steel Works that not more than four men were to be allowed to work in a labor gang without a special permit, signed by the General Superintendent of the Works, this special permit to extend for one week only. It was arranged that as far as possible each laborer should be given a separate individual task.[47]

True to his concept of the economic man, Taylor held that a worker's only motivation for accomplishing a "scientifically determined" task was an extra bonus, 30 to 100 percent above the going rate. He insisted on the importance of this bonus in all his writings and constantly recommended that the piece rate, once determined by the time study, should not be ordinarily cut for any reason if the confidence of the worker was to be kept intact. Scientific management could thus eliminate soldiering first, by being able to prove the fact of soldiering, and second, by providing a high enough economic incentive. These twin ideas have dominated industrial management to a large degree since the death of Frederick Taylor.

The years between 1881 and 1890, when Taylor left Midvale, may be called the "years of achievement." Relatively freed from personal anxiety, he was now able to direct his tremendous energy toward revising and incorporating a theoretical solution into a practical system. These nine years brought a body of innovative achievement that is exceptional by any standard. By 1883, at the age of twenty-seven, Taylor had received his master's degree in mechanical engineering, through home study, from the Stevens Institute of Technology. By 1884, after a period of only six years, he had advanced from the position of unskilled laborer to that of chief engineer of Midvale. This was also the year in which he married Louise M. Spooner, a girl he had known since his childhood. Though he still worked hard, the frantic work activity of the weekends and the midnight runs through the deserted streets of Germantown were a thing of the past. By 1886, the superintendent of Midvale, Davenport, had adopted "crazy" Taylor's general methods for the entire works. Indeed, he was slowly winning a grudging respect from his fellow executives, who eventually began to concede "that in the madness of a man who gets two forgings turned where only one had been turned before, there must be a gleam of method, and that it might be a good thing for the works in general to go crazy to this extent."[1]

This chapter then considers Taylor's work, or his system, if one will, and how it differed from the traditional methods of the average factory. Here it must be remembered that even Taylor's engineering work, with small exceptions, was geared toward making his solution concrete: how to predetermine scientifically that elusive quantum of work which each worker should turn out daily. His investigations in metal cutting were begun with this one object in mind: the cutting speed of a machine, the feed and depth of the cut, the appropriate tool, could no longer be left to the subjective judgment and discretion of the individual machinist.

6 MIDVALE: THE INNOVATIVE PERIOD

The one best way, the only scientific combination of these variables, had to be found:

. . . our problem is to take the work and machines as we find them in a machine shop, and by properly changing the countershaft speeds, equipping the shop with tools of the best quality and shapes, and then making a slide rule for each machine to enable an intelligent mechanic with the aid of these slide rules to tell each workman how to do each piece of work in the quickest time.[2]

The object was to resolve three crucial questions—shape of tools, speed, and feed—with answers now to be provided by the management with the aid of slide rules rather ". . . than they were formerly by the machinists, each one of whom ran his own machine, etc., to suit his foreman or himself."[3] The technical problem was a complicated one, including as it did twelve variables: the quality of the metal to be cut; the diameter of the work; the depth of the cut; the thickness of the shaving; the elasticity of the work and the tool; the shape or contour of the cutting edge of the tool, together with its clearance and lip angles; the chemical composition of the steel from which the tool is made; the heat treatment of the tool (whether a copious stream of water or other cooling medium is used on it); the duration of the cut; the pressure of the chip or shaving upon the tool; the changes of speed and feed possible in the lathe; and the pulling and feeding power of the lathe. In spite of the considerable inconvenience to the shop, Taylor received Sellers' permission to start experiments along these lines in 1881. Although the experiments were not completed until twenty-six years later, the basic ones were carried out in Taylor's Midvale period. The sheer magnitude of the task and Taylor's conscientious comprehensiveness and utter devotion to detail stagger the imagination when one compares the fact that the German Society of Engineers, conducting the same types of experiments in 1901, limited themselves to about 220 experiments and did not include more than four variables. Similarly, between 1902 and 1903, when eight manufacturing firms in England, acting jointly with the Manchester Municipal School of Technology, conducted these experiments, they considered only the joint effect of four or five variables. Taylor conducted between thirty and fifty thousand recorded experiments and many others of which no record was kept, using almost 800,000 pounds of steel and iron.[4] The important steps in these investigations, as described by Taylor, are as follows:

In 1881, the discovery that a round-nosed tool could be run under given conditions at a much higher cutting speed and therefore turn out much more work than the old-fashioned diamond-point tool.

In 1881, the demonstration that, broadly speaking, the use of coarse feeds accompanied by their necessarily slow cutting speeds would do more work than fine feeds with their accompanying high speeds.

In 1883, the discovery that a heavy stream of water poured directly upon the chip at the point where it is being removed from the steel forging by the tool would permit an increase in cutting speed, and therefore in the amount of work done of from 30 to 40 per cent.

In 1883, the completion of a set of experiments with round-nosed tools; first, with varying thickness of feed when the depth of the cut was maintained constant; and, second, with varying depths of cut while the feed remained constant, to determine the effect of these two elements on the cutting speed.

In 1883, the demonstration of the fact that the longer a tool is called upon to work continuously under pressure of a shaving, the slower must be the cutting speed, and the exact determination of the effect of the duration of the cut upon the cutting speed.

In 1883, the development of formulae which gave mathematical expression to the two broad laws above referred to. Fortunately, these formulae were of a type capable of logarithmic expression and therefore suited to the gradual mathematical development extending through a long period of years, which resulted in making our slide rules, and solved the whole problem in 1901.

In 1833, the starting of a set of experiments on belting.

In 1883, the measurement of the power required to feed a round-nosed tool with varying depths of cut and thickness of shaving when cutting a steel tire. This experiment showed that a very dull tool required as much pressure to feed it as to drive the cut. This was one of the most important discoveries made by us and as a result all steel cutting machines purchased since that time by the Midvale Steel Company have been supplied with feeding power equal to their driving power and vary greatly in excess of that used on standard machines.

In 1884, the design of an automatic grinder for grinding tools in lots and the construction of a tool room for storing and issuing tools ready-ground to men.

From 1885 to 1889, the making of a series of practical tables for a number of machines in the shops of the Midvale Steel Company, by the aid of which it was possible to give definite tasks each day to the machinists who were running machines, and which resulted in a great increase in their output.

In 1886, the demonstration that the thickness of the chip or layer of metal removed by the tool has a much greater effect upon the cutting speed than any other element, and the practical use of this knowledge in making and putting into everyday use in our shops a series of broad-nosed cutting tools which enabled us to run with a coarse feed at as high a speed as had been before attained with round-nosed tools when using a fine feed, thus substituting, for a considerable portion of the work, coarse feeds and high speeds for our old maxim of coarse feeds and slow speeds.[5]

As Taylor mentions earlier in his work *On the Art of Cutting Metals*, the rough tables used at Midvale were replaced by the slide rules developed between 1899 and 1902, which made it practical for a workman to use Taylor's formulas and laws. The experiments on cutting metals that were conducted after he left Midvale resulted in the discovery that tools made from chromium-tungsten steels when heated to the melting point would do from two to four times as much work. The development of high-speed steel, called the Taylor-White process, was held to be an extremely important one, saving the machine industry of the

United States hundreds of millions of dollars per year, and in the view of some, contributing to the American victory in the First World War: "By means of these high-speed tools the United States during the World War was able to turn out five times the munitions that it otherwise could have done in the same time."[6] Yet to Taylor this was only accessory to his real aim. He said:

While many of the results of these experiments are both interesting and valuable, we regard as of by far the greatest value that portion of our experiments and of our mathematical work which has resulted in the development of the slide rules; i.e., the patient investigation and mathematical expression of the exact effect upon the cutting speed of such elements as the shape of the cutting edge of the tool, the thickness of the shaving, the depth of the cut, the quality of the metal being cut and the duration of the cut, etc. This work enables us to fix a daily task with a definite time allowance for each workman who is running a machine tool, and to pay the men a bonus for rapid work.[7]

In these earlier days, Taylor's reputation was primarily based on his engineering accomplishments; Taylor himself, however, considered them only a part of his whole system of management. At a joint meeting of the British Institution of Mechanical Engineers and the A.S.M.E. at Birmingham in 1910, at which Taylor was present, the subject of discussion was "High Speed Tools and Machines." Extensive references were made to Taylor's work. In due course, Taylor himself rose to speak:

"The proceedings of the American Society," he said, "have been burdened to such an extent with what I have said on the subject of high-speed steel and similar topics, that I feel it would be improper for me to make any further remarks on that point. I do, however, welcome the opportunity of speaking upon the far broader subject of which the art of cutting metals and the proper use of machine tools is but one of the small elements, namely, the great opportunity, as well as the duty, which lies before us as engineers of taking such steps as will, during the next few years, result in a very material increase of output of every man and every machine in their manufacturing establishments. The importance of obtaining this increase of output is that, in my mind, it presents the only opportunity open to us, measurably speaking, of settling the great labour problem which faces both of our countries. I say without hesitation that in the average establishments in America, not in all the establishments, it is possible to double the output of the men and the machines just as they stand now, and I believe the same is true throughout this country. It gives us the opportunity at the same time to give the men what they want most—higher wages, shorter hours, better working conditions; and, on the other hand, to give the companies what they most need—a lower labour cost, so that they might be able more successfully to compete at home and abroad."[8]

With the development of the slide rules, he had reached one of his goals, "that of taking control of the machine shop out of the hands of the many workmen, and placing it completely in the hands of the management, thus superseding 'rule of thumb' by scientific control."[9]

Taylor's object, total control over the job and its performance, could be endangered by many factors; a workman might fail to perform his task because something went wrong with the machine, or because he was delayed by a slipping belt, or had to wait for the instructions, tools, or materials needed for a new job. For the full utilization of the time study of the man and the machine and the full implementation of scientific management, *all* the conditions of the job had to be standardized at the highest possible level of efficiency. Take the example cited earlier, the standardization of tools. It would be far simpler, Taylor maintained, to have all the tools ground by one man, in one central shop, to few simple but rigidly exact shapes than to allow each machinist to spend a part of his working day at the grindstone, grinding his tools with wrong curves and wrong angles "merely because bad shapes are easier to grind than good."[10]

We have already described the workers' response to such radical measures of standardization. Their uneasiness and latent sense of impoverishment are evident throughout the congressional hearings called in 1912 to examine Taylor's system. The following exchange between a workers' representative and a foreman witness is one of innumerable examples scattered throughout the bulky records of the congressional investigation:

Mr. Jennings:
Yes, but under the old system when a man got a good lathe tool or a good planer tool, wasn't it the custom to take good care of that tool, and didn't he think almost as much of it as he did of the dollars he earned?
Mr. Mackean:
Yes, that is very true.[11]

Other innovations proceeding from the logic of the new control followed: the establishment of a repair shop with standardized procedures for the inspection and repair of machine tools and belting; the setting up of a central planning room which scheduled the route of each assembly and subassembly in advance—the forerunner of the assembly line technique; the introduction of a refined cost-accounting system; the systematization of purchase and inventory control; the use of printed job and instruction cards that informed the management how much of a man's and a machine's time was devoted to each product; the replacement of the multifunctional single foreman with four or five supervisors each of whom had a special function (the only Taylor concept to have been completely discarded). These innovations became standard shop practice, and with slight modifications have remained so to this day. The blueprint of a system for the planning, coordination, and control of human cooperation as it relates to the production of goods was thus marked out and filled in with many of its characteristic details; and yet its revolutionary importance, undeniable in the context of job and factory, has remained obscure in the historical record. None of these innovations in itself was spectacular; more often than not, only certain small changes in organization were involved. But, as Hugh Aitken has expressed it, "History has done Frederick Taylor less than justice for these inconspicuous innovations have probably exercised a more far-reaching influence on industrial practice than has the conspicuous innovation of stop-watch time study."[12]

A bare outline of the elements of scientific management is perhaps not sufficient for an appreciation of their revolutionary importance in industrial history. Fortunately, we have an exhaustive description of the management methods in one factory both *before* and *after* the introduction of scientific management—the Watertown Arsenal. It was in the Watertown Arsenal that worker protest over the introduction of the new methods led to the setting up of the frequently mentioned Congressional Committee to Investigate the Taylor and Other Systems of Shop Management.[13]

In the period between 1909 and 1912 when scientific management was introduced, the Watertown Arsenal, situated eight miles west of Boston, consisted of five main buildings —the smith shop, the machine shop, the erecting shop, the foundry, and the administration building—and employed five-hundred civilians in addition to its military personnel.[14] Though the Watertown Arsenal (one of five under the Department of Ordnance) manufactured a wide variety of smaller articles such as gun forgings for mobile artillery, frames for pack saddles, artillery targets, and armour-piercing projectiles for seacoast guns, its principal product was gun carriages for seacoast and field whose production involved the manufacture and assembly of some 4,500 different components. Technically, the arsenal was hardly modern and had more than its share of obsolete equipment; its management, however, was very similar to, neither better nor worse than, the average industrial establishment in the country.[15]

Under the old management system when an order was received by the arsenal, the correspondence office, directly under the commanding officer, would prepare a shop order in general terms naming the product and the quantity to be manufactured. Copies of the order were then sent to the foremen, who were thereafter held responsible for filling the order. A foreman had to get the drawings to find out what he had to make, compile a list of the parts to be manufactured, and make up a file of raw materials to be converted into products. In addition to these duties, he was responsible for the supervision of the workers and the maintenance of shop discipline. The foreman then had to write out the job cards for the workers and the requisitions for the materials, sending for the materials when he needed them. The stresses under which a foreman labored were many and heavy.

Burdened with clerical duties, the foreman was left with very little time for supervision of the workers. In lieu of advance planning, material delivered to the shop was simply left near a convenient (or inconvenient) door. When a worker finished a given job, he would go to his foreman for another job assignment, find the material, and either alone or with assistance move it to his machine. He would then track down the drawings and work specifications and go after the required tool. These haphazard preliminaries were doubly expensive in that they demanded no skill on the part of a worker trained to manufacture, and furthermore, all the while the machine tool lay idle. Once the machinist had collected his material, his drawings, and his tools, it was then his "duty" to study the drawings and plan a way of doing the job.[16]

The machinist would grind his own tools, select his own speed and feed, and, if the belting was defective, repair it himself before starting the work. There was no coordination of work, since the foreman had no means of knowing when he could expect the delivery of the raw or semifinished materials. There was practically no stock on hand, and most of the material was bought only after an order was received.

The dates of delivery were so uncertain that frequently there were inordinate delays, with the result that in order to keep the workmen busy, they were given "busy work" with the idea of putting it aside once the material for the pressing jobs was received.[17]

The waste of materials was enormous, since the foremen customarily requested larger quantities than were actually needed, thinking it a good idea to have a little surplus that could be used here and there on odd jobs without being accounted for. Or an anxious foreman, his original order late in coming, often simply made a duplicate requisition. Odds and ends of material would thus accumulate and come to light only when the yearly inventory was made. If a rush order came in, and if, for example, a three-and-a-half-inch piece rod was called for and was unavailable, the foreman would be apt to order a four-inch piece turned down to three-and-a-half inches, resulting in increased wear on the machine, increased waste of man-hours, and loss of material.[18] These traditional practices, practically universal in Taylor's lifetime, had still not been completely eradicated more than a decade later. Thus, a French worker writing in 1929 of his experiences in an American factory run under the old system of management, gives the following description:

The factory I had entered was not exactly a machine shop. The product being manufactured was brushes for dynamos, but I was employed in the tool shop that was to make and keep in shape the material necessary for manufacturing them. I was in a crew of workers occupied in making a new contrivance to carry winding spools from which copper wire would be fed to a cable-making machine.

As this work had just begun, I found myself in the midst of preliminaries. The foreman was occupied with tracing freehand designs in chalk on the cement floor. Once the designs were traced, straight lines having been drawn with the aid of a piece of wrought iron that happened to be lying there, the foreman took a steel protractor to measure the various angles that had thus been determined, just as if such a measuring instrument could actually check up a crude sketch in chalk. During this time I was a spectator, and though I did not greatly admire his procedure, you may know that I took note of it with much interest . . . . I had become acquainted with the "rule-of-thumb."

Being inclined to a certain amount of indulgence, I tried to persuade myself that this empirical method might have its advantage through the check on the final result it constantly afforded. I knew that it would be necessary to construct at least ten of the contrivances in question, and the procedure of completing one might guarantee that the others would operate satisfactorily; it would be a sort of first experiment, after which there would be nothing to do but go quietly ahead with the construction of others.

Alas, my indulgence was wasted, for while they were constructing the first spool holder, no one took note of the data thus collected, not even the workers who would have to repeat the same work in the days that were to follow. The result was that in one instance I was asked, two days afterward: "Do you remember at what angle we fastened on this piece?" And naturally as I did not remember any more than did the others, the tentative trials I had witnessed in the beginning all had to be repeated.

A great number of identical parts being necessary for these contrivances, simple logic required that they should all be prepared at the same time, once their dimensions had been settled. But this simple idea did not seem to occur to anyone in this land of the Taylor System, and the foreman was content to say to any of his workmen, "Oh, you haven't anything to do? Well, make a dozen of this piece!"—without his worrying over whether a dozen would be enough or whether it would not be necessary to make more in a few days again.

In the making of this device several steel bars of a certain size were needed. There happened to be bars of the proper dimension lying half hidden among some scraps of wood, tin cans, etc., in the factory lot. Now though unable to start work on them immediately, the foreman discussed their utilization with a couple of us one day and finally said: "Go down into the lot, get those steel bars, and cut them all through the middle." I suggested then—the reasoning Frenchman coming to the surface—"Instead of cutting them at hazard in the middle, can't we cut them at once into the proper lengths that will be needed?" "Oh, go ahead and cut them in the middle. It's simply to keep some other crew from getting them; once they are cut, nobody will take them away from us."

This little scene will give an idea of the order reigning in the distribution of materials for work.[19]

Coming back to the Watertown Arsenal, let us see how an order from the Ordnance Department was processed under the new Taylor system of management.[20] The order, say for gun forgings, was sent by the commanding officer to the engineering division, which then prepared a bill of materials, a list of parts, the suborders, and a set of drawings. The bill of materials was sent to the property division, where a balance of stores department examined it and made notations on it as to whether or not the materials required were at hand. One copy of this bill of materials was sent to the purchasing department, which purchased the material marked not on hand. Other copies of the bill along with the drawings and the suborders went to the shops where the work was to be initiated: thus, in the design of new gun carriages, a suborder for patterns was sent to the pattern shop, a suborder for castings to the foundry, a suborder for forgings to the smithy, and so forth. When any of these suborders was completed, a report was submitted to the planning room and a shipment of the required pieces made to the machine shop if the planning room gave the signal that the machine shop was ready to work on them. In the meantime, the planning room had already received from the engineering division the order, the bill of materials, the list of parts, and the required drawings. From this information, the planning room determined the operations necessary to complete each part and the sequence in which these were to be carried out. These decisions were compiled on a master route and schedule sheet from which various smaller cards were prepared for use in the shops. These cards included:[21]

a. A *job card* for each operation, giving the name and sub-order number of the part, the code number of the machine to be used and the location of the machine, and leaving space for the time necessary to complete the operation. These cards served two purposes: (1) to inform the worker of the job specifications; and (2) on their return to the planning room after the completion of the operation, to provide the necessary information for the calculation of the labor and overhead costs.

b. A *move card* for each part which accompanied the article throughout the manufacturing process from one work station to another. Since the move card was sent back to the planning room after the completion of each move before being sent on to the next work place, it enabled the planning room to ascertain at any moment where the article was, how long it had been there and which operations were still required to bring it to completion.

c. *Move tags,* small labels attached to each part containing instructions for the unskilled "move men" who were actually responsible for the physical transfer of materials and products.

d. *Instruction cards* containing detailed instructions to the workmen as to how the operation was to be performed— speed, feed, and so forth—and giving the time allotment from the time study.

Each suborder carried a number. All the material was purchased under that number, all labor was performed under it, and all final costs were computed with reference to it. When a worker began work on a certain article, the time was stamped on his job card when it was issued and when it was returned. The same cards were thus used to calculate wages as well as to keep track of costs. A special department for the inspection and repair of machines was set up to carry out periodic inspections and make necessary repairs, outside the normal working hours, whenever possible, so as not to hinder the flow of work. Most of the traditional duties of the foreman were performed by the planning room and the engineering division, and the foreman's functions consisted of checking up on the delivery of materials, obtaining special tools and fixtures, and making certain that the workers understood and followed instructions from the planning room. The introduction of the new management system thus also meant a change in the social structure of the work groups.

A discussion of Taylor's innovations at Midvale would not be complete without mentioning his strictly engineering achievements. During this time, he not only took out patents for automatic grinders, false tables, chucks, forging and tool-feeding mechanisms, and boring and turning mills but designed a revolutionary steam hammer that kept its alignment by the elasticity of its parts. Dependence upon the principle of elasticity enabled him to build a hammer that, for its weight, had far greater power than any hammer that had ever been built.[22] Its novelty lay in the fact that it repudiated the then current theory that large bodies must move slowly. Whereas all previous hammers of this class had been designed to keep their alignment by great mass and stiffness, Taylor's was designed to keep its alignment through the elasticity of its parts. Its construction reflected Taylor's typical working style—thoroughness, merciless attention to details, and dogged perseverance. First, he devoted two years to collecting, from all over the world, exhaustive data on hammers until he was able to isolate those instances in which some of the parts of each of the various hammering machines had never broken. He then copied the design of each of these, "collecting one element from one machine, another from another, another from a third. . . ." There was one part of the hammer, however, which was vulnerable in every design he found. On this he focused his ingenious attention until he was able to put together a hammer comprising all the parts already existing which had not broken, plus one "of his own design and patent," which he trusted to hold. And it did—lasting years without a breakdown.[23]

In these pages we have attempted to give a short summary

of the specific nature of Taylor's innovations. However, to do full justice to the subtitle of this study, these innovations have also to be placed in historical perspective. Lyndall Urwick, a distinguished practitioner and historian of scientific management, sympathetic to Taylor personally, has made the following assessment:

What Taylor did was not to invent something quite new, but to synthesize and present as a reasonably coherent whole ideas which had been germinating and gathering force in Great Britain and the United States throughout the nineteenth century. He gave to a disconnected series of initiatives and experiments a philosophy and a title; complete unity was not within his scope. As an inventor and technical engineer of genius, the bulk of whose practical career was passed in American machine shops in the last two decades of the nineteenth century, his outlook was largely limited to production and primarily to machine shop practice. It was left to others to extend his philosophy to other functions and especially to Henri Fayol, a Frenchman, to develop logical principles for the administration of a large-scale undertaking as a whole.

It detracts nothing from Taylor's greatness to see him thus as a man who focussed the thought of a preceding age, carried that thought forward with a group of friends and colleagues whose united contribution was so outstanding as to constitute a "golden age" of management in the United States and laid the intellectual foundations on which all subsequent work in Great Britain and many other countries has been based. But it is impossible to understand Taylor's achievement or the significance of Scientific Management for our society, unless his individual work is seen against the background of this larger whole of which it is only a part.[24]

Considering the nature of innovation and the innovative process, we would suggest that this assessment understates both the fact and the impact of Taylor's achievement. With Homer Barnett, we see innovation as "any thought, behaviour or thing that is new because it is qualitatively different from existing forms."[25] Basically, innovation is a recombination of existing parts into a new, configurational whole. Taylor's work was thus not a part of a "larger whole" but a new whole in which the various existing ideas about factory organization had been recombined. Taylor's work of course had antecedents in many countries —all innovations have antecedents, and in this special sense every innovation is derivative.

A cursory research into the history of the scientific approach to work and its organization reveals a steadily rising interest from the second half of the seventeenth century. In 1667, Thomas Sprat (1635–1713), Bishop of Rochester and Deacon of Westminster, in his book *The History of the Royal Society of London, for the Improving of Natural Knowledge,* talks of an approaching increase in production once the experimental methods of natural science are applied to the work methods of the crafts-man.[26] Adam Smith's pin-making example has already been noted. The man closest to Taylor in spirit, however, was Charles Babbage (1792–1871), a mathematician best known for his design of the "calculating engine," who anticipated the analytical part of the time study. Similarly in France, there were instances of the scientific approach to work as evidenced in the following chronological listing:

1. A minister of Louis XIV, Colbert, was the initiator. At his call, in the second half of the seventeenth century, physicists and engineers made the first experimental researches on human work. A short time after its creation, the French Academy of Sciences invited "all scientists to study the work done by the workmen in their workshops."

2. De la Hire (1640–1718) showed the relation existing between the physical strength of the worker and his weight, and concluded that sloping boards were the rational way to elevate heavy loads.

3. Amontons (1663–1705) conducted experiments on the "specific speed for men and horses" and collected data on the daily amount of work.

4. Vauban, Marshall of France (1633–1707), for the first time in history let the times be taken which were required by soldiers for the carrying of loads of earth in building

fortifications. In one of his books, Vauban wrote: "I am certain that nobody who has even a small use of management, will deny that four men properly supervised will do more than the six others left to themselves."

5. Belidor (1693–1761), a military engineer who analyzed the works of Vauban in a book published in 1729, called *The Science of Engineering in Fortifications and Civil Architecture,* stated that ten hour's work of a man stimulated by his interest are worth at least fifteen of another who has his day regulated.

6. In another book, *Architecture Hydraulique* (Paris, 1750), the same author gave an example of time analysis quite similar to modern methods. He also studied the problems of the rational workday, the utility of separating planning from performance.

7. Peronnet (1708–1796), founder of the School of Building Engineering, applied scientific management methods based upon an exact study of elementary operations. In 1738, when serving as a young engineer in Alençon, he analyzed the work done at the pin factory of Loigle, in Normandy. His studies were summarized in two reports which he presented to the Academy of Sciences in 1739 and 1740. These reports were used by Adam Smith to formulate his fundamental principles of economy.

8. Coulomb (1736–1806), an army engineer, at the end of the eighteenth century studied the work done by workers chosen from among those who did the hardest kind of work. He showed in his *Memorandum on Human Strength,* published in 1798, that the useless movements of a workman are one of the principal causes of fatigue, that proper instruction should eliminate these movements, that heavy work should be divided into short intervals of action and rest. He enumerated for the first time all the physiological factors of a man's work.

9. Dupin, a professor of mechanics, noted on January 15th, 1829, in an opening lecture, that "wheras a huge effort toward perfecting machinery has been made, very little had been done toward perfecting the workman." With another physicist, Porcelet, he started a campaign for rational methods and work analysis in industry, believing it to be the only way to protect workmen against

overwork. He was obtaining a certain success when political events in 1830 stopped the movement.

10. In the middle of the nineteenth century, an important step was taken toward scientific methods of work analysis by Marey, who created a graphic method by which all kinds of phenomena could be inscribed on a smoked paper cylinder. It was his idea that this invention could be used for professional work analysis. In 1896, Fremont used Marey's methods for the analysis of anvil work, nailing and filing.[27]

This is admittedly a very abbreviated account of the antecedents of Taylor's work—a comprehensive history of human work still awaits its historian. When the evidence of prior work in his field was brought to Taylor's attention toward the end of his life, he is reported to have said, "How very incredible that such examples should have been fruitless and that such work should even have been totally forgotten."[28] His comment is a good starting point for a brief discussion of the role of the cultural environment in innovation and a review of the external conditions that are most relevant to an individual's innovative potential.

Innovation flourishes first of all in societies or in historical periods in which it is expected and welcomed.[29] A society that views the notion of progress positively and supports innovation as a means of solving problems is more conducive to innovative activity. Today in the West, one is apt to take this mood for granted, forgetting that this characteristic attitude is almost unique to European civilization and its offshoots. And even in Europe, this has been a comparatively recent development (rooted near the end of the seventeenth century), one of those signposts so often used to date and measure our "modernity."

The older view that harked back to a "golden age," saw innovation as an unnecessary derivative, a poor copy of an ancient idyllic state, a deviation. In an early seventeenth-century work, for example, "striving for innovating" and "abuse" were used practically synonymously.[30] Francis Bacon, in his essay "Of Innovations," elegantly expressed the world view of his period, when he compared innovations to strangers, more admired than loved.[31] The notion of progress gradually attained respectability, however, and by Taylor's time, in nineteenth-century America, innovation, especially in the technological sphere, was the order of the day.

Another catalyst to innovative activity, historically, has been the collapse of traditional controls or ruling authorities during periods of political and social upheaval. In such transitional periods, innovative initiatives that suggest new balances of social and economic as well as political power and offer new ways of easing the dislocations of war, revolution, economic boom, or depression are at a premium. In an earlier chapter, we considered this factor in the context of the post-Civil War period of American history and have suggested its close relationship to the body of Taylor's innovative work.

The innovative process itself, as noted earlier, basically consists of two mutually dependent elements: the *analysis* of a conventional configuration and a *recombination* that discovers new potentialities of a different configuration.[32] The analysis itself is not a conventional one but has a new and different starting point both in historical time and in individual life experience. Thus, there can be little doubt that though men had worked for thousands of years, Taylor was the first one who really *saw* them work. The recombination depends on the availability to the innovator of a prototype which, on first glance, may seem to have very little to do with the problem at hand. This prototype may never have been clearly defined; it may be barely conscious or buried indeed in the far reaches of memory. The difference between the innovative process we are describing and routine problem solving may be clarified schematically (Figure 1):

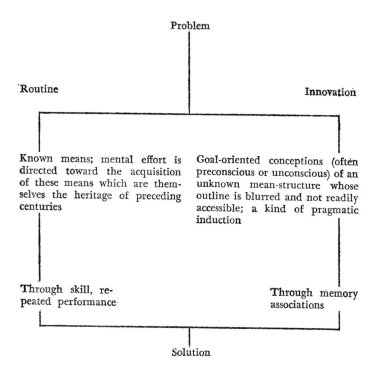

Problem

Routine   Innovation

Known means; mental effort is   Goal-oriented conceptions (often
directed toward the acquisition   preconscious or unconscious) of an
of these means which are them-   unknown mean-structure whose
selves the heritage of preceding   outline is blurred and not readily
centuries   accessible; a kind of pragmatic
                                           induction

Through skill, re-   Through memory
peated performance   associations

Solution

The main work in this process of innovative recombination is the search into one's past for apt prototypes. The "search" may by systematic, even ritualized, or it may be barely conscious, recognizable only in the pleasant shock of relevant, resonant discovery. It is similar to the search for a forgotten word, a process so vividly described by William James:

The state of our consciousness is peculiar. There is a gap therein; but no mere gap. It is a gap that is intensively active. A sort of wraith of the name is in it, beckoning us in a given direction, making us at moments tingle with a sense of our closeness, and then letting us sink back without the longed-for term. If wrong names are proposed to us, this singularly definite gap acts immediately so as to negate them. They do not fit into its mould. And the gap of one word does not feel like the gap of another, all empty of content as both might seem necessarily to be when described as gaps. . . . The rhythm of a lost word may be there without a sound to clothe it; or the evanescent sense of something which is the initial vowel or consonant may mock us fitfully, without growing more distinct.[33]

We can easily recognize the prototypes of Taylor's innovations, especially the time study, in his childhood and adolescence: the diary listings of the arrival and departure times of the trains in Europe, for example, the experimentation with his legs to find the "right" length of walking step, the measurements and "strict laws and formulas" accompanying his games. Taylor himself places the prototype of time study in his period at Exeter:

The first piece of time study that I ever saw made by anyone was made in the study of just that thing, a study of the mental capacity of boys. When I was at Phillips Exeter Academy Mr. George W. Wentworth was the professor of mathematics, and he worked off his first geometry while it was in manuscript and his first algebra on my class, the class of '74. . . . I, as a student, wondered how it was possible (that right along steadily, right through from the beginning to the end of the year, as we went on from month to month) that old bull, Wentworth, as he was called, gave us a lesson which it always took me two hours to get. For the two years I was there I always had to spend two hours getting that lesson, and finally we got onto his method. We were very slow in getting onto it however. Mr. Wentworth would sit with his watch always hid behind a ledge on the desk, and while it was there we did not know what the darn thing was used for. About once a week or sometimes twice a week he went through the same kind of exercise with the class. He would give out a series of problems and insisted that the first boy who had them done should raise his hand and snap his fingers. Then he would call his name. He went right through the class until just one-half of the class had held up their hands. We always noted when he got half way through the class and the middle boy would snap his fingers he would say, "that is enough; that will do." What he wanted was to find out just how many minutes it took the average boy in the class to do the example which he gave. Then we found that Wentworth timed himself when he first tackled those problems. He got his own time for doing those five examples, and the ratio between his time to do the examples and the time of the middle boy of the class enabled him to fix the exact stunt for us right along. . . . That was the first instance of a time study of mental operations which I had ever seen.[34]

The workable recall and use of prototypes into history-making innovations is of course not automatic. It depends, in part, upon the "availability" of certain critical portions of an innovator's life history—such as Taylor's Exeter period. It can be argued, in fact, that such periods are more readily available to the play of a restless mind precisely because they have harbored a strong conflict; a conflicted past lives on in the present. This is not to contradict the concept of repression. It simply interprets a crisis not as an isolated instant but as part of a temporal space. Thus, much of the Exeter crisis may have been repressed in Taylor's later life, but the conflict-free areas of that period—details of a baseball game or a class in mathematics—would tend to remain much more vivid. In analogy, such a crisis in a life history is like a searchlight, blinding if faced directly, but illuminating, in some detail, the surrounding area of darkness. Thus, the particular kind of innovative process that is characterized by creative memory depends upon the accessibility of its prototypes, which in turn, seems to be heightened if the period in which the prototype is embedded is marked by crisis.

In conclusion we must reemphasize the fact that most of Taylor's innovations were designed as part of a whole new system for the reorganization of work which followed a certain historical and personal logic. Taylor's system offered a novel solution to the problems raised by vast and rapid technological and industrial change, not the least of which were the gradual eclipse of the small-scale unit as the dominant unit of production and the increasing inadequacy of the old personalized style of management. At the same time, it claimed to be the most efficient method for the management of these very changes. In the context of social and economic upheaval which followed the Civil War, the innovations of scientific management, although they minimized the importance of the associational and ego needs of the worker, claimed to allay the worker's sense of material insecurity by promising him a larger share of the goods that were themselves to be increased manifold through the application of the new system. On the personal level, the system of innovations was related to and appears to have been a "solution" for an intense inner conflict which animated Taylor, as it were, with a new sense of wholeness. Thus, Taylor's innovation does not alone derive from its historical or personal antecedents but rather from the fateful coincidence of the life history of a gifted and conflicted man with a critical moment in the history of his world.

By 1890, Taylor, then thirty-four years old, seemed to be well set for a highly successful and brilliant career in industry. Although his personal mentors of the earlier years had left Midvale—Sellers was ousted from the management in 1887 by the new owner, and Davenport had gone to the Bethlehem Steel Company in 1888—Taylor had the full confidence of the new owner, Charles Harrah. And in 1890, an even more glittering opportunity came his way.

Some members of President Cleveland's inner circle, financiers linked with Standard Oil interests, were organizing a company known as the Manuafacturing Investment Company.[1] These men, headed by William Whitney, then Secretary of the Navy, included Colonel O. H. Payne of New York, Don M. Dickinson, and Daniel Lamont, Secretary to the President. The company's object was to capitalize upon a new process invented by a German chemist, Andrew Mitscherlich, for the conversion of forest products into fiber suitable for the making of paper. This process, whose patents were acquired by the Manufacturing Investment Company, utilized the waste products from the manufacture of saw logs into lumber, the slabs, edgings, sawdust, and bark that were otherwise burned.

The possibilities of the new process for the conversion of this waste material seemed enormous, and the organizers had already begun to erect one plant in Madison, Maine, and another in Appleton, Wisconsin, when Whitney called Taylor for a conference in Washington, D. C. He asked him to manage these two mills and, once they were properly organized and running, to erect new mills in other parts of the country for the further development of the new conversion process and product diversification. It was through Midvale's defense business that Whitney had come to hear from government inspectors of Taylor and his successful management innovations. He offered Taylor a significantly larger salary than he had been re-

THE TIME OF TROUBLES   7

ceiving as chief engineer at Midvale; and Taylor, confident that he would have a real chance to test his methods in practice, accepted the offer. On May 26, 1890, he signed a contract which specified that from that date until October 1, 1890, he should devote as much time as possible to the affairs of the new company and from October 1, 1890, to October 1, 1893, full time. Though his resignation from Midvale took effect on October 1, he and his wife maintained their home in Germantown until the spring of 1891, making frequent trips to Madison, Maine, and to the company's financial office in New York. In the spring of 1891, the Taylors closed their home in Germantown and took the first of their many trips to Appleton, Wisconsin. Although his work shuttled Taylor back and forth between Maine and Wisconsin, he and his wife decided to build a house in Maine and to settle down there.

As general manager of the Manufacturing Investment Company, Taylor was in a position to introduce his system into a newly established industry and through the success of that industry, to help secure the general acceptance of his methods for modern industrial management. Taylor failed, however, and this failure at the Manufacturing Investment Company was to be the first of many disappointments of his middle years. The reasons for this failure lay both in the external circumstances bearing on his work as well as in his difficulties with his employers, fellow executives, and with the workers—an importunate combination that was to occur so often as to lead one to believe Taylor was marked by fate's particular ill will. William Fannon, a worker under Taylor, gives us the following report in his *Recollections:*

Mr. Taylor had hardly taken hold and got the organization permanently started before we all discovered that the enterprise was to be very largely a disappointment for the reason that, first, the price paid for the patents was a large one in view of the fact that later it developed that these patents were not as strong or as much a controlling factor as was anticipated they would be. When the company bought these patents, they believed that all other companies wishing to cook wood in a digester would have to pay Manufacturing Investment Company a royalty for the use of the lining of the digester and considered the final victory over the most hazardous part of the sulphite business . . . . Mills [were built] by other people who were not obliged to pay the Manufacturing Investment Company royalties and a process was established and became a commercial success which was where the fiber was not as good as the fiber made from the Mitscherlich process; . . .

Then, the next unfortunate experience was that, in the company's anxiety to get these mills started, they did not take sufficient time to locate in the best locations, for there were other water powers that they might have secured which were far better than the ones they did secure and were equally as well, if not better, located for the supply of forest productions.

An additional unfortunate thing occurred. In their desire to get these mills going, there was a competitive spirit started between Admiral Goodrich and Admiral Evans as to who would get his mill going first producing fiber. The Appleton Mill succeeded in making the first fiber, which was on March 15, 1891; but, in the haste to get these mills going, there were some unfortunate mistakes made in the designing of the mills by the architect or engineers, some of which were beyond the control of Mr. Taylor, as they were already made before he took charge.

In this same rush, Mr. Taylor also made some mistakes, as did all the other men. All seemed to contribute some to the making of mistakes, due largely to their anxiety to get started, and acted in an impulsive way. In addition to this, there was the inexperience as to what was needed in this new process; which, added to what is written above, helped to make the proposition a disappointment.

Then, on top of all this, they just about got started right when the [financial] Panic of 1893 showed in a most forcible way that the profits that had been promised by the original promoters and accepted as a fact by the organizers of the Manufacturing Investment Company were far below what was anticipated; and, indeed, it was difficult to make a new dollar from an old one.[2]

His difficulties with the workers were foreseeable. They resented the "city man" with his newfangled notions of running a mill, mistrusting even the improvements he made for their benefit. For example, "barkers" who stripped the bark from the logs with revolving steel discs were put inside cages in order to prevent serious accidents should passersby knock against them. The men resented this and thought it tantamount to "making a monkey out of a man."[3] There followed the first of many newspaper attacks which Taylor, ever fearful of "exposure" and resentful of criticism, could not learn to take with any degree of equanimity.[4]

By far his greatest disappointment, however, was his failure to get on well with his employers, the financiers who had organized the company. They disapproved of his habit of "making money fly," and ever thereafter Taylor nourished a great distaste for the business methods of financiers. These men were not especially evil or especially greedy in this respect; they were perhaps above the norm for American capitalists of the period; but . . . none of them was Sellers. In Taylor's own account:

Personally my experience has been so unsatisfactory with financiers that I never want to work for any of them. If there is a manufacturer at the head of any enterprise, such as shipbuilding or construction work of any kind, and he is a large minded man, that is the man whom I want to be under. As a rule, financiers are looking merely for a turnover. It is all a question of making money quickly, and whether the company is built up so as to be the finest of its kind and permanently successful is a matter of complete indifference to almost all of them. A good example of the utter lack of "proper pride" of the manufacturer is to be seen in the present managers of ———. They are among the leading financiers in Philadelphia and New York, and absolutely refuse to spend a cent for the much needed physical improvements or for improvements in management. All they are looking for is the chance to unload on someone else and get out whole.[5]

Taylor came to include financiers in his chamber of horrors along with professors, theologians, and Germans, for reasons that were both personal and social. First, they (and some other executives at the Manufacturing Investment Company) were "aloof" and "aristocratic." Scudder Klyce, who at one time cherished the ambition of being the philosopher of scientific management, writes in his *Recollections:*

I remember that in the second interview Taylor, for the only time in either conversation or letters to me, adversely criticized the character of a specifically named man. To mention that incident will I think throw much light on Taylor's instincts or fundamental traits. He condemned Rear-Admiral R. D. Evans most unmercifully. Now, Evans was a pretty able man, and in most respects had superficially at least done excellent work . . . . But Evans was fundamentally both an aristocrat and a liar. Taylor specifically objected to him that he was not truthful; that was easy enough for anybody to see. But Taylor said that there was something else about Evans he couldn't name, which was far worse than that. I suggested the name "aristocrat" to him, as describing what he said Evans was:—a man who thinks that his dictum is right, and because it is his, law, simply because he happens to be himself, or to hold a formal job. . . . Taylor instantly decided that that name was exactly suitable to Evans. Now, Evans was not aristocratic to any marked degree: no one ever dreamed that he was pathologically so, or insane. But so completely was Taylor a democrat—so unbalancedly so, perhaps—that he violently objected to Evans because he was the opposite.[6]

The nature and personal implications of these violent feelings against "aloof aristocrats," to the point of "forgetting" the very word aristocrat, have already been discussed. Franklin Taylor threw a long shadow indeed.

Taylor's attitude toward financiers, however, was influenced not only by personal but also by social factors. He was an engineer, and a conscientious member of the American Society of Mechanical Engineers; his stated antipathy for the financiers was in part based on arguments advanced by fellow engineers and articulated so eloquently by Thorsten Veblen in his writings around 1900.[7]

In the period between 1865 and 1910, American engineers were vitally concerned with their status.[8] Engineering education in American universities was still a relatively new phenomenon, and the engineers were fighting for equal status with the other academically trained professions. In the engineers' view, members of their profession had provided the underpinnings of economic growth—transportation grids and communication systems—for which the nation was indebted to them. They had helped build the arteries of the industrial system—roads, bridges, canals, railroads—besides running the system itself.

In short, the engineers pictured themselves as the critical actors in industrialization. Their self-image was one of men who made things work, who avoided the waste of time, capital, and labor. They saw themselves as the mediators in the struggle between capital and labor and were convinced that the best of their profession, men who combined scientific training with business orientation, were the ideal captains of industry. Since to the engineers, finance and speculation represented nonproductive activity, they felt their antagonism toward financiers to be completely justified. Endowed with such a staunchly vigorous professional identity, it is hardly surprising to find engineers competing with the men who employed them—an enlivened probability in the case of a man of Taylor's single-minded determination and competence.

It must be admitted that in the "Age of Robber Barons" many of the engineers' points were reasonable, for very few of the financiers of that period had much interest in the ". . . realities of what underlay their structures of stocks and bonds and credits. Later on, a Henry Ford might introduce an era of intensely production-minded captains of industry, but the Harrimans, Morgans, Fricks, and Rockefellers were far more interested in the exciting manipulation of huge masses of intangible wealth than in the humdrum business of turning out goods."[9]

Before the depression of 1893, Taylor had accepted an amendment to his contract by which he agreed to a reduction in his salary in exchange for several thousand dollars worth of common stock and, in installments, several thousand dollars worth of preferred stock. By 1893, however, Taylor had had his fill of trouble, and had decided on ". . . getting my skirts clear of this company."[10] Though Whitney made generous offers in order to keep Taylor with the company—promising to make him a millionaire within a few years—Taylor's antipathy had become much too intense to allow him to stay.[11] Taylor wrote of his resignation to a friend:

I think that you will be pleased to hear that I have succeeded in getting out of the Manufacturing Investment Company. I have not been relieved from the debt of $30,000 of which I spoke to you but I have a written contract with them agreeing to take it up. While I come out of the company with a loss of $25,000 I think I'm lucky in not having the debt hanging over me. Besides this, I feel that the time has arrived when I can honourably leave the company, as our western mill is now doing finely (for a Mitscherlich mill) and our Madison mill, mechanically speaking, is all straightened out and we are progressing fairly with the piece-work system. Both mills are left with a well drilled corps of superintendents and if the company are sensible enough to keep them together they will certainly have fair success in business. . . .

This is now the only paper or pulp mill in the United States which is running on piece-work, so far as I know, but I feel surely that it will not long remain so. Our mill at Madison is rapidly getting on to piecework in the same way as our western mill and I have not the least doubt but other paper and pulp mills will very soon follow suit. I am quite sure that if it had not been for piece work in the western mill we should have failed before now, as even with the piece-work and driving as hard as we are now doing the profits are not what they should be for so large an investment, as the Mitscherlich process of making sulphite pulp is an enormous fraud.

We expect to remain in Madison all through this summer during which time I hope to have a thorough rest. This is the first time that I have been free for over two weeks at a time for twenty years.[12]

Taylor's situation was grim indeed. He was now thirty-seven years old, jobless in a period of general financial uncertainty and disorder, most of his savings wiped out and the rest invested at a time when no return was possible. Furthermore, he felt a sense of responsibility for the men he had brought with him into the Manufacturing Investment Company, men like William Fannon and Carl Barth (later to become his chief lieutenant in the management movement) whom he had "failed."[13] These factors along with the strain of years of overwork and a mounting sense of his own failure culminated in a breakdown, one (and perhaps the first one) of the "two or three nervous breakdowns" he later claimed in a letter to a friend to have suffered.[14]

He now decided that it was unwise to carry on the double burden of executive and proseletizer for his ideas—of running a factory and introducing his system of management. He chose to concentrate on the latter, and set himself up as a consulting engineer. The rubber stamp he prepared for himself reads:

Fred W. Taylor, M.E.
Ross Street, Germantown, Philadelphia
 Consulting Engineer
Systematized Shop Management and
Manufacturing Costs a Specialty

He fixed his fee at $35 a day, later raising it to $40. The next four and a half years in his new profession were marked more by failure and frustrations than accomplishment: the meager jobs that came his way fell far short of the success he had hoped for.

In September 1893, he left for Boston to work for his first client, the Simonds Rolling Machine Company in Fitchburg, Massachusetts, which manufactured steel balls for bicycle bearings. Taylor had come in contact with the owners when he acquired some company stock in exchange for surrendering some rolling machinery patents he held. The job was a minor one, the introduction of a new accounting system, and he completed it by the middle of 1894 when he faced the first real test of his new profession, the reorganization of the machine shop of the Cramp's Shipyards in Philadelphia, where he proposed to standardize (1) belting, (2) automatic tool grinding, (3) the tools room, stores room, and toolmaking, and (4) machine speed.[15] The opposition of the management—"those financiers" again—was to thwart his plans. Taylor perceived clearly enough that "wherever scientific methods are introduced those who direct the company should be prepared to lose some of their valuable men who cannot stand the changes and also for the continued indignant protest of many of their old and trusted employees who can see nothing but extravagance in the new ways, and ruin ahead,"[16] but the management was not thus "prepared." And Taylor, unskilled in either diplomacy or compromise, made no headway in the particularly traditionalist atmosphere of the Cramp's Shipyard. His increasing inability to control his hostility toward "those financiers" undoubtedly played a major role; forever anticipating their opposition, he antagonized them with his belligerence and imperious impatience. Thus he left after six months, frustrated, another "failure" chalked up on the record—and yet his spirit, according to Copley, was apparently "unwounded."[17]

That this failure did not have the same psychological consequences as the ones earlier we may attribute, at least in part, to Taylor's first mentor and, if one will, his protective deity, William Sellers. During his employment at

Cramp's Shipyards, Sellers agreed to share the expenses of determining the suitable tool steel, and thus Taylor spent the winter months of 1895 working at a lathe in Sellers' company in Philadelphia, once again in the benign and affirming presence of the man who had shown faith in him while he was still a young man. In his testimony before the House Committee, Taylor speaks of these months as follows:

Perhaps I can make it clearer to you by telling you that I worked the whole winter of 1895, I think it was, in running a machine myself. I went back and ran a machine for the whole winter in making a series of experiments in developing the "art of cutting metals," which I described to you in my direct testimony, and during this time I worked more steadily on the lathe than I had ever worked in my whole lifetime as a workman. I worked the same hours as the other workmen, and I tell you it was the easiest and happiest year I have had since I got out of my apprenticeship—that year of going back and working on a lathe. I worked hard from the machinist's standpoint and harder than I had ever worked before in my life as a mechanic. I was known to be a manager, and the men knew I was in there conducting some of the series of experiments that I have told you about on the art of cutting metals, and yet some of the men came to me and begged me not to set too fast a pace or the other fellows might have their rate cut as a result.

I give you my word, Mr. Chairman, that during that winter there was never a day that I was overworked, and I was physically soft; I was a comparatively middle-aged man and had not done any work by hand for twelve or fourteen years, and yet I was not in the slightest degree overworked.[18]

After Cramp's, Taylor did some minor work organizing the accounting practices of William Deering & Co. and Northern Electrical Manufacturing Co. of Madison, Wisconsin. A more extensive job, and certainly the only bright spot of these years, was the work he did in 1896 in Johnstown, Pennsylvania, for the Lorain Steel Company and its allied concern, the Johnson Company. In a letter to a friend, he wrote:

We have been here since about the first of March and shall not get away until some time during the fall. I am engaged in systematizing the many departments of Johnson Company who make most of the rails for the steel railways of the country, and who also have a large electrical works, iron, steel, foundries etc., and are very satisfactory people to deal with.

We came here expecting to have a miserable time as this is a small Pennsylvania village. Mrs. Taylor has, however, fixed things so that we have had an uncommonly pleasant and agreeable stay. Altogether I think that we find this one of the most agreeable places that we have ever stayed in. There is fine bicycle riding and law tennis whenever I find the time for it.[19]

Meanwhile, in spite of meager success as a consultant, Taylor's professional reputation among the engineers was steadily growing. In 1893, he had read his first paper, "Notes on Belting," before a meeting of the American Society of Mechanical Engineers. In 1895, there followed his first paper on management, "A Piece-Rate System," with the subtitle "A Step Toward Partial Solution of the Labor Problem." Taylor was still years away from formulating a comprehensive system of management; this paper was rather in the tradition of earlier papers read before the Society such as Kent's "A Problem in Profit Sharing," Towne's "Gain Sharing," and Halsey's "The Premium Plan of Paying for Labor," which reflected the engineer's growing interest in management problems and particularly in the problem of wages and productivity.

In November 1896, the leading men of Simonds Company, dissatisfied with its present management, invited Taylor to Fitchburg for a conference, and asked him to take over its management. For Taylor this was a big opportunity, both to introduce his system and to redeem his reputation as an able manager. He asked for absolute control until

April 1898, and tackled the job with his characteristic enthusiasm, buying more company stock in a dramatic demonstration of confidence in his own abilities and asking his old associates (in this case, Gantt) to come with him. In some respects, however, the experience proved more horrendous than anything he had faced so far. We can reconstruct what happened in Fitchburg from the following letter to his friend, A. R. Couder, dated November 22, 1897:

. . . As I have, however, been attacked personally in the most disagreable manner by the gang that has been fighting me here, and as they have done everything in their power to injure me by talking at random against me all over the country this must be my excuse for going into matters which are partly personal to such an extent.

As you probably know, a man named Geo. W. Weymouth has been the manager of the Simonds Rolling Machine Co. in Fitchburg for some seven or eight years past and during this time he has had absolute sway paying simply no attention whatever to the directors and orders given him by the Board of Directors.

This utter disregard of their orders became so serious that last December they employed me on a contract basis lasting until next April to carry out their wishes as to the organization and management of the company. I was put in absolute and entire charge of the manufacturing and from the time I came here entirely superseded Weymouth in this respect.

It appears now that even before I had arrived at the works to take charge of it he had decided to form a rival company. . . . This went on through the whole of last winter and spring and, although I was certain [illegible] and called the attention of the Directors to them, no one really knew anything definite about his intentions until, on the 28th of June, he resigned on three days notice, and with him every foreman and assistant foreman in the place, as well as the Superintendent, all of the salesmen, and the head man in the office. This was the first that the Directors or anyone connected with the company knew of their intentions. They did this, of course, hoping to put the Simonds Company into such a hole that they would be obliged to shut down or else, as Weymouth hoped, discharge me and go back to the old system of management. There was however only one out of the nine directors besides Weymouth himself who considered any such course for more than five minutes. Weymouth was the most disappointed man.

The new concern is a grand failure and at the meeting of the Stockholders of the Simonds Company which occurred some weeks ago he appeared and wanted to patch up the break and come back again but the same Board of Directors was chosen and my management was entirely endorsed by them.

Owing to the severe competition in the bicycle ball business, however, the price of balls has fallen to one half what it was last season, and this of course stops the payment of dividends. Young Mr. Simonds, who is a very nice young fellow but has no experience what ever in business, naturally wants dividends, and Weymouth has told him, as he has everyone else connected with the company, that if he were only managing the company now they would be paying just as large dividends, as ever.

He has also spread no end of lies broadcast about me, saying I never have made success of anything, that I had always been fired wherever I have been, that I had no friends, and was a very general kind of damned fool. Mr. Simonds has therefore written letters to a number of my previous employers in order either to verify or disprove the above statements.

The chief work which I have been doing has been to change the running of the establishment from Day Work to the piece-work, and although this work is not yet [illegible: "advanced"?], still we are turning out nearer three times as much work per man than twice as much as we were under the Day Work management. We have also made very large improvements in the machinery in the direction of cheapening the output and spend about $100,000 for new machinery and buildings, which come right out of the earnings of the company.

I have never been able to accomplish as much in so short a space of time in the way of saving money through piece work and improved management as has been done here, and in spite of all the foremen and superintendents leaving as they did on the 1st of July we are now manufacturing cheaper and better then we did with the old gang, not because they are more experienced but because they are more loyal and heartily in favor of the new system of management.

I enclose herewith a copy of a letter which young Simonds has written broadcast to all the people, as far as I can find out, for whom I have done any work. You will note that in this letter he states that my present management of the company is unsatisfactory to the Stockholders. This is certainly a most unwarranted statement as my management at the recent annual meeting was endorsed by an almost unanimous vote of the Stockholders, and you can understand what a bad thing it is for me to have a statement of this sort written promiscuously to all of my previous employers telling them that my present management was not giving satisfaction. Neither the money nor success that I can possibly have from this company will at all pay me for the damage which such a statement as this inflicts upon my reputation and feel most bitter that this should have been done, and particularly since I have been working myself sick for this company for the past nine months.

Several of my friends to whom these letters have been sent have been kind enough to forward me their answers and I enclose you copies of the two most important of these answers which certainly entirely vindicate my management for the period covered between the years 1878 and 1893. If you hear any of these slanderous reports about me I will be very much obliged indeed to you for contradicting them.[20]

This letter is one of many in a similar vein that Taylor wrote to his friends and previous employers. Its tone clearly indicates that Taylor, usually so taciturn in his letters, was under great emotional strain. To make matters worse, in the same year his seventy-three-year-old mother had a stroke that paralyzed her. This combination of acute personal and professional anxiety led, in our opinion, to the second of his "nervous breakdowns," a contention supported by Copley who reports that "at Fitchburg the symptoms of a weakened nervous system, mainly in the form of dyspepsia and insomnia, began to manifest themselves . . . too insistently for him to disregard entirely."[21] Although Taylor had already left a few months earlier, the Simonds Company, unable to meet its competition, had to shut down temporarily in 1898. This was a blow to Taylor, for it seemed to be a repetition of the Manufacturing Investment Co. episode. He was worried not only about his reputation but especially because he had induced so many others, including friends, to "go in" with him, whom he had again "failed."[22]

In the midst of his troubles at Simonds, Taylor received a letter from his old chief of Midvale days, Russel Davenport, now the second vice-president at Bethlehem Steel Company, with whom he had kept in touch over the years. The letter reads:

My dear Taylor:

I have been requested by President, Mr. R.P. Linderman, to communicate with you in reference to the possibility of arranging to secure your services at an early date in connection with the proposed establishment of a piece-work system in our Machine Shop.

I should like therefore to hear from you at your early convenience as to whether your present engagements will allow you to consider this question, and if so when you can make it convenient to come to Bethlehem and have a preliminary talk with Mr. Linderman.[23]

The letter meant another chance to repair his confidence in himself and his methods and an undreamed-of opportunity to work on a scale that had not hitherto been possible. Before meeting Linderman, Taylor had a talk with Davenport in which he was briefed on the situation prevailing at Bethlehem.

Bethlehem Iron Co. (renamed Bethlehem Steel Co. in 1899) had been started around 1860 in Bethlehem, Pennsylvania, by two brothers who simply bought a farm and established a blast furnace on it.[24] Under the direction of the well-known mechanical engineer, John Fritz, who made great contributions to the development of the Bessemer process, the company grew steadily in size and importance. As with Midvale, the greatest impetus to its growth came from its good share of the then burgeoning defense business—in Bethlehem's case, the supply of forgings for heavy cannon and armour plate to the navy. Up to the mid-1880s, the ownership of the company had been shared by some leading local families, the Lindermans, the Sayres, and the Wilburs; with the growth initiated by defense contracts, however, outside capital had to be brought in. And when Taylor went to Bethlehem, although a Linderman scion was still the company's president, effective power had passed into the hands of the Philadelphia financier, Joseph Wharton, who owned one quarter of the company stock and a majority of its bonds. With a nominal capitalization of $5,000,000, Bethlehem's value was placed at about $15,000,000, and it employed from 5,000 to 6,000 workers, making it one of the biggest industrial enterprises of that period.

After his talk with Davenport, Taylor had a brief meeting with Linderman and then went to see Wharton, in order to ensure himself of the backing of the most powerful man of the company. The meeting was a satisfactory one. Taylor described it to Davenport as follows:

While I was in Philadelphia about ten days ago I dropped in to see Joseph Wharton and find his views regarding piece-work. He told me that he had urged upon the Board of Directors several times during the last five years the necessity of running the Bethlehem Steel works on piece work, and that he was very heartily in favor of the same. I told him however that it involved paying from 33 to 50% higher wages in order to get out properly really hustling piece-work. He said at first that this was out of the question. After talking with him for some time however and explaining that men would not work extraordinarily fast for ordinary wages he seemed convinced on this point. At any rate he said he was heartily in favor of having piece-work.

I suggested that you were as well qualified as anyone in the country to introduce piece-work and I took upon myself to recommend your transfer to the head of the manufacturing department. He, however, was absolutely noncommital on this point, neither acquiesced nor the contrary. . . . I write you this in order that you may know the way I stand in this matter. I have not, however, said anything about it to Mr. Linderman.[25]

It seems clear that Taylor was hoping to replicate at Bethlehem the authority-subordination relationship of Midvale in which his innovative mind had first flourished —with Davenport as his immediate superior, and Wharton (in place of Sellers) as the powerful man behind him. In this constellation there was very little room for the president, Linderman. Taylor wrote to Linderman on the same day, forecasting the trouble that was bound to come with his arrival at Bethlehem:

Referring to the conversation which the writer had with you sometime since regarding piece-work in your machine shop, I beg leave to write herewith a memorandum of what appears to my mind to be certain elements necessary to the successful introduction of this system.

It is practically certain that any move toward piece-work will be strongly opposed by all of your workmen and probably also by most of your foremen and superintendents. It appears to the writer therefore important that the management of your company should fully realize the nature of the changes to be made and the obstacles to be overcome.

Before piece-work can be successfully introduced I believe it to be necessary that many of the details connected with the running of the machines and the management of the work of your shop which are usually left to the individual judgment of your workmen should be standardized and taken entirely out of their control. . . .[26]

Having delivered himself of this warning, Taylor went into Bethlehem in his usual way, buoyed with confidence and hope, asking Wharton for stock in the company—with the declaration, "I am a very firm believer in the future

possibilities of the company and, therefore, wish to partici-
pate as greatly as possible in the gains if there are any."[27]
He was accompanied by those veteran followers who knew
well the vicissitudes of the Taylor trail, among them Gantt,
Barth, and Merrick. His first task at Bethlehem was to
try to have Davenport made Superintendent of Manufacture where he would be directly associated with Taylor
and working with him. Accordingly, in one of his first
recommendations to Linderman, Taylor noted:

The first step in my judgment toward this end should
be to establish a new office or position in your works,
namely, that of Superintendent of Manufacture. . . .
It is hardly a strained comparison to say that the management of your manufacturing departments as at present
conducted, by a General Superintendent without the aid
of a Superintendent of Manufacture, is analogous to the
state of affairs which would exist if our fleet of ships off
Santiago de Cuba were without an Admiral, and their
daily evolutions were directed by the Secretary of the Navy
from Washington by wire. . . .
It would seem then as though you were especially in need
of a strong man who can unite all of your heads of departments; and who, if possible, is reasonably familiar with
your manufacture, and if practicable, for many reasons,
this man should be selected from among your employees
rather than from outside. . . . I went over carefully with
each of your leading employees the nature of the position
to be filled, and then asked each one to name a man whom
they thought best fitted for the office. . . . I am sorry, however, to be obliged to report that your employees are not
all united in recommending any one man for this position.
It is the opinion of the writer that Mr. Davenport is the
best available man for this position for the following reasons: First, he will have from the start the hearty cooperation of all of your leading manufacturing departments.
This is evident from the list of those who favor him. Second, he has demonstrated his fitness for the position by
filling a similar one at the Midvale Steel Works in a
satisfactory manner. Third, he is probably more familiar
with the operation and performance of all of your manufacturing departments than anyone who could be found.

Fourth, he will greatly strengthen the executive force of your works, which is the weakest part of your organization, without any increase of your salary list. . . .

I can quite appreciate that the transfer of Mr. Davenport from his present position would be an inconvenience to you in your business department, but in my judgment the weakness of the present manufacturing organization is so serious and the need of securing the best possible man for this position so great, that it would justify almost any sacrifice in your other departments.[28]

Davenport was duly installed as superintendent; and assured of the full backing of Wharton, Taylor went on to do some of his most productive work since he left Midvale.

Taylor's work at Bethlehem was twofold, the introduction of his management principles first in the yard, and then in the machine shop. The description of the first part of this task, known as the "story of Schmidt," became a classical example of scientific management, and was used frequently by Taylor as an illustration in his writings and speeches. We tell it here in his own words:

One of the first pieces of work undertaken by us, when the writer started to introduce scientific management into the Bethlehem Steel Company, was to handle pig iron on task work. The opening of the Spanish War found some 80,000 tons of pig iron placed in small piles in an open field adjoining the works. Prices for pig iron had been so low that it could not be sold out of profit, and it therefore had been stored. With the opening of the Spanish War the price of pig iron rose, and this large accumulation of iron was sold. This gave us a good opportunity to show the workmen, as well as the owners and managers of the works, on a fairly large scale the advantages of task work over the old-fashioned day work and piece work, in doing a very elementary class of work.

The Bethlehem Steel Company had five blast furnaces, the product of which had been handled by a pig iron gang for many years. This gang, at this time, consisted of about 75 men. They were good, average pig iron handlers, were under an excellent foreman who himself had been a pig iron handler, and the work was done, on the whole, about as fast and as cheaply as it was anywhere else at that time.

A railroad switch was run out into the field, right along the edge of the piles of pig iron. An inclined plank was placed against the side of a car, and each man picked up from his pile a pig of iron weighing about 92 pounds, walked up the inclined plank and dropped it on the end of the car.

We found that this gang were loading on the average about 12½ long tons per man per day. We were surprised to find, after studying the matter [time study], that a first class pig-iron handler ought to handle between 47 and 48 long tons per day, instead of 12½ tons. This task seemed to us so very large that we were obliged to go over our work several times before we were absolutely sure that we were right. Once we were sure, however, that 47 tons was a proper day's work for a first-class pig iron handler, the task which faced us as managers under the modern scientific plan was clearly before us. It was our duty to see that the 80,000 tons of pig iron was loaded on to the cars at the rate of 47 tons per man per day, in place of 12½ tons, at which rate the work was then being done. And it was further our duty to see that this work was done without bringing on a strike among the men, without any quarrel with the men, and to see that the men were happier and better contented when loading at the new rate of 47 tons than they were when loading at the old rate of 12½ tons.

Our first step was the scientific selection of the workman. In dealing with workmen under this type of management, it is an inflexible rule to talk to and deal with only one man at a time, since each workman has his own special abilities and limitations, and since we are not dealing with men in masses, but are trying to develop each individual man to his highest state of efficiency and prosperity. Our first step was to find the proper workman to begin with. We therefore carefully watched and studied these 75 men for three or four days, at the end of which time we had picked out four men who appeared to be physically able to handle pig iron at the rate of 47 tons per day. A careful study was then made of each of these men. We looked up their history as far back as practicable and thorough inquiries were made as to the character, habits, and the ambition of each of them. Finally we selected one from among the four as the most likely man to start with. He was a little Pennsylvania Dutchman who had been observed to trot back home for a mile or so after his work in the evening about as fresh as he was when he came trotting down to work in the morning. We found that upon wages of $1.15 a day he had succeeded in buying a small plot of ground, and that he was engaged in putting up the walls of a little house for himself in the morning before starting to work and a night after leaving. He also had the reputation of being exceedingly "close," that is, of placing a very high value on a dollar. As one man whom we talked to about him said, "A penny looks about the size of a cart-wheel to him." This man we will call Schmidt.

The task before us, then, narrowed itself down to getting Schmidt to handle 47 tons of pig iron per day and making him glad to do it. This was done as follows. Schmidt was called out from among the gang of pig iron handlers and talked to somewhat in this way:

"Schmidt, are you a high-priced man?"

"Vell, I don't know vat you mean."

"Oh, yes, you do. What I want to know is whether you are a high-priced man or not."

"Vell, I don't know vat you mean."

"Oh, come now, you answer my questions. What I want to find out is whether you are a high-priced man or one of these cheap fellows here. What I want to find out is whether you want to earn $1.85 a day or you are satisfied with $1.15, just the same as all these cheap fellows are getting."

"Did I vant $1.85 a day? Vas dot a high-priced man? Vell, yes I vas a high-priced man."

"Oh, you're aggravating me. Of course you want $1.85 a day—every one wants it! You know perfectly well that that has very little to do with your being a high-priced man. For goodness sake answer my questions, and don't waste any more of my time. Now come over here. You see that pile of pig iron?"

"Yes."

"You see that car?"

"Yes."

"Well, if you are a high-priced man, you will load that pig iron on that car tomorrow for $1.85. Now do wake up and answer my question. Tell me whether you are a high-priced man or not."

"Vell—Did I got $1.85 for loading dot pig iron on dot car tomorrow?"

"Yes, of course you do, and you get $1.85 for loading a pile like that every day right through the year. That is what a high-priced man does, and you know it just as well as I do."

"Vell, dot's all right. I could load dot pig iron on the car tomorrow for $1.85, and I get it every day, don't I?"

"Certainly you do—certainly you do."

"Vell, den, I vas a high-priced man."

"Now, hold on, hold on. You know just as well as I do that a high-priced man has to do exactly as he's told from morning till night. You have seen this man here before, haven't you?"

"No, I never saw him."

"Well, if you are a high-priced man, you will do exactly as this man tells you tomorrow, from morning till night. When he tells you to pick up a pig, and walk, you pick it up and you walk, and when he tells you to sit down and rest, you sit down. You do that right straight through the day. And what's more, no back talk. Do you understand that? When this man tells you to walk, you walk; when he tells you to sit down, you sit down, and you don't talk back at him. Now you come on to work here tomorrow morning and I'll know before night whether you are really a high-priced man or not."

This seems to be rather rough talk. And indeed it would be if applied to an educated mechanic or even intelligent laborer. With a man of the mentally sluggish type of Schmidt it is appropriate and not unkind, since it is effective in fixing his attention on the high wages which he wants and away from what, if it were called to his attention, he probably would consider impossibly hard work.

What would Schmidt's answer be if he were talked to in a manner which is usual under the management of "initiative and incentive"? Say, as follows:

"Now, Schmidt, you are a first class pig iron handler and know your business well. You have been handling at the rate of $12\frac{1}{2}$ tons per day. I have given considerable study to handling pig iron, and feel sure that you could do a much larger day's work than you have been doing. Don't

you think that if you really tried you could hand[...]
of pig iron per day, instead of 12½ tons?"

What you think Schmidt's answer would be to th[...]
  Schmidt started to work, and all day long, and a[...]
intervals, was told by the man who stood over [...]
a watch, "Now pick up a pig and walk. Now sit d[...]
rest. Now walk, now rest," etc. He worked when [...]
told to work, and rested when he was told to rest[...]
half-past five in the afternoon had his 47½ tons [...]
on the car. And he practically never failed to work [...]
pace and do the task that was set him during th[...]
years that the writer was at Bethlehem. And thro[...]
this time he averaged a little more than $1.85 pe[...]
whereas before he had never received over $1.15 pe[...]
which was the ruling rate of wages at that time in B[...]
hem. That is, he received 60 per cent higher wages [...]
were paid to other men who were not working on [...]
work. One man after another was picked out and tr[...]
to handle pig iron at the rate of 47½ tons per day unt[...]
of the pig iron was handled at this rate, and the men [...]
receiving 60 per cent more wages than other work[...]
around them.[29]

  The often-repeated story of Schmidt has been quoted h[...]
at such length because it best conveys the essence [...]
Taylor's personality and his style as a manager. It a[...]
raises an important question: How can Taylor's avowal [...]
cooperation as the basic tenet of scientific management [...]
reconciled with the authoritarian streak that dominate[...]
the story? On the face of it, it would seem that Taylo[...]
interprets cooperation as orders from the manager anc[...]
unquestioning obedience from the workers—"when he [...]
tells you to walk, you walk, when he tells you to sit down [...]
and rest, you sit down . . . and what's more, no back talk." [...]
He would, however, have made the following distinction, [...]
namely, that cooperation does not mean the scrapping of [...]
an authority-subordination pattern in the factory but [...]
merely the elimination of arbitrariness in authority. [...]
Scientific management lays out certain rules and procedures [...]
to be followed to reach a certain goal; the manager simply [...]

transmits these rules to the workers, he does not originate them. Taylor's favorite analogy for this cooperation was the relationship between a doctor and a slightly obtuse patient.

Taylor's more critical task, and the purpose for which he was specifically employed, was to reorganize the No. 2 machine shop along the lines of his system. The only existing organization was the typical factory arrangement of the period, with the shop divided into rough geographical sections with a foreman in charge of each. Taylor's first recommendation to Linderman thus read:

In most manufacturing establishments it is customary to leave many details which seriously affect the quality and quantity of the output entirely in the hands of the foremen, gang bosses or even the individual workmen. Such details for example as the care of belting, the shape of the cutting tools, and the method of dressing, tempering, grinding, storing and issuing the same, the quality of the tool steel from which they are made, and the quantity to be kept on hand; the speeds and feeds used on the machine tools, etc, etc.

It is the writer's viewpoint that the efficiency of the shop depends quite as much upon proper attention to these details as it does upon the nature of the machine tools which are used. If this is a fact, it is evident that it is a matter of the greatest importance that each of these details should receive the most careful study and attention, and that in each case a STANDARD should be adopted and maintained throughout the works.[30]

Instead of the tables used at Midvale, which gave the proper speed, feed, and cut of the machines, a slide rule, developed by Barth, was put into practical use for the first time. This, in turn, made the setting up and enforcement of standards essential.

The slide rules cannot be left at the lathe to be banged about by the machinist. They must be used by a man with reasonably clean hands, and at a table or desk, and this man must write his instructions as to speed, feed, depth of cut, etc., and send them to the machinist well in advance

of the time that the work is to be done. Even if these instructions are sent to the machinist, however, little attention will be paid to them unless rigid standards have not only been adopted but enforced throughout the shop for every detail, large and small, of the shop equipment, as well as for shop methods.[31]

It was at Bethlehem that Taylor took the first steps in establishing functional foremanship as a system of organization and in developing it into the regular planning department that the technical innovation of the slide rule demanded. Here, the format of his instruction card was finalized. The time card made its first appearance. And the mnemonic system of classification and symbolization (previously applied only to stores and accounts) was applied to tools. It was also at Bethlehem that many other details of scientific management such as balance of work sheets, order slips, and so forth, were fully systematized.[32]

It was at Bethlehem that Taylor continued his experiments on tool steels and, in association with Manuel White, made his discovery of high-speed steel at the end of 1898. The essence of the discovery was that while chromium-tungsten tools were not effective when heated to temperatures between 1,500°F and 1,750°F, their cutting efficiency actually *increased* when the heat was raised above 1,750°F and, indeed, was the greatest just before the melting point. This new heat treatment of the tool steel, as we have noted, resulted in a much greater output from the machine tools, which could be now run at much higher speeds. It is significant that even before the discovery was patented, Taylor wrote to his old chief Sellers in Philadelphia offering its use for the benefit of Sellers' company.[33] Eventually, however, Taylor sold the right to Bethlehem in exchange for a fixed percentage of the fees paid for it—which mounted, in time, to more than $50,000.[34]

Despite the unusual financial prosperity and productivity

of these years, the Bethlehem episode was Taylor's greatest setback. The cause lay not only in the increasing opposition amongst the great majority of Bethlehem's executives and owners but also in Taylor's diminishing ability to deal with their opposition. Though the trouble with Linderman (whom he considered a typical financier) started soon after his arrival, he could afford to ignore it as long as his operational relationship with Davenport and his confidence in Wharton's support were sustained.

I got into a big row with the owners of the company on that labor question. They did not wish me, as they said, to depopulate South Bethlehem. They owned all the houses in South Bethlehem and the company stores, and when they saw we were cutting the labor force down to about one-fourth, they did not want it. They came to me and said so frankly, "We don't want that done," they said. I said: You are going to have it, whether you want it or not, as long as I am here. You employed me with the distinct understanding that that is what I was going to do. You agreed to it, and got me here for that purpose. You had a unanimous vote. I would not come here if there was a single man that did not want what I was going to do. "Well, we did not think you could do it." I said: I don't care what you thought. Your remedy is at hand. Tell me any night you want me to go, and I go tomorrow morning. On the other hand, Mr. President, just counter-mand one of my orders and I will go tomorrow morning, but while I am here I am going to do what I came to do, whether you like it or not. If you did not want that done, it was up to you to say so when I put it in writing. You agreed to it and said you wanted it. It is going to be done.[35]

There is an uncorroborated story that some of the directors assembled one day and tried to heckle Taylor into submitting his resignation. Taylor, however, still backed by Wharton, let them know in no uncertain terms, that he was aware of their purpose but that if they wanted to get rid of him they would have to fire him, and "what was more, they one and all could go to blue blazes."[36]

Taylor's written communications to Linderman, after all

the company president, were especially peremptory, tactless, and full of pique:

. . . Your company is not paying sufficiently large salaries
to keep the good men which it has, and you therefore
cannot hope to attract from other works the additional
men most urgently needed to carry on the improved scheme
of management which the writer is introducing.

. . . Unless adequate steps are taken to correct the above
trouble it is an extravagance on your part to pay the
writer the wages which he is receiving, and that the writer
on his part cannot afford to waste his time and risk his
reputation in training good men at your expense merely
to have them taken away and used by other companies.[37]

Today Mr. Davenport called my attention, for the first
time to a drawing of the foundation for your new Steam
Hammer which is being put up. The foundation, as
designed, is so entirely opposite of what I believe a steam
hammer foundation should be, that I wish to most clearly
disclaim all responsibility for the same. I have not been
consulted about this by anyone, and therefore, will not
assume the slightest responsibility, either direct or indirect,
regarding it.[38]

It is a curious psychological fact, and one for which the
writer can find no explanation, that of all the parties who
have visited the works and are acquainted with what has
been done here, the only ones who have failed to con-
gratulate the writer upon the results accomplished are with
one or two exceptions the leading officers of the company.[39]

The violence of his response was steadily mounting. As his
official and often worshipful biographer, Copley, admits:

As time went on, he exhibited a fighting spirit of an
intensity almost pathological. Men in his own little group
were shocked by some of his outbursts. "If I know that a
man is going to stab me," he said, "I'll stab him first, and
if he hits me once, I'll hit him twice." . . . Made morbidly
sensitive to kicks by years of taking them, he now and then,
to some extent, appeared to lose his head. Men would come
to him and say: "You ordered a four-inch belt. Should
it not be three inches?" "Make it four and a half," he
would retort. "Question me, do you? Then I'll give you
worse and more of it."[40]

Clearly a crisis, psychological and professional, was in the offing, and finally did occur in early 1901. Taylor complained of poor health and "nervous strain" and was advised by friends to get out completely and "take some satisfaction in life."[41] The old symptoms of a "nervous breakdown" appeared once again—"I have since last summer had very poor health. Mrs. Taylor was operated upon for appendicitis in the spring, and the worry and anxiety over this coupled with the regular strain due to introducing new methods rather overworked my nerves so that my stomach has given me a great deal of trouble."[42] At Bethlehem too things were coming to a head. Taylor asked Wharton for a conference, and afterwards, on April 4, 1901, wrote a letter to Linderman (enclosing a copy to Wharton) which read:

Dear Sir,

I was employed by your company some three years ago to introduce a new system of management, accounting, etc., into your works.

My progress in this work has on the whole been slow. One of the chief causes being that I have lacked the authority to see that my directions were properly carried out.

There are also many minor details of your plant which must be modified in order to successfully introduce my system of management, and it is obviously necessary that I be given the requisite authority to see that these details are arranged in harmony with the new system . . . .

I do not want any authority in any matters except those immediately affecting my system of management and accounting, but I respectfully request that the various officers of the company be instructed to carry out all orders which may be given them by me in relation to these subjects.[43]

Having cleared the letter first with Wharton and under the impression that he had his full support, Taylor went off for a short golfing vacation where he received the following letter from his assistant, Gantt:

You would be interested to know that the number of rumours that are floating around here about people's resignations, etc. The whole works are full of them, and even the town. They are hardly worth repeating to you, but serve only to illustrate the fact that the whole place is stirred up.[44]

When he returned from his vacation, Taylor found the following brief epistle awaiting him on his desk:

Dear Sir,

I beg to advise you that your services will not be required by this company after May 1st, 1901.

Yours truly,

[signed]   Robt. P. Linderman
                                    President[45]

Along with Taylor, all his associates, Gantt, Barth, and the rest, were summarily dismissed. Davenport, because of his association with Taylor, was also forced to resign, and the grestest experimental application of the new management was brought to an abrupt halt. For the moment, in his own eyes, Fred Taylor was a failure.

Failures, and their attendant disappointments, have always been a common condition of human life. They are not limited or particular to any one period of life but are liable to occur, in varying degrees of intensity, in all stages of the life cycle. Failure makes a demand, a demand to master the attendant disappointment. To the extent that modern society is predominantly work oriented, a failure in a man's career development can lead to a serious personal crisis that must be faced and mastered.[1] The magnitude of such a crisis depends on one's emotional investment in the area of work, for a failure can often reopen old conflicts and threaten the ego mastery of earlier developmental stages. Failure, paradoxically, does not preclude success—that is, career achievements which by customary objective criteria spell success may be experienced subjectively by an individual as a sense of failure. This, of course, reflects the gap between expectations and actual achievements, a gap between what one wants to be and what one is. For most human beings who have known this discrepancy, the pain of failure is made bearable by familiar work or trusted social relationships, as well as by their participation in collective social rituals that provide psychological support by constantly reaffirming and reintegrating them as members of a community. The lives of some creative men, however, reveal that the consequences of adult failure have been much more serious, precipitating a psychological crisis of the first magnitude.

Often, these are lonely men in whom the intensity of crisis reflects the extent of their isolation—as if their communal bonds lay more in the past than in the present. Such men often have had a close, almost "symbiotic" childhood relationship with one of their parents. Often, they have received the exaggerated admiration of one or both parents, and thus from early childhood on, have a sense of being someone special, of being chosen. In some cases, this parental admiration is combined with demanding

8

FAILURES AND DISAPPOINTMENTS

harshness—a constellation which forces a child's emotional investment inward. This, in turn, may result in a heightened—narcissistic—sense of self. For such a child, this narcissism is both a shield and the Damoclean sword; in Freud's words, "A strong egoism is a protection against falling ill, but in the last resort we must begin to love in order not to fall ill, and we are bound to fall ill if, in consequence of frustration, we are unable to love."[2] Such a person, then, faces a greater threat from failure, especially if other avenues of self-fulfillment, like the ability (in Nietzsche's phrase) to "plant a garden of love," are closed. We shall come back to this a little later.

The trend of the foregoing remarks is easily discernible. Did Taylor have such a childhood constellation leading to a heightened sense of self that would explain the magnitude and the severity of his reaction to the failure at Bethlehem? Although this question is not central to this particular study, a post-Freudian biographer finds it impossible to ignore.

The data on Taylor's childhood relationship with his parents are scant. However, on the basis of the existing data—Taylor's personality as it comes through the historical record and the contemporary clinical literature on this problem—it is probable, call it informed speculation, that the relationship between Emily and Frederick Taylor was of the kind just described. The portrait of Emily Taylor in an earlier chapter—her leadership in the suffragette movement, her moralistic strictness, and her domination of the Taylor household—is resonant with the description of other mothers met with in clinical literature whose relationship with their sons is such that the son abandons the expectation of emotional nurture from his mother in favor of ambition and a desire to achieve:

Such mothers are frequently seductive, especially when they characteristically develop heightened defensive reactions, that is, additional defenses against their hostility toward men. . . . As a defense against the fears of their incestuous desires they attempt to drive their sons—and often succeed—into an intense idealization of the ego ideal which may also be then coupled to a severe, meaning punitive, superego.[3]

Career failure thus hits hardest those men who have an intensely idealized ego ideal (who one wants to be), and a disappointment (of the scale of Taylor's on his dismissal from Bethlehem) leads, at least temporarily, to the impairment of this ego ideal and gives rise to feelings of absolute unworthiness.

Occasionally, within the limitations imposed by a biography, one must complement the available data with informed speculation in order to present a coherent and plausible picture; for the certainty of "what was" one has sometimes to substitute the probability of "what very well may have been." Hence the foregoing small excursion into "originology." Our main interest, however, is to acknowledge the dimensions of Taylor's disappointment and to clarify the process of recovery which later contributed to his emergence as the "prophet" of scientific management. Clinical descriptions of the dynamics of disappointment and subsequent recovery are scant. An illuminating source for understanding this phenomenon is the "private writing"—the correspondence and journals of those creative men who have suffered major disappointments in their adult lives. An examination of such diaries and letters suggests a rough sketch of the dynamics of this process of failure and mastery of disappointment in adult life.

We have noted that one of the effects of massive disappointment is to break down the ego ideal—a disintegration that the individual perceives as a radical lowering of self-esteem. A confession of failure takes the form of self-directed accusations. Oscar Wilde was a man known above all for his brilliance, wit, and vanity ("I summed up all systems in a phrase and all existence in an epigram"). His brilliant career cut short by his conviction for homosexuality, he levels these reproaches at himself in a letter from prison:

I let myself be lured into long spells of senseless and sensual ease. I amused myself with being a *flaneur,* a dandy, a man of fashion. I surrounded myself with the smaller natures and the meaner minds. I became the spendthrift of my own genius, and to waste an eternal youth gave me a curious joy. Tired of being on the heights I deliberately went to the depths, in the search for new sensations. What the paradox was to me in the sphere of thought, perversity became to me in the sphere of passion. Desire, at the end, was a malady, or a madness, or both. I grew careless of the lives of others. I took pleasure where it pleased men and passed on. I forgot that every little action of the common day makes or unmakes character, and that therefore what one has done in the secret chamber one has some day to cry aloud on the housetops. I ceased to be Lord over myself. I was no longer the Captain of my Soul, and did not know it. . . . I ended in horrible disgrace. There is only one thing for me now, absolute Humility.[4]

Every self-reproach has an element of punishing oneself for sins committed or imagined, a quality of "moral masochism."[5] Wilde's imagery testifies eloquently to this element:

Out of my nature has come wild despair; an abandonment to grief that was piteous even to look at: terrible and impotent rage: bitterness and scorn: anguish that wept aloud: misery that could find no voice: sorrow that was dumb. I have passed through every possible mode of suffering. Better than Wordsworth himself I know what Wordsworth meant when he said:

Suffering is permanent, obscure and dark
And has the nature of Infinity.

But while there were times when I rejoiced in the idea that my sufferings were to be endless, I could not bear them to be without meaning. Now I find hidden away in my nature something that tells me that nothing in the whole world is meaningless and suffering least of all. That something hidden away in my nature, like treasure in a field, is Humility.[6]

Self-reproach is one of the facets of disappointment. The

other one is bitterness directed outward, against those held responsible for causing the pain. Thus only two months after Wilde's professions of humility, with a capital "H," he was writing, "I go out with an adder in my heart and an asp in my tongue, and every night I sow thorns in the garden of my soul."[7]

The inward-directed reproach and the outward-directed one often go together, alternating with the mood of the sufferer; the common element is the isolation of the individual thrown back upon his own resources. Whether he lashes out against himself or against "others," he is alone. A letter of Nietzsche shows how deeply interwoven these themes can be:

It is absolutely necessary that I should be misunderstood; nay, I would go even further and say that I must succeed in being understood in the worst possible way and despised. The fact that those "nearest to me" should be the first to do this was what I understood last summer and the following autumn, and by that alone I became filled with the glorious consciousness of being on the right road. . . . In so far as the general trend of my nature is concerned, I have no comrades; nobody has any idea when I most need comfort, encouragement, or a shake of hand. . . . And if ever I complain the whole world thinks it is entitled to exercise its modicum of power over me as a sufferer—they call it consolation, pity, good advice, etc.

But men like myself have always had to put up with the same sort of thing. . . .[8]

Of these two facets of disappointment, we have already seen evidence of the latter in Taylor's bitterness against the aristocrat-financiers, who did not support him and whom he always held responsible for his failures. Writing to a friend after his dismissal from Bethlehem, he describes their perfidious ingratitude:

Altogether with the sale of patents and forming of combinations, etc., I have been able to gather in about $— so that I do not propose to do much more of the exceedingly disagreeable work I have had for the last six to eight years in organizing manufacturing companies, in which I was in hot water from the time I started to work, till I got through, with never any thanks, until after my work was all done and I had gone into a new set of quarrels.[9]

Perhaps it is true that the men who ran Bethlehem, and especially the president, Linderman, did not understand Taylor and the importance of his innovations. But it seems equally true, as evidenced in Taylor's violent reactions to actual or imagined slights and in his tactless notes to Linderman, that Taylor wanted to be misunderstood. Or, to put it another way, he wanted to be punished. Nor was this a new theme. Taylor's aggression and hostility toward those in positions of authority, a grasping aggression that sought to take possession of those same authority figures and to overpower them, was always a kind of testing. The hidden motive of this far from playful game was to see if his superior was strong enough, man enough, father enough, not only to withstand it but to punish it. For only then could he be loved—as Sellers was at Midvale. But a succession of his superiors—Brinley at Midvale, the "financiers" at Manufacturing Investment Company and at Cramp's Shipyards, Linderman at Bethlehem—did not "love him enough" to punish him. His hostile mistrust for these "aloof," "aristocratic" men then increased, his "fighting spirit" intensified to pathological proportions, until his superiors had to act. When the punishment finally came, Taylor would interpret it as an act of weakness on the part of a superior who could not stand his ground but retreated by casting him (Taylor) away.

In Taylor's case there is no evidence of self-accusation. The fact is not surprising, for with the exception of the most introspective of men, these accusations are silent ones, present rather in a sense of vague unease and periods of self-criticism.

The defenses employed against the lowering of self-esteem are, however, only partially adequate and are usually followed by depressive reactions. The form of this depression depends on the whole developmental sweep of an individual's life history and on his ego strength. It may be a fleeting one, mildly chronic, or an acute one, precipitating a complete breakdown. Taylor's "nervous breakdown" with its attendant physical symptoms—insomnia and stomach trouble—signaled his depression.

We now turn to the process of recovery. What are the factors that encourage and sustain the mastery of depression? The first one is the individual's capacity for radical candor—his capacity to confront himself emotionally, to recognize both the failure and the depression and to try to redefine his aspirations and abilities. Abraham Zaleznik quotes the following passage from the *Diaries of Harold Nicolson* (written when Nicolson was asked to resign his post as Parliamentary Secretary) as an illustration of this kind of fundamental self-assessment:

"But I mind more than I thought I should mind. It is mainly, I suppose, a sense of failure. I quite see that if the Labour leaders have been pressing to have my post, there is good cause why they should have it. But if I had more power and drive, I should have been offered Rab Butler's job at the Foreign Office, which I should dearly have loved. As it is, I come back to the bench below the gangway having had my chance and failed to profit by it. Ever since I have been in the House I have been looked on as a might-be. Now I shall be a might-have-been. Always up till now I have been buoyed up by the hope of writing some good book or achieving a position of influence in politics. I now know that I shall never write a book better than I have written already, and that my political career is at an end. I shall merely get balder and fatter and more deaf as the years go by. This is an irritating thing. Success should come late in life in order to compensate for the loss of youth; I had youth and success together, and now I have old age and failure. Apart from all this, I mind leaving the ministry, where I did good work and had friends.

This space indicates the end of my ambitions in life.

'Omnium consensu capax imperii nisi imperasset.' (Tacitus on the Emperor Galba: 'Had he never been placed in authority, nobody would ever have doubted his capacity for it.')"[10]

Another factor in the process of self-recovery and the transcendence of failure is the support sought in, and often provided by, human relationships. One becomes excessively dependent on and grateful for small acts of kindness from friends and relatives, reading into such acts meanings that may not exist, all in an imperative effort once again to redirect emotional energy outward. But these very relationships, so vital to recovery, may be strained to the breaking point. The sufferer's feelings of unworthiness may become desperate enough to preclude a casual and spontaneous acceptance of love; he demands greater and greater proof of love, and indeed, finally the unlimited parental love of early childhood. Theodor Reik tells the story of a man who asks his mistress if she would still love him if he suddenly became poor. "Of course," she replies. The man is not satisfied. Would she love him if he accidentally became a cripple? "Yes," she reassures him. Still not satisfied, he asks if she would love him if he became deaf, blind, and insane. The limits of her patience reached, she explodes, "Why on earth should I love an impoverished, crippled, blind, insane, deaf idiot?"[11] The man has reached his goal for he can now whisper to himself, "My mother would have, in spite of everything."

The human relationships from which the needed support may be derived are not temporally limited; they may be part of the immediate present or actual in warm memories of childhood. Dostoevsky, awaiting trial and suffering severe depression, writes to his brother:

The time goes by most irregularly, so to speak—now too quickly, now to slowly. Sometimes I have the feeling that I've grown accustomed to this sort of life, and that nothing matters very much. Of course, I try to keep all alluring thoughts out of my head, but can't always succeed; my early days, with their fresh impressions, storm in on my soul, and I live all the past over again. That is the natural order of things.[12]

The reliance on these relationships, on any bond of trust and love, in the recovery from depression is most poignantly described in one of Nietzsche's letters to a friend:

We grow older and therefore lonelier; the love that leaves us is precisely that love which was lavished upon us like an unconscious necessity—not owing to our particular qualities but in spite of them. The curtain falls on our past when our mother dies; it is then for the first time that our childhood and youth become nothing more than a memory. And then the same process extends; the friends of our youth, our teachers, our ideals of those days, all die, and every day we grow more lonely, and ever colder breezes blow about us. You were right to plant another garden of love around you, dear friend![13]

Where intimacy with family or friends or lovers has been denied, depression can end in tragedy. The biography of James Forrestal,[14] a man successful on Wall Street and in government service, is a case in point. Forrestal's capacity for intense, single-minded work was apparently developed at the expense of human intimacy. So radical was his isolation that the major disappointment of his life, his resignation as Secretary of Defense, led to psychosis and suicide. And Nietzsche, above all, in his consummately personal letters, has documented the need for human sympathy in periods of depression:

. . . and even now the whole of my philosophy totters after one hour's sympathetic intercourse even with total strangers! It seems to me so foolish to insist on being right at the expense of love, and not to be able to impart one's best for fear of destroying sympathy. *Hinc meae lacrimae.*[15]

The capacity to work, and to lose oneself in one's work, it seems is not enough for self-recovery, and one comes back again to Freud's dual criteria—*"love* and work." Disappointment isolates, failure invokes loneliness, and the need once again to invest oneself in other people becomes paramount.[16]

Taylor too turned to human relationships in his effort to recover and cast off the slough of depression. His actions after leaving Bethlehem are like steps back into the warm corners of his childhood and youth. He adopted three children of a distant relative of his wife's—two boys and a girl—the same family constellation of his own childhood. He left the town of Bethlehem, and went back to Germantown to live in a house very near "Cedron," where he spent the first eleven years of his boyhood.[17] Every evening he would walk down to his parents' Ross Street house to visit his invalid mother. He once again went back to "Uncle William" Sellers, not to work for him but in an effort to renew a trusted association.

Sellers agreed to let Taylor continue his metal cutting experiments in his machine shop under the direction of Carl Barth. Sellers, however, was now an old man, and his young managers were unsympathetic to Taylor's ideas. Constant friction was the result, and in 1903, Sellers called Barth, pleading advancing age for his disinclination to countermand or pacify his managers on Taylor's behalf. So the experiments had to be stopped, but the disappointment was a minor one. Of far greater importance to Taylor at that stage of his life was the mere association with the man who had first guided and supported him. It was in Philadelphia, under the protective shadow of his first sponsor, that Taylor decided that he "could no longer afford to work for money" and would spend the rest of his life in the propagation of his system. By the end of 1903, the crisis had passed.

There is a third factor that may play a crucial role in the transcendence of failure and the mastery of disappointment. As mentioned earlier, the very cause of depression in some restless and creative persons—the narcissistic sense of self—has in it also the source of the remedy. Failure threatens the ego ideal and results in lowering of self-esteem. Narcissism, self-love, we use the terms synonymously, functions to repair the damage to the ego and the ego ideal. Even in the depths of depression the creative person seems to be saying, "The best way to show the world that I cannot yet be written off is by undertaking even more ambitious projects and bringing them to fruition. I cannot give up now."

With all this was mingled a certain self-pity, for I felt that I was dying and believed that I was bidding the public my last farewell. Far from fearing death, I watched its coming joyfully. But I was reluctant to leave my fellowmen before they had learned my true worth, before they knew how deserving I should have appeared of their love if they had known me better.[18]

This is Rousseau recovering from depression and girding up for some of his best work. Similar sentiments are expressed by Nietzsche, before writing *Zarathustra*,[19] and by Wilde as he slowly overcame the depression caused by his disgrace and prison.[20]

Taylor's decision henceforth to be the prophet of scientific management bespeaks, in part, this combination of self-love and ambition. His abandoning the practice of scientific management and taking it up as a cause was thus also a way of maintaining that scientific management and by implication Taylor himself were not failures but were yet to show their "true worth" to the world. His retreat to Germantown and to his mother, to his renewed association with William Sellers, his adoption of children, his giving up the practical tasks of his vision to don the reformer's mantle, these were all interconnected acts, mutual elements in a restitutive process designed to master the psychological crisis precipitated by his ultimate career failure at Bethlehem.

We have examined the dimensions of the psychological crisis precipitated by Taylor's career failure and the process of recovery which allowed him to emerge from this crisis in his new dual role as an industrial reformer and as the prophet of a creed that promised complete harmony between workers and managers. We have considered Taylor's actions mainly from the point of view of his personal development. However, the psychohistorical method, outlined in the opening chapter—the method that has guided this entire study—includes three additional coordinates for the interpretation of the "meaning" of an action or event: it must also be considered with reference to the life stage of the individual at the time of the event; to the relevant values, attitudes, and expectations of his society or community; and to the relevant historical development of that community.

Erikson's concept of the human life cycle has described human development not as a smooth continuum but as a succession of intimately related crises or turning points.[1] In analogy, human growth is more like the cocoon-butterfly than the sapling-tree. Each developmental stage of the life cycle then is marked by a crisis. Whereas in childhood these crises are unambiguously related to physical growth and to what Freud called the "vicissitudes of the libido," in adulthood their psychosexual aspects may appear somewhat attenuated.

The span of years we call "middle age" is long (ever more so with increasing life expectancy) and variable. Sometime during these years, typically in the forties, the mid-life crisis occurs—in a scarcely noticeable malaise or in acute conflict. Sexually, it manifests itself in women in the menopause and in men in what has often been called the male climacteric. Human biology simply gives notice, so to speak, that one is growing old. Eliot Jacques has maintained that the psychological impact of this is critical —that the mid-life crisis often means a confrontation with the fact of death and intimation of personal mortality.[2]

For philosophers like Bergson, death is the source of man's uniqueness as well as his dismay, since, alone among the animals, man realizes he is going to die and must learn to live with his finiteness. For Kierkegaard, the acceptance of death and mastery of anxiety created by the fear of death is the beginning of a true religious sense. Yet for most men, at least until mid-life, death is merely an abstract concept. As Freud noted:

Our own death is indeed unimaginable, and whenever we make the attempt to imagine it we can conceive that we really survive as spectators. Hence the psychoanalytic school could venture on the assertion that at bottom no one believes in his own death, or to put the thing in another way, in the unconscious every one of us is convinced of his own immortality.[3]

We find the same insight in the story of the demon and the righteous king in the Indian epic, *Mahabharta*. The demon puts a final question to the king, whose correct answer would bring back the king's brothers from the realm of death: "What is the strangest thing in the world?" And the king answers correctly, "The strangest thing is that each man, seeing others die around him, is still convinced that he himself is immortal."

It is in mid-life that this conviction of immortality is often suddenly shaken—contributing to a depressive crisis which Dante has expressed in the words:

In the middle of the journey of our life, I came to myself within a dark wood where the straight way was lost. Ah, how hard it is to tell of the wood, savage and harsh and dense, the thought of which renews my fear. So bitter is it that death is hardly more.[4]

We would venture to add that this confrontation with the unalterable fact of one's own mortality may be precipitated by an experience or sense of failure in this stage of life. There is evidence in the recollections of his friends that at Taylor's middle age whenever he was in the presence of any talk of illness or death, he would suddenly become withdrawn and silent, seemingly suffering.[5]

Each stage of the human life cycle, in Erikson's theory, is characterized not only by its threat to individual vitality but also by a specific positive developmental task whose relative resolution is another step in the growth of ego integrity. In this sense, the crisis of mid-life is one of generativity versus stagnation. Generativity, defined as the "concern in establishing and guiding the next generation" includes, besides procreativity, the concepts of productivity and creativity.[6] Generativity thus has both a personal element—the care of one's offspring—and a social element —the concern for future generations. Taylor's adoption of three children then and, more significantly, his decisive assumption of the role of preacher of scientific management together with the espousal of more exalted goals than the mere increase in productivity—namely, the elimination of strife and the creation of cooperation between capital and labor—can thus also be interpreted as a successful response to the mid-life crisis, as mastery of its depression and resolution of the psychosocial task of generativity.

The theme, then, is an archetypal one, of crisis and renewal, which is vividly present in much of the world's great literature (indeed, it is the central preoccupation of the somber Russian masters) if it has not yet found its place in the clinical journals. After working through this crisis, Taylor's whole personality seems to have become more gentle and self-confident—certainly the tone of the letters of his later years is more serene. His friends seem to have noticed this change. Copley writes:

. . . toward the close of his engagement at Bethlehem, he was seen at his worst, in that he was betrayed into outbursts of vindictiveness, or what seemed to be such. But this was merely as the coming up of storm clouds that are quickly dissipated in the prevailing geniality of a summer day. Then as he was released from first-hand or every-day contact with the shop and its clashing wills, and time continued to work its changes in him, his nature steadily mellowed. And with this mellowing came an intensification of his hatred of "antagonism and strife" and of his desire to substitute for it the spirit of "friendly cooperation and mutual helpfulness."[7]

It would have been desirable to place Taylor's early retirement from active work in a social matrix, in order to know the extent to which such a decision was customary or exceptional. There is not enough information on the career patterns of Taylor's social group, retirement ages, or the nature of postcareer occupations or hobbies to permit useful generalization. Yet we do know that Taylor's step was in the historical Quaker tradition of turning from "work" to "good works." His grandfather had retired at the age of thirty-eight, while his father had left the legal profession at an even earlier age. In a sense, Taylor was returning to the ways of his forebears— whether these were also the ways of his contemporaries is an open question.

The period between 1902 and 1910 was, if not the happiest, at least the calmest period of Taylor's adult years. Although he had given up working for money, he had by no means lost the habit of work. Relatively freed from the personal attacks that had intruded upon his middle years, and settled into family life, he found a measure of serenity in what had been until then such a turbulent life.

The mornings were set apart for work—which now consisted of writing, keeping up with his correspondence, and counseling the growing number of his followers engaged in introducing his system into different factories throughout the country. In the afternoons, he played golf and was at the disposal of his wife. And the evenings belonged to the family. The family gathered in the living room after the evening meal, and, like his father before him, Taylor read aloud. Copley has recorded his preferences:

No morbid stuff of any kind. Standard fiction such as the works of Scott and Dickens. Tales too, of school life. Outdoor stuff in plenty. Cowboy tales of the "Hopalong Cassidy" order, and records of pluck and grit such as Dillon Wallace's *The Love of the Labrador Wild.* A piece of writing that particularly delighted him was one entitled *The Will of Charles Lounsbury,* in which, among other things, was bequeathed to young men "all boisterous inspiring sports of rivalry" and "disdain of weakness and undaunted confidence in their own strength."[8]

His emphasis on robust health and activity and the concomitant fear of physical weakness or illness was reflected not only in his choice of reading material but also in the upbringing of the children. The entire family had to have periodic checkups with the doctor, whose instructions, on Taylor's insistence, had to be put down in writing. The recollections of his elder son, Kempton Taylor, offer an insight into Taylor as a father:

He earlier showed the most radical methods in straightening out the weakness of the young. My brother and I were by nature weak and by training indifferent to outdoor sport. He had the coachman play ball with us. Yet he never believed in extravagance lavished on the young, for our first baseball gloves cost 25¢ each, and we were always held a trifle behind our friends in the acquisition of worldly material. . . . I remember the indignation with which Papa greeted the presence of brother and me in a party of girls, and our hot shame at being ordered home. Papa never stood on ceremony. He heard of a ball team in our neighborhood composed of boys considerably older than ourselves and immediately told us to go and play with them. What a painful task was this one of self-introduction to a group of unknown boys, and what an unfeeling monster Papa seemed.

We moved to Boxly [Taylor's home during his last years] in the spring of 1902 and the next fall we all started in at new schools. We were both rather disinclined to push ourselves into school activities, so Papa had us don our football clothes, walk a mile to the playfield, and join a squad of boys five or six years older than ourselves. For several months we commuted in this fashion to and from the football field while our older playmates dressed in the locker rooms. This was in accordance with Papa's oft-repeated maxim: "Get into the game!" Whether we were of use to that football squad made little or no difference. Activity was the all-important principle, and activity was demanded as vigorous in the classroom as on the playing field.[9]

In values and methods of child rearing, the generations had come full circle—in this paternal absolutism we see once more the dominance of Taylor's maternal inheritance.

Taylor's own physical exercise during this period was his regular game of golf, a game which he had taken up at the age of forty. And once again, a familiar pattern—golf was not merely recreation, but to be exploited in constant experiment to increase his "efficiency" at the sport. In addition to his invention of the two-handed putter (used croquet style), he experimented with the weight and length of other clubs to get the right balance, and eventually evolved a driver that was ten inches longer than the normal one and had a much thinner lower shaft. He applied the principles of motion study to his swing and hit upon an effectively deviant playing style:

He addressed the ball almost in a line with his stance, raising one shoulder and bending one leg in a manner which aroused such epithets as "watch spring" and "human grasshopper." With this curious stroke he drove a tremendously long ball.[10]

Taylor was not oblivious to others' amusement at his expense on the golf course, and furthermore, he was able to take it with good grace. A sense of humor has ever been the greatest ally of mental serenity, and Taylor seems not to have been without his own variety of dry humor which came more and more to the surface during these years. In a letter to a golfing friend who had joked about his swing, he wrote:

Your mind seems to run entirely to implements, while mine has been working rather in the direction of motion study. I wish it were possible to convey to you an adequate impression of some of the beautiful movements that I have been working up during the past year. The only possible drawback to them is that the ball still refuses to settle down quietly into the cup, as it ought to, and also in most cases declines to go either in the direction that I wish or the required distance. Aside from these few drawbacks, the theories are perfect.[11]

Soon after Taylor had moved back from Bethlehem to Germantown, he started writing the first paper which was to give a complete outline of his system. "Shop Management" was read before the Saratoga meeting of the American Society of Mechanical Engineers in 1903. Although limited notice was taken of it at the time, it was a significant landmark in the management movement, for it helped to convert two Philadelphia manufacturers, James Dodge and Wilfred Lewis, and thus inspired the reorganization of two factories after Taylor's methods. And these two factories, in turn, served as "demonstration models."

Wilfred Lewis, a boyhood friend of Taylor's, had organized the Tabor Manufacturing Company, which produced molding machines, in 1900. Taylor, as an old friend, had partially funded the new company. The company, however, lost money; and the situation was further aggravated when its workers went on strike. When Lewis solicited Taylor for extra funds, Taylor was willing to come through this time only on the condition that the company be run under the principles of scientific management. Lewis agreed, and accordingly, Barth, who had just left William Sellers Company, was hired to reorganize the plant with Taylor serving as an unpaid advisor. At the same time, James Dodge, the president of the American Society of Mechanical Engineers and the owner of the Link-Belt Company, wanted to introduce scientific management into his company. Dodge had been using "high speed" steel and was further impressed by Taylor's paper on "Shop Management." Once again, in May 1903, Barth was sent to the new client, later dividing his time between the two companies. Another of the old Taylorites who came to Link-Belt was Merrick, the time-study expert at Bethlehem. The movement had at last obtained a real foothold from which it could venture out in search of new conquests. These two companies, besides serving as demonstration models to people interested in the actual workings of scientific management, were also used as training schools for men interested in scientific management as a career, some of whom Taylor paid from his own pocket to learn his methods. Many of these men later became prominent figures in the management movement. One was Horace Hathway, a twenty-six-year-old engineer who was hired to assist Barth at Link-Belt and later moved to Tabor. So successful was he in assimilating Taylor's methods that within four years he had become the vice-president of the Tabor Company. These new men, Hathaway and Cooke, along with the older Taylorites, Gantt, Barth, and Thompson (who had worked with Taylor in the Manufacturing Investment Co.) were to become his leading disciples; they were the core of the scientific management movement.

Meanwhile, Taylor's reputation as an engineer, based partly on his discovery of "high speed" steel, had been steadily growing. In December 1905, he was elected President of the A.S.M.E. for the following year. In his presidential address he chose to read a paper based on his metal-cutting investigations. "On the Art of Cutting Metals," which was published by the A.S.M.E. in 1907, gained immediate renown both in America and Europe; translations appeared in France, Germany, Austria, and Russia within two years. Henri Le Châtelier, professor of metallurgy in France, and later Taylor's chief partisan and disciple in that country, wrote of the monograph as follows:

The near future will show us the service which has been rendered to the mechanical arts by this generous publication of researches pursued with such uncommon perseverance. But even now we can admire without reserve the scientific method which has controlled this whole work. It is an example unique in the history of the mechanic arts. We have all admired the researches of Sir Lothian Bell on blast furnaces and those of Sir William Siemens in the regenerative furnace; but notwithstanding the high scientific value of the work of these two great engineers, on reading their papers neither of them leaves an impression on the mind which can be compared with that of Mr. Taylor's paper. It is a model which every young engineer will have to study.[12]

The impact of "On the Art of Cutting Metals," with its clearly articulated objecive of management reform, drew greater attention to Taylor's earlier paper on shop management which was now belatedly translated into the European languages. Scientific management was arousing the interest of more and more manufacturers. Barth's clientele was increasing to include Yale & Towne, Smith & Furbush, and Erie Forge Companies. Gantt, who after his dismissal from Bethlehem, had set himself up as an independent consulting engineer, had also been steadily expanding his operations. Taylor, at the end of his term as president of the A.S.M.E. in 1907, continued to follow closely and supervise the work of his disciples, and gave his undivided attention to the spread of the cause.

To the people who wrote to him expressing an interest in scientific management—and these included engineers, industrial and college executives, army and navy officers— he issued invitations to visit him at his home, Boxly. A typical invitation (to Professor Hollis of the Harvard Engineering School) reads:

I should very much appreciate the opportunity of showing you, in some of the manufacturing establishments which are managed under our system, the means which we adopt for rapidly developing successful men in the various lines of management. A few hours spent in actual observation would show more than any amount of talk or writing. If it is possible for you to come to Philadelphia, it is needless to say that it would be a very great pleasure to have you come to my house, and afterward visit two or three of our manufacturing establishments.[13]

There was now a small but steady stream of men who

came to meet Taylor and hear about scientific management. Taylor set aside certain days on which he arranged to speak to these groups at home and then to take them to see scientific management in action in the demonstration shops—the Tabor and Link-Belt Companies. His lecture, which gradually became a standard one, stated the new creed—namely, that true industrial harmony lay in the cooperation of workers and employers to increase productivity and wages and that this end could be achieved by the application of scientific methods of management.

The movement, however, was not yet all conquest. Though interest in it was steadily growing there was still much opposition among the manufacturers. Taylor was aware of this; referring to the deprecating reports and rumors about his system, he wrote to a friend in 1908:

I am also enclosing for you a quotation which is typical of the reports which are spread abroad regarding nearly every company in which our system of management is introduced. It is a curious fact that when these reports are received, they are generally believed, and those who received them rarely take the trouble to write to the owners of the company, inquiring as to the truth in the matter. For some reason, the average man who is interested in management seems to be particularly delighted when he receives a rumor that our management has been put out of business.

I can hardly understand the cause for this general antagonism to what we are doing. It is entirely comprehensible when the system is being introduced in any company, that those who are asked to change their ways should, to a certain extent, object to the bother and nuisance, but why people generally should take the attitude that they do I fail to see.[14]

This "antagonism" was only a small cloud on an otherwise bright horizon. Scientific management was gaining in credibility and respectability, attracting attention and followers in government and academic circles.

Brigadier General Crozier, the chief of the Ordnance Department, had contacted Taylor in 1906 and expressed an interest in the possibilities of his system for use in military arsenals.[15] Their correspondence continued for two years as Taylor patiently answered Crozier's questions. Fearing the opposition of labor and their power as constituents to exert pressure on the Congress against the introduction of scientific management into a government establishment, Crozier was understandably cautious. The first tentative attempt to take time studies was made by the commandant of the Rock Island Arsenal in 1908, but it was quickly dropped when the workers protested and appealed to their congressmen. The next attempt, a more successful one, took place in the Watertown Arsenal; Barth was hired for the reorganization, later to be assisted by Merrick.[16] And elements of scientific management were being introduced into the navy yards as well. On the West Coast, a naval constructor, Holden Evans, had written to Taylor in 1906, asking for copies of his A.S.M.E. papers. He studied the papers carefully, was converted, and became Taylor's chief disciple on the West Coast. In his naval yard in California, he conducted some time studies and made suggestions (which were approved) for changing over from day work to piece work. On the East Coast, Taylor's friend, Admiral Goodrich, who had worked with him in the Manufacturing Investment Company, was the commandant of the Brooklyn Navy Yard. He effected some reforms along the lines of Taylor's system and arranged for Taylor to meet the then Secretary of the Navy under Theodore Roosevelt, Truman H. Newberry. Although Newberry did not commit himself in any way, Taylor's disciples such as Barth and Hathway began to find work in the navy yards, a development that came to a stop with the change in administration in 1909.

With his election to the presidency of the A.S.M.E., Taylor had become widely known in academic circles. Many universities invited him to lecture; and in 1906, he was awarded the degree of Sc.D. by the University of

Pennsylvania. In 1910, the Amos Tuck School of Administration and Finance at Dartmouth under Harlow Person made scientific management the basic element of their curriculum. Similarly, Dean Edwin F. Gay of the Harvard Graduate School of Business Administration (established in September, 1908) visited Taylor in Philadelphia early that year, followed up the meeting with correspondence, and decided to make scientific management the prominent feature of the first-year course.[17] Taylor was at first opposed to the teaching of management in business schools, on the grounds that it was more appropriate for engineering schools. He relented in his opposition, however, and came to Harvard in April 1909, to give a series of three lectures on "Workmen and Their Management," a series that he repeated in successive winters until 1914.

Although Taylor's movement had spread steadily among professionals by 1910, it had not yet caught the attention or imagination of the lay public. The situation changed abruptly with the publicity provided in 1910 by Louis D. Brandeis and the Eastern Railroad Case.

In the spring of that year the railroads operating in the area north of the Potomac and Ohio Rivers and east of the Mississippi granted their employees a wage increase and immediately asked the Interstate Commerce Commission for an increase in freight rates. The eastern shipping concerns organized to fight this increase and contacted the "people's lawyer," Louis Brandeis, to prosecute their case. Brandeis decided to base his argument on the inefficiency of the railroads:

In September 1910, I entered, as unpaid counsel for the Trade Associations of the Atlantic Seaboard, on what is known as the first Advance (Freight) Rate Investigation before the Interstate Commerce Commission.

As the hearings developed I became convinced that one of the great causes of the lack of net income, of which the railroads were complaining, was the lack of efficiency and of an intimate knowledge of the cost of operation which in competitive industrial businesses had been developed. There came to mind discussions which I had had on the subject of efficiency with Mr. Harrington Emerson some years before, and certain statements he had made upon the relative efficiency or inefficiency of the various railroads. I also had in mind, among other things, a pamphlet on Shop management by Mr. Taylor, which in some way had come to my attention years before, and by which I had been much impressed when I read it. I also had in mind an evening I had spent with Mr. H. L. Gantt discussing the methods of developing efficiency by him in one of the cotton mills. And I had generally in mind those efforts in improved efficiency which certain of my clients, who were manufacturers, had been conducting.

I then arranged to see Mr. Emerson, and talked with him concerning the possibilities of presenting to the Interstate Commerce Commission the facts concerning possible increases in efficiency and railroad management.

Mr. Emerson gave me such data as he had available, and I questioned him carefully as to such other persons who, in his opinion, would be most helpful along these lines. He spoke to me of Mr. Gantt, and particularly of Mr. Taylor; and from his office I called up Mr. Taylor asking for an interview. It was cheerfully granted, and I immediately went to Philadelphia to discuss the situation with him. This interview was followed by several others. And it was largely through Mr. Taylor or Mr. Gantt that I got in touch with Mr. Cooke, Mr. Barth, Mr. Hathway, Mr. Dodge, Mr. Towne, and others directly interested in what came to be called Scientific Management; and secured their cooperation in adequately presenting the subject before the Interstate Commerce Commission.[18]

At a meeting of the men mentioned in this letter, the generic name scientific management was given to Taylor's methods of management which had heretofore been called "task and bonus" or the "Taylor-Emerson system." The most dramatic testimony of the Hearings came from Brandeis:

We will show you, may it please your honors, that these principles applicable to all businesses, are applicable to practically all departments of all businesses, and that the

estimate which has been made that in the railroad operation of this country an economy of one million dollars a
day is possible is by no means extravagant; and you will
see as we develop the science and develop its application
in varied businesses that that estimate is, if anything, an
underestimate instead of an overestimate.[19]

The "million dollar a day savings" idea immediately
caught the fancy of the press. Though Taylor had not appeared as a witness in the Rate Hearings, his name had
constantly been mentioned as the "father" of the movement responsible for such "miracles." The public spotlight now shifted to the fifty-four-year-old prophet. By his
account:

Since December 1st, ten different editors of magazines
have been over to my house to look into the general principles of scientific management, and to see it in operation
in Philadelphia, and many articles are now being written
on it. A great many articles have also appeared in the daily
papers, although the railroads, through concerted action,
have done much to stop the publication of articles in the
daily print.[20]

Hundreds of articles on scientific management appeared
in newspapers and magazines in the following years. In
1911, "The Principles of Scientific Management" appeared,
first in the *American Magazine* (preceded by a biographical sketch of Taylor by Ray Stannard Baker), and then
in book form. This slim volume, probably the single most
important book in the history of management, had by 1915
been translated into eight European languages and Japanese.[21] Requests for speeches, articles, and advice, along
with the steady stream of visitors, now poured into Philadelphia to hear Taylor expound his theory of scientific
management. He was now at the height of his fame.

This flood of notice and praise was marred, however, by
the increasingly disparaging criticism that began to appear
in editorial articles and correspondence columns in the
national press. Some members of the engineering fraternity
resented what appeared to be Taylor's virtual monopoly

of the subject of management. Thus, in response to an article on scientific management in *The Century Magazine*, the editor of *Engineering* wrote:

Will you forgive me if I express grave regret that in its treatment of the subject of "scientific management" (I refer to Will Irwin's impressively announced article) "The Century Magazine" should apparently confirm an ill-informed and unfortunate interpretation which is now being industriously circulated by the magazines of lower standing.

The misinterpretation to which I refer is that the Taylor system, scientific management and the efficiency system are synonymous coextensive terms. . . .

I hope sincerely that in the article which is announced to follow the publication in your March issue, due recognition will be given to the splendid work in the promotion of the industrial efficiency that has been done by the really scientific workers, not devotees of any formulated system which must be taken entire or let entirely alone (as Taylor insists his system must be). . . . I hope, especially, place will be given to the part played in the development of scientific management by H. L. Gantt who has done so much to humanize the Taylor system and to make it bearable by adapting it to recognition of more of the factors met with in problems of management. I hope, most of all, that tribute will be paid to Harrington Emerson, the greatest philosophical mind of them all, who has not put forth any "system," but has led industrial and economic thought in the discovery and definition of the principles and laws underlying the science of management.[22]

A letter from a professor of mechanical engineering at Columbia was more blunt:

In the first place, Mr. Will Irwin is not an engineer, and has no business writing on engineering topics, however complete may be his command of magazine English. Second, there is no such thing possible as the science of management, new or old. Third, there are many other people far more important than Mr. Fred W. Taylor, and the article indicates that Mr. Will Irwin believes in the greatness of Mr. Taylor because Mr. Taylor himself admits it.[23]

The relative importance of Taylor's contribution to the

field of scientific management as a whole has occasionally been questioned. Although this is not the appropriate place to examine in detail the contribution of other prominent figures in scientific management such as Carl Barth, Henry Gantt, Frank Gilbreth, and Harrington Emerson, we must at least suggest the nature of Taylor's relations with these four leading practitioners. Barth and Gantt, both of whom had been intermittently associated with Taylor ever since Midvale, considered themselves loyal followers, Barth serving as the orthodox and Gantt as the unorthodox disciple. Their work was based directly on Taylor's innovations—upon which Barth was to elaborate, and which Gantt used as a point of departure for further experiment.

Gilbreth, a successful building contractor with a national reputation who came under Taylor's influence after reading his paper "Shop Management," published his own *Motion Study* (one of the more important books in the literature of scientific management) in 1911, and was to become one of the best-known spokesmen of the movement. Gilbreth's letters to Taylor, far from questioning Taylor's leadership, reveal the fervent admiration of a disciple. After a meeting with Taylor in 1908, he wrote:

I am absorbing the ideas that you have given me as fast as I am mentally capable, but I am afraid that the whole thing will result in my having "Tayloritis."[24]

Or, urging Taylor to write a textbook on management:

I am not guessing—I am sure that I am right, that you are so far beyond all of us in the Laws of Management that you cannot see our viewpoint.[25]

In 1908, he declared his lifework to be the spread of Taylor's system:

I intend to devote the rest of my life to installing the Taylor system for two purposes—one, the greater efficiency in any business—two, to assist in solving the industrial strife between employer and employee.[26]

Harrington Emerson was the only one of the leading

figures in management who was outside the Taylor orbit, in the sense that he had never been associated with Taylor. Though not an engineer, he had adopted the profession of management consultant—which he called "efficiency engineering." He too made use of Taylor's methods of factory reorganization—planning, routing, scheduling, standardizing—and added some elements of his own such as the "Emerson Bonus Plan." Although he did not follow the Taylor system *in toto*, he acknowledged his debt to the "father of management" in such deferential letters as, "I would rather have your approval of what I am trying to do than any other man living or dead."[27] He sent his book on efficiency to Taylor, inscribing the flyleaf:

In a haphazard way I had been doing standard practice work for many years. I heard you speak, and I suddenly understood. Since that day, continuously deriving inspiration from you, I sought in my practice the fundamentals on which it rests
The fair deal
Intelligent line
Intelligent staff
Highest individuality, in performance and reward.
All these are other names for the truths and precepts you have instinctively taught.[28]

On the other side of the ledger, the critics not only tried to diminish the importance of Taylor's individual contribution, but attacked scientific management for its alleged "red tape," its arbitrariness, its pressuring and exploitation of the workers, its "all or nothing" attitude. In a long letter to his future biographer, Copley, Taylor tried to answer some of these charges:

One of the most frequent criticisms of scientific management is that we (those of us who are introducing our system of management) insist "imperatively and arbitrarily" upon using certain details; that we insist on a certain "ritual" which swamps the establishment with a system. To show you the absurdity of the claim that the details of the system are held absolutely sacred and of more importance than the essence of it, I would refer you to my testimony before the Congressional Committee, and I am giving the needed references in the pages accompanying this letter—There you will see that instead of laying great stress upon the details of scientific management, we lay the greatest stress upon just the opposite, namely upon the spirit which must pervade both the working people and those on the management side; and I explicitly state that scientific management does not consist of a great mass of details of any kind. . . .

This accusation, that we are passionately devoted to "red tape," comes from the fact that, in such an establishment (for example) as a machine shop, there is of necessity a very large amount of mechanism used in applying scientific knowledge to the every day work of every workman. And the enemies of scientific management try to discredit it by sneering at this mechanism and calling it "system" and "red tape," and they also lie almost universally as to the cost of this "red tape." They make the assertion that it costs far more than can be saved by it.

In justification of the statement made by these men, that I personally look upon this red tape as "sacred" and insist upon jamming it into every company with which I have anything to do, I will make this statement.

That for many years past, I never undertook to systematise a company unless I was absolutely sure that the owners of the company *wanted* scientific management, and *wanted it very badly*. They had to convince me that they were very anxious to have scientific management in order to get me to work for them. And before starting to work for them, in every case I took them to see some other company which was running under scientific management, and showed them all of the details, that is, the so-called "red tape" and "system." And I then called their attention to the fact that in changing from the system of management under which they were then running, to the new system of management they would have to use details somewhat similar to those which I had shown them. I carefully explained, however, in all cases, that no two companies ever had the same mechanism or details, because their work demanded a modification in the details—that is, in the mechanism. After this, I invariably made a clear cut bargain with them that whenever there was a conflict of opinion between themselves and myself as to what details should or should not be used in introducing the new system of management, *my* decision must be final, and that they would agree to put in the details which I believed to be necessary . . .

Now, I almost invariably have had the same experience, particularly with men who had been managers themselves of their own business for a great many years; that when I told them that I wished them to use such and such mechanism, they came back at me with the statement that they had something else in their company which was equally good, and when I insisted that the mechanism which they liked might be even better than our mechanism for the other type of management, but that it was not suited and would not dovetail in properly with the mechanism which we had found best suited to scientific management, then many of them honestly thought that I was prejudiced and made a "fetish" of details.

These men had no notion of the fact that the greater the number of the elements which are used in management, the more necessary it is that all of these details should harmonize one with the other, and that a great part of our experience and study, throughout thirty years, had been in getting together a series of details or elements which did dovetail properly in, one with another, and work harmoniously, instead of clashing.

And I do not hesitate to say that any man who was installing a new system of management, and who did not insist that the final decision as to the details to be adopted in the new system should rest with the man who is systematizing the company would make a complete failure of his work . . . .

If a man who had a Pierce-Arrow automobile, for example, were to go to the Packard Company and say to them, "I should like to have one of your automobiles, but I already have a Pierce-Arrow car, many of the parts of which suit me exactly. Will you not therefore kindly use the parts of the Pierce-Arrow car which I will point out to you, in furnishing me with a Packard?" The Packard people would answer, "If we are to be responsible for the working of our car, we must have the final say as to just what parts are put into the car."

This is precisely what those of us who are introducing scientific manufacturing into manufacturing establishments say: that if the responsibility for the success of the system is to be ours, we must have the final decision as to the details, and not the owners of the company. The fact is, however, that there are hundreds of companies now crying for the service of men who are capable of introducing scientific management with all of its details, just as they are, and who cannot get experts to work for them . . . .

Admiral Edwards, in his article (The Fetish of Scientific Management) repeats the various denunciations of our system that came from the labor leaders, of which the following is a sample quotation:

. . . That the daily task idea is simply another step toward enervating work and exhausted vitality.

This is the most serious accusation which has been made against scientific management, namely, that it is a system for merely speeding up workmen, causing them to overwork, and finally leaving them with no more pay than they originally had. And I most sincerely hope that while you were visiting the various companies engaged in scientific management, you yourself studied the motions of the workmen and talked with them, to satisfy yourself as to whether this most cruel accusation is true. It is the worst falsehood that has been told against scientific management, because it is directly the opposite of the truth.[29]

For a while Taylor, in his role as a reformer, was able to meet the criticism philosophically, "I have found that any improvement of any kind is not only opposed, but aggressively and bitterly opposed, by the majority of men, and the reformer must usually thread a thorny path."[30] But the sniping continued, and in spite of the efforts of his disciples to reassure him—"the reformer [is] always misunderstood and misrepresented"[31]—Taylor had (as we have seen) a low tolerance for sustained hostility. The situation steadily worsened. The attacks on him multiplied as organized labor now entered the fray, and scattered sniping developed into a broad fusillade.

Early in 1911, the Executive Council of the A.F.L. adopted a resolution denouncing the "premium bonus system" and urged its affiliates to resist the spread of what they called the "speeding" system.[32] Samuel Gompers sarcastically held forth against Taylorism:

So, there you are, wage-workers in general, mere machines —considered industrially, of course. Hence, why should you not be standardized and your motion-power brought up to the highest possible perfection in all respects, including speeds? Not only your length, breadth, and thickness as a machine, but your grade of hardness, malleability, tractability, and general serviceability, can be ascertained, registered, and then employed as desirable. Science would thus get the most out of you before you are sent to the junkpile.[33]

Gompers' statement reveals the workers' deepest anxiety —namely, the fear of losing their freedom of choice, of becoming appendages to the machines, of being regimented by technical logic and mechanical requirements, in short, of being dehumanized.

The union leaders also believed that scientific management was bent on destroying the trade-union movement by reducing the number of skilled workers to a minimum and imposing low wages on all those thus thrown into the army of the unskilled. Unions like the Molders Union and the International Association of Machinists took up the battle against Taylor's system, especially in government establishments, such as the arsenals, that could put pressure on congressmen. No stakes were too high from the point of view of the unions. As the president of the machinists' union put it, ". . . either the machinists will succeed in destroying the usefulness of this system through resistance, or it will mean the wiping out of our trade and organization, with the accompanying low wages, life-destroying hard work, long hours, and intolerable conditions generally."[34]

Taylor had always insisted that scientific management was to benefit management and worker equally. Thus, in answer to a labor leader's attack in 1916, he wrote:

You are absolutely wrong in your description of what my

views regarding management are. Nothing could be further from what you state my views to be.

It ought to be perfectly evident to any man that no other human being would devote the whole of his life and spend every cent of his surplus income for the purpose of producing higher dividends for a lot of manufacturing companies in which he has not the slightest interest and of which he has never heard before.

As you know, I retired from money-making business in 1901 and have never received a cent of pay for any work that I have done in the interest of Scientific Management. On the contrary I have devoted nearly all of my time and money to furthering the cause of Scientific Management. This is done entirely with the idea of getting better wages for the workmen—of developing the workmen coming under our system so as to make them all higher class men—to better educate them—to help them to live better lives, and, above all, to be more happy and contented. This is a worthy object for a man to devote his life to.

It would seem to me a farce to devote one's whole life and money merely to secure an increase in dividends for a whole lot of manufacturing companies. On the other hand, I realize (as you don't seem to realize) that it is utterly impossible to get the maximum prosperity for workmen unless their employers and owners of the establishments in which they work cooperate in the most hearty ways to bring about this end. I am sure it can be only brought about by friendly, kind cooperation. Realizing this it becomes a part of my duty toward the working people (to whose interests I am devoting my life) to induce manufacturers to come into this scheme of hearty cooperation. Therefore, in all my writings and in everything I say I must emphasize the gain which comes to the manufacturers quite as much as the gain which comes to workmen, otherwise it would be impossible to get the manufacturers to cooperate.

You perhaps do not realize that in introducing Scientific Management a great and new burden falls upon the management and in order to make the management take up this new burden they must also see a profit for themselves as well as for the workmen.

You and I differ absolutely and radically in one thing, which you do not seem as yet to realize, that is, you fundamentally believe that war between workmen and their employers is the only road to success for the workmen, whereas I believe (equally firmly) that the road to success lies through the warmest kind of friendly cooperation.[35]

Though proworker, Taylor was certainly antiunion, believing that unions had no place in scientific management, which could much better serve the "true" interests of the workers:

You speak of the trade unions and my attitudes toward them. What you say is far from correct. I am *not* an autocrat by birth, training, and experience. I have worked as a workman and lived right among workmen for many years and have many of my best friends now among the workmen, so that this characterization is far from true.

As you know, my principal object during my life time has been the welfare of the workmen. But I believe that their welfare is vastly better conserved through the establishment of laws and the control of laws than by autocratic authority. Throughout my writings and in everything I say I speak against autocratic authority and in favor of the rule of law. My object has been to get scientific management into as great a number and as great a variety of industries as possible before I die . . .

As you know, I am heartily in favor of unions where a hog employer or an employer careless of his workmen's rights is up against the old-fashioned type of organization, but that my contention has been and still remains that a union is absolutely unnecessary and only a hindrance to the quick and successful organization of any manufacturing establishment. And I am sure that an establishment runing under the principles of scientific management will confer far greater blessings upon the working people than could be brought about through any form of collective bargaining.[36]

Taylor, however, became manifestly upset by the union campaigns against him. This was dramatically illustrated when labor lobbying succeeded in getting Congress to appoint a special committee in 1911 to study and report on "The Taylor and Other Systems of Shop Management." At the end of his testimony, Taylor, under the relentlessly hostile questioning of union leaders is reported to have lost his self-control, so much so that this part of the testimony had to be stricken from the record.

Thus, during the last three years of his life Taylor was reputedly a disappointed and disheartened man.[37] The hostile attacks of the labor unions were only one of the causes. There was strife among his followers who had organized themselves into the Society for the Promotion of the Science of Management (later known as the Taylor Society). Disputes arose, both territorial and "ideological," with each disciple appealing to the leader for a ruling in his favor, while Taylor himself cherished futile hopes of patching the fissures in the movement. To Barth he wrote:

It has been my experience that almost all troubles in life, particularly those between friends, are the result of misunderstandings. Now it seems to me of the very greatest importance that no radical difference should arise between any of our particular group of men, who are all working together for the same broad object.[38]

He withdrew more and more from the hub of the movement he had created. His wife fell ill in December 1911, and most of his time and energy were devoted to her care. Her illness ("nervous prostration") lasted for three years, and for long periods Taylor did not have more than three hours free for his own work.[39] Although the movement was indeed spreading and Taylor himself was receiving great honors—an honorary doctrorate from Hobart College, an offer of the presidency of M.I.T.—he was depressed. Fearing the creeping of old age and looking back on his life, he apparently experienced nagging despair and doubt of its worthwhileness. He wrote to a childhood friend:

Every minute of my day here is filled up now, and yet somehow I don't seem to accomplish much of anything. Studying the growth of grass plots is a great time consumer and although I believe the work to be valuable, still it may —like many other things I have undertaken—prove after all to amount to but little.[40]

He appealed to doctor to help him get rid of the obsessive thoughts which were again troubling him.[41] But he knew his own therapy—ceaseless activity: ministering to his wife, answering his correspondence, experiments in grass growing —and in a letter to a friend he specifically acknowledged the curative aspect of work, counting it as his greatest blessing that "I have enough work to occupy all my spare time."[42] His self-image as the misunderstood prophet became ever more complete. Copley relates how this prosaic man who had always expressed an antipathy for literature, conceived a great liking for a piece of emotional writing, full of hyperbole—Herbert Kaufmann's *The Dreamers:*

Their vision lies within their souls—The world has accoladed them with jeer and sneer and jibe, for worlds are made of little men who take but never give—who share but never spare—who cheer a grudge and grudge a cheer. Through all the ages they have heard the voice of Destiny call to them from the unknown vasts. They dare uncharted seas, for they are the makers of the charts. With only cloth of courage at their masts and with no compass save their dreams, they sail away undaunted for the far, blind shores . . . . They are the chosen few—the Blazers of the Way.[43]

On March 10, 1915, Taylor entered a hospital with pneumonia. He was there for nine days before he died. The manner of his death, as reported by Copley, has a startling dramatic—and psychological—consistency with the manner of his life. Every morning, he would get up and systematically wind his Swiss watch at the same hour. On the ninth day, he was heard to wind his watch at half-past four in the morning, an unusual hour. When the nurse entered his room half an hour later she found that he was dead.

In this study, we have developed two themes—specifically, the life history of Frederick Taylor in the context of his cultural setting and historical time, and theoretically, the problem of the relation between personality development and innovation. Both of these themes, the historical and the theoretical, are parts of the whole piece and can be separated only for purposes of analysis. These themes were briefly sketched out in the introduction; here, in conclusion, we will review them, in light of the evidence, from a more general perspective.

As we have seen, Taylor's innovation in the sphere of work, namely, scientific management, had a critical, even "curative," impact on two levels of history—the private and the public. In a period of intense inner crisis in his own life history it became the focus for his devoted, if idiosyncratic, intelligence and his fastidiousness, and enabled him to work out his anxieties about authority and subordination and to reintegrate his defenses, thereby regaining a sense of wholeness that had been temporarily lost. And yet we must reemphasize that Taylor's life history merits a biography not because his system of innovations was a "solution" to neurotic conflict—that alone would be merely another case for the clinical record—but because it met the needs of industrial management at a time when traditional ways were fast becoming obsolete. What holds our attention is the fateful coincidence of an orginal man's conflicted life history with a critical moment in the industrial and social history of his world.

From a historical standpoint, Taylor's enduring importance would seem to derive from his leadership in the introduction of the scientific method into the area of work. Indeed, the development and spread—not to mention the popularization—of scientific method is the most characteristic innovation of the nineteenth century. As Alfred North Whitehead put it, "The greatest invention of the nineteenth century was the invention of the method of inven-

10 IN CONCLUSION

tion."[1] Reasoned application of the method seemed to certify progress, to ensure that henceforth progress would not have to depend on the chance cropping up of infrequent genius or sporadic superhuman will, but that ordinary men, armed thus, could with methodical patience, systematically and predictably mine the deeper veins of knowledge—in science, in technology, as well as in general scholarship.[2] Taylor's application of the scientific method to work, and in particular to industrial work, thus meant a revolutionary change, with subtle but devastating implications, from amateurism to professionalism in factory organization and management. The rise of a new profession, industrial engineering, and a host of new managerial functions is only the most obvious manifestation of this revolution.

His second, related, great achievement was to apply, with his own particular radical focus, the Positivist approach best expressed in Comte's "savoir pour prévoir, prévoir pour prévenir"* to the organization of work. Henceforth, it was to be a self-evident proposition that all the problems that might hinder the precise and effective functioning of a factory organization were not to be left to the chance ingenuity or momentary inspiration of the worker but were to be confronted and resolved in advance, to be forestalled on the basis of knowledge already available.

The way in which this radical vision was translated into the system of scientific management is a more controversial subject. The specific contributions of Taylor's system are on an altogether different level; they are more closely connected with a particular historical period and hence much more vulnerable to history. To a very great extent, Taylor is responsible for the managerial philosophy that prevails today, which can be summed up as follows: To increase productivity, 1. break the work process into

* Know to foresee, foresee to forestall.

the smallest possible components; 2. fit jobs into structures that clearly emphasize the duties and boundaries of each job rather than its part in the total process; 3. wherever possible use individual or small group monetary incentive system, gearing pay to the output; 4. subtract skill and responsibility from the job to make them functions of management.[3]

Critical studies have demonstrated the pitfalls inherent in this kind of rationalistic engineering. In fact, the results of factory reorganization along these lines all too often diverged markedly from expectations. Experiments with job enlargement, as opposed to job diversification, suggest that beyond a certain point, further division of labor yields diminishing returns. Further on-the-job research has made it abundantly clear that an exclusive preoccupation with revision of the technical system—the technology of the job, its physical and mechanical requirements—may have adverse effects on the social-psychological system of which the worker is also a part, and hence a negative influence on overall productivity.

These arguments with Taylorism have to do with the matter of means; with Taylor's ends there is no quarrel. All who reject Taylor's system for its ignorance or depreciation of the social and psychological dimensions of work gear their arguments and justify their cases with reference to a common goal—increased productivity. The concept of increased productivity has become the lodestar of modern work, replacing such concepts as morality, expiation of sin, individual self-realization, aesthetic fulfillment, and community well-being that, singly or together, defined and guided work in other historical epochs. Efficiency, with which Taylor's name is primarily associated —this efficiency, expressed in measurable, quantifiable terms—has thus already become a core element of the new technological identity.

Beyond this, what is the role and relevance of scientific

management in our time? Alain Touraine, in a study of the Renault enterprise, has suggested that industrial work evolves in three phases.[4] Phase one, the old system, is characterized by skilled work or craftsmanship, universal all-purpose machines, direct participation of the craftsman in the production process, and the worker's commitment not only of his technical knowledge but of a whole range of subjective judgment to his work. Phase two, the transitional system, is characterized by mechanization and increasing specialization, the replacement of universal machines with single-purpose machines, a new emphasis on rationally coordinated labor rather than individual skill, and hence, the increasing monotony of work, which is typically little more than the tending of the machines. The third phase, automation, excludes any direct participation of the worker in the production process. His job, as part of a technical system, is now merely to record and control. The character and rhythm of the work process are not determined by human skill, nor by the machine, nor by the nature of the product, but by the way the whole technical system is organized.

All forms of work do not necessarily have to pass through all three phases. Some industries have never come through phase one, others have passed directly from the first to the third phase, while the dominant characteristic of many is the second phase. Even in a single factory, the three phases often coexist: the power plant is in the third phase, certain machine shops are in the second, while some shops, such as pattern or dye making, have all the hallmarks of the first phase. Touraine's model is, however, useful and pertinent to research on human behavior in a factory context, since it explicitly takes the technical system into account. The variable psychological demands of each phase on the individual worker—or, in our terminology, the dimensions of the ego aspect of work—have too often been ignored in behavioral research.

Many of the techniques of scientific management are circumscribed by the characteristics of the second, transitional, phase in which the worker is the major factor governing output, as well as a major cost element. All those techniques of this production system which focus on the worker and on maximizing his efficiency—motion-study to rationalize and improve his movements and methods, time-study to bring order to formerly unpredictable performance, incentive payment schemes to stimulate effort— have a certain logical coherence.[5] With the perfection of technology in the automation stage, however, the worker has ceased to be a major cost factor; he no longer controls output; and furthermore, his manual movements are irrelevant to his principal function as monitor—all of which renders many of Taylor's techniques obsolete.[6] Nonetheless, Taylor's claim to greatness, as we have argued, does not rest on his invention of these specialized techniques but rather on a less tangible and much more radical *idea:* a new approach to the entire problem of human work and its organization.

The second theme of this study—its theoretical focus— has been the relation between personality and innovative work. To recapitaulate the formulations of Chapter 6, innovation is both a process and a product. It means (1) a change that requires at the same time selective intelligence and comprehensive imagination, (2) a clear break with the established way of thinking or doing things, and (3) the creation of a new idea or capability. The difference between innovation, as defined here, and creativity may be more semantic than substantial. Creativity itself is not a clear concept, variously denoting a product or ability, or a psychological process by which novel and valuable products come into existence. It is generally agreed that in both the innovative and the creative processes two kinds of thought are involved: convergent thinking, which emphasizes analysis and reasoning, and divergent thinking, which stresses the richness and novelty of ideas.[7] Both are necessary, although their relative importance in intellectual or social problem solving varies widely. In popular usage, the term innovation has heretofore implied a high proportion of "convergent" thinking and been reserved for technical and economic areas, while creativity has implied rather more "divergent" thinking and tends to be associated with artistic and "pure" scientific phenomena. Yet Taylor's case dramatically demonstrates that any boundary between the two is, at best, arbitrary.

It seems that creativity does indeed depend on personality in a number of ways—innate talent, learning (both in the sense of emotional development and cognitive growth), specific training, the richness of the unconscious and access to it, the available means of expressing giftedness. Still, as Kurt Eissler suggests, it may be that creativity is basically a biological puzzle which cannot be solved by the means now at the disposal of psychology.[8] And, on the other hand, there are, in addition to personality factors, a host of historical and environmental factors affecting innovation or creativity, some of which we considered in Chapter 6. In spite of the vast amount of literature it has generated, the creative process eludes those who would categorize it absolutely. It remains an enigma, illumined here and there in the private and public record of uncommon lives that await the attention of evermore systematic biography.

Psychoanalysis has been principally concerned with artistic creativity. In part, this reflects the dominance of "divergent" thinking that is held to be closely bound up with the unconscious and the preconscious layers of personality; and, in addition, interpretations guided by the psychoanalytic method reveal the depths and themes of inner conflict and the existence of unconscious desires in the artistic creation itself. Yet, once again, Taylor's life suggests that it is not only in artistic creation but in the formulation of a scientific system of thought as well—as in scientific management—that inner conflict finds expression in radical originality.

In those psychoanalytic researches and monographs that have stressed the role of unresolved neurotic conflict as the critical element in creativity, there is still a range of opinion as to the dynamics of this relationship. There is a hypothesis for almost every clinical syndrome: creativity as restitution for object loss, creativity in the service of narcissism, creativity as a means of dealing with heightened aggressive impulses, creativity as a means of ego restoration or ego survival, and, in rare cases, creativity as sublimation;[9] or creativity as the expression of heightened body sensitivity and perception, creativity as "regression in the service of the ego."[10] Although the interpretations of the dynamics vary, the evidence of case histories and life histories persuasively supports the consensus that (in Harry Slochower's phrase) unease and dis-ease are essential conditions for the original mind. Or, as Nietzsche put it in powerful poetry. "One must harbor choas within one's self to give birth to a dancing star."[11] An "essential" condition for creativity, of course, means a necessary, not a sufficient, condition. Although there is still no trustworthy answer to the question whether the relationship between conflict and creativity is causal or merely coincidental, the history of Taylor's life and work would support the view that holds the study of inner crisis as a key to the problem of creativity.

Some have suggested the relativity of psychopathological phenomena—namely, that there is an instrumental (not moral or therapeutic) distinction to be made between the sickness of a genius and that of an average person.[12] Eissler, in his studies of Leonardo da Vinci and Goethe, argues that psychopathological episodes in the lives of geniuses may, in their very trauma and in the event of cure, serve to dissolve rigidities that block the creative process, thus leaving the personality freed and renewed. These are, in a sense, healthy diseases,[13] the psychopathological episode sparking creative work. In Goethe's case, and in many others, as soon as some distance from the neurotic episode was won, an original and creative function took over. This pattern of breakdown followed by psychological reintegration and the emergence of an "original function" also holds true in Taylor's case. The two periods that witnessed the single-minded elaboration and deployment of his peculiar genius—Midvale and Bethlehem— were both preceded by periods of "chaos within." And his "original function" of prophet and reformer was an integral part of his mastery of the final failure at Bethlehem in 1901.

The innovative personality, however, becomes a leader— artistic, scientific, ideological, or religious—only when his inner crisis dovetails with an historical crisis, when an original resolution of his own identity struggle also serves the needs and captures the imagination of the wider community. The life and work of Frederick Taylor, an example *par excellence* of innovative leadership, are also a striking illustration of the dynamics of this process.

CHAPTER 1

1. Harlow S. Person, "F. W. Taylor as a Seeker of Truth," *Journal of Efficiency Society*, 4 (April 1915): 8. For other tributes by Taylor's followers, see *Frederick Winslow Taylor, A Memorial* (New York: Taylor Society, 1920).

2. Quoted in Ray S. Baker, "The Gospel of Efficiency," *The American Magazine*, Vol. 71 (March 1911): 563.

3. Quoted in O. Sheldon, "Taylor, the Creative Leader," *Bulletin of the Taylor Society*, Vol. 9, No. 1 (February 1924).

4. Frank B. Copley, *Frederick W. Taylor, Father of Scientific Management*, 2 vols. (New York: Harper and Bros., 1923), I, p. xxii.

5. V. I. Lenin, *Collected Works* (Moscow: Progress Publishers, 1965), Vol. 27, 259.

6. Erik H. Erikson, *Insight and Responsibility* (New York: Norton, 1964), p. 148.

CHAPTER 2

1. See the 1872 Catalogue of the Phillips Exeter Academy in Professor Tuft's *Recollections* in the Taylor Collection, Stevens Institute of Technology, Hoboken, New Jersey.

2. Frank B. Copley, *Fredrick W. Taylor, Father of Scientific Management*, 2 vols. (New York: Harper and Bros., 1923), Vol. 1, p. 79.

3. *Ibid.*, p. 80.

4. See Taylor's testimony in United States Congress, House, Special Committee, *Hearings to Investigate the Taylor and Other Systems of Shop Management*, 3 vols. (Washington, D.C.: Government Printing Office, 1912), Vol. 3, p. 1427.

5. See Samuel Haber, *Efficiency and Uplift* (Chicago: University of Chicago Press, 1964), p. 6.

6. Erik H. Erikson has emphasized this clinical approach in his writings. In addition to "On the Nature of Psycho-Historical Evidence: In Search of Gandhi" (*Daedalus*, Summer 1968, pp. 696ff.), see "The Nature of Clinical Evidence" in *Insight and Responsibility* (New York: Norton, 1964); "Relevance and Relativity in Case History," in *Childhood and Society*, 2nd ed. (New York: Norton, 1963); and *Young Man Luther* (New York: Norton, 1958).

7. Quoted in Edward D. Baltzell, *Philadelphia Gentlemen* (Glencoe, Ill.: Free Press, 1958), p. 265.

8. Nathaniel Burt, *The Perennial Philadelphians* (Boston: Little, Brown, 1963), p. 116. See further C. Weygandt, *Philadelphia Folks* (New York: Appleton, 1938).

9. *Ibid.*, p. 101.

10. Letter to Morris W. Cooke, December 3, 1910, Taylor Collection.

11. Letter from Franklin Taylor, (month illegible) 28, 1872, Taylor Collection.

12. Copley, *Frederick W. Taylor*, Vol. 1, p. 53. Many of the details of Taylor's childhood are based on Copley's biography.

13. Burt, *Perennial Philadelphians*, p. 517.

14. H. W. Bulkeley, *A Word to Parents* (Philadelphia, 1855), p. 13. Quoted in John Demos, "The Rise of the Concept of Adolescence in America: 1800–1920," unpublished manuscript, 1964, p. 4. For a survey of the child-rearing practices and the child-rearing advice of the period, see R. Sunley, "Early Nineteenth-Century American Literature on Child Rearing," in Margaret Mead and Martha Wolfenstein, eds., *Childhood in Contemporary Cultures* (Chicago: The University of Chicago Press, 1955), pp. 155 ff. See further Elaine V. Damis, "The History of Child Rearing Advice in America from 1800 to 1940," unpublished honors thesis, Radcliffe College, 1960.

15. Copley, *Frederick W. Taylor*, Vol. 1, p. 65.

16. Letter to Morris Cooke, Taylor Collection.

17. Copley, *Frederick W. Taylor*, Vol. 1, p. 53.

18. Erikson, *Childhood and Society*, p. 252.

19. Birge Harrison, *Recollections*, August 25, 1915, p. 2, Taylor Collection.

20. *Ibid.*, p. 3.

21. Copley, *Frederick W. Taylor*, Vol. 1, p. 87ff.

22. *Ibid.*, p. 67.

23. *Ibid.*, p. 72.

24. William Fannon, *Recollections*, Taylor Collection.

25. *Hearings*, Vol. 3, p. 1387.

26. *Ibid.*, p. 1388.

27. *Ibid.*, p. 1395.

28. Quoted in Burt, *Perennial Philadelphians*, p. 30.

29. Peter Blos, *On Adolescence* (Glencoe, Ill.: Free Press, 1962), p. 11.

30. Anna Freud, *The Ego and the Mechanisms of Defense* (London: Hogarth Press, 1954), p. 159.

31. G. Stanley Hall's *Life and Confessions of a Psychologist*, quoted in N. Kiell, *The Universal Experience of Adolescence* (Boston: Beacon Press, 1967), pp. 184–185.

32. Demos, "The Rise of the Concept of Adolescence," p. 8.

33. *Ibid.*, p. 10.

34. Letter to Morris Cooke, Taylor Collection.

35. Emily Taylor to Frederick Taylor, September 29, 1873, Taylor Collection.

36. Franklin Taylor to Frederick Taylor, undated, Taylor Collection.

37. Letter from Franklin Taylor, February 22, 1874, Taylor Collection.

38. For this aspect of post-Freudian psychoanalysis, see Heinz Hartmann, *Ego Psychology and the Problem of Adaptation* (New York: International Universities Press, 1958); and H. Hartmann *et al.,* "Comments on the Formation of Psychic Structure," *The Psychoanalytic Study of the Child,* Vol. 2 (New York: International Universities Press, 1946). See further, Erik H. Erikson, "Identity and the Life Cycle," *Psychological Issues,* Vol. 1, No. 1 (New York: International Universities Press, 1959).

39. Erikson, *Young Man Luther,* p. 14.

40. *Ibid.,* pp. 19ff., italics added.

CHAPTER 3

1. Birge Harrison, *Recollections,* August 25, 1915, p. 2, Taylor Collection, Stevens Institute of Technology, Hoboken, New Jersey.

2. Frank B. Copley, *Frederick W. Taylor, Father of Scientific Management,* 2 vols. (New York: Harper and Bros., 1923), Vol. 1, p. 76.

3. Emily Taylor to Frederick Taylor, September 29, 1873, Taylor Collection.

4. Frederick W. Taylor, Lecture on "Success," Taylor Collection.

5. See Edward C. Kirkland, *A History of American Economic Life* (New York: Crofts, 1936). See further Henry Gibbins, *Economic and Industrial Progress of the Century* (Philadelphia: Linscott, 1903); and Thomas C. Cochran and William Miller, *The Age of Enterprise* (New York: Macmillan, 1949).

6. Gibbins, *Economic and Industrial Progress,* Chapter 57.

7. Cochran and Miller, *Age of Enterprise,* p. 131.

8. *Ibid.,* p. 230.

9. Leland Jenks, "Early Phases of the Management Movement," *Administrative Science Quarterly,* 5 (1960): 424.

10. J. S. Whitney, Paper on Apprenticeship and Report of the Discussion, Philadelphia Social Science Association papers, 1878–1889, p. 13.

11. Cochran and Miller, *Age of Enterprise,* p. 264.

12. *Ibid.,* p. 231.

13. L. Blodget, Paper on the Social Condition of the Industrial Classes of Philadelphia, Philadelphia Social Science Association Papers, 1878–1889.

14. The discussion of apprenticeship in Philadelphia is based on A. B. Burk, "Apprenticeship As It Was and Is," Philadelphia Social Science Association Papers; and Whitney, Paper on Apprenticeship.

15. Quoted in Burk, "Apprenticeship," p. 5.

16. Whitney, Paper on Apprenticeship, p. 19.

17. Burk, "Apprenticeship, As It Was and Is," p. 12.

18. See Taylor's testimony in United States Congress, House, Special Committee, *Hearings to Investigate the Taylor and Other Systems of Shop Management*, 3 vols. (Washington, D.C.: Government Printing Office, 1912), Vol. 3, p. 1427.

19. Copley, *Frederick W. Taylor*, Vol. 1, p. 90.

20. *Ibid.*, p. 91.

21. Frederick W. Taylor, "Workmen and Their Management," unpublished lecture manuscript, 1869, Harvard Graduate School of Business Administration, Boston, Massachusetts, pp. 13–14.

22. Frederick W. Taylor, "A Comparison of Methods of Discipline," unpublished lecture manuscript, c. 1906, p. 7, Taylor Collection.

23. Letter to Cooke, Taylor Collection.

24. Copley, *Frederick W. Taylor*, Vol. 1, p. 88.

25. Taylor, Lecture on "Success," p. 8, Taylor Collection.

26. Jenks, "Management Movement," p. 446.

27. Copley, *Frederick W. Taylor*, Vol. 1, p. 72.

28. Letter to Cooke, Taylor Collection.

29. Taylor, "A Comparison of Methods of Discipline," p. 7, Taylor Collection.

30. *Hearings*, Vol. 3, p. 1411.

31. *Ibid.*, p. 1413, italics added.

32. The historical data on the Midvale Steel Company are taken from Copley, *Frederick W. Taylor*, Vol. 1, pp. 106–115.

33. *Ibid.*, p. 114.

34. Letter to Cooke, Taylor Collection.

35. Harlow S. Person, Foreword to Frederick W. Taylor, *The Principles of Scientific Management* (New York: Harper and Bros., 1947).

36. Copley, *Frederick W. Taylor*, Vol. 1, p. 108.

37. Talcott Parsons, "The Father Symbol: An Appraisal in the Light of Psychoanalysis and Sociological Theory," *Social Structure and Personality* (New York: The Free Press, 1964), p. x.

38. *Ibid.*

39. Erikson, *Young Man Luther* (New York: Norton, 1958), p. 124.

40. Copley, *Frederick W. Taylor*, Vol. 1, p. 158.

41. Franklin Taylor to Frederick Taylor, January 30, 1873, Taylor Collection.

42. Frederick W. Taylor, "The Study of Classics," unpublished manuscript, Taylor Collection.

43. Letter to Cooke, Taylor Collection.

44. Copley, *Frederick W. Taylor*, Vol. 1, p. 111.

45. *Ibid.*, p. 129.

46. Taylor, "Workmen and Their Management."

47. Letter from the Dean of the College of Engineering, University of Illinois, August 29, 1908, Taylor Collection.

48. Taylor, Lecture on "Success," Taylor Collection.

49. *Ibid.*

50. *Ibid.*

51. *Ibid.*

52. *Ibid.*

53. Copley, *Frederick W. Taylor*, Vol. 1, p. 108.

54. *Ibid.*, p. 134.

55. *Ibid.*

56. Taylor, "Workmen and Their Management."

57. Taylor, Lecture on "Success," Taylor Collection.

58. Copley, *Frederick W. Taylor*, Vol. 1, p. 135.

59. Taylor, Lecture on "Success," Taylor Collection.

60. *Ibid.*

61. Copley, *Frederick W. Taylor*, Vol. 1, p. 130.

62. *Ibid.*, p. 124.

63. *Ibid.*, p. 120.

64. *Ibid.*, p. 238.

65. Frederick W. Taylor, "On the Art of Cutting Metals" (New York: A.S.M.E., 1907), p. 34.

66. Copley, *Frederick W. Taylor*, Vol. 1, p. 232.

67. *Ibid.*

68. Memo from Steele to Deering, in the Steele correspondence, Taylor Collection.

CHAPTER 4.

1. Abraham Zaleznik, *Human Dilemmas of Leadership* (New York: Harper & Row, 1966), p. 24.

2. United States Congress, House, Special Committee, *Hearings to Investigate the Taylor and Other Systems of Shop Management*, 3 vols. (Washington, D.C.: Government Printing Office, 1912), Vol. 3, pp. 1411ff.

3. Frank B. Copley, *Frederick W. Taylor, Father of Scientific Management*, 2 vols. (New York: Harper and Bros., 1923), Vol. 1, p. 168.

4. *Ibid.*

5. *Ibid.*, p. 167.

6. *Hearings*, Vol. 3, p. 1434.

7. *Ibid.*, p. 1428.

8. See Sigmund Freud, "Charakter und Analerotik," and "Bemerkungen über einen Fall von Zwangsneurose," *Ges. Werke*, Bd. 7 (Frankfurt: Fischer, 1966). See further "Das Öknomische Problem des Masochismus," *Ges. Werke*, Bd. 13.

For later descriptions, see Otto Fenichel, *The Psychoanalytic Theory of Neurosis* (New York: Norton, 1965). See further David Shapiro, *Neurotic Styles* (New York: Basic Books, 1965), Chapter 2; and Helene Deutsch, *Psychoanalysis of the Neuroses* (London: Hogarth Press, 1932), Part 3.

An excellent summary of the present psychoanalytical thinking on the obsessional neurosis is to be found in Anna Freud, "Obsessional Neurosis: A Summary of Psycho-Analytical Views as Presented at the Congress," presented at the conclusion of the 24th International Psycho-Analytical Congress, Amsterdam, July 1965, in *International Journal of Psychonalysis*, 47 (1966).

9. Anna Freud, "Obsessional Neurosis," p. 117.

10. *Hearings*, Vol. 3, p. 1414.

11. Shapiro, *Neurotic styles*, p. 31.

12. Frederick W. Taylor, Lecture on "Success," p. 6, Taylor Collection, Stevens Institute of Technology, Hoboken, New Jersey.

13. Letter to Cooke, Taylor Collection.

14. Copley, *Frederick W. Taylor*, Vol. 1, p. 170.

15. Wilfred Lewis, *Recollections*, November 25, 1915, Taylor Collection.

16. Frederick W. Taylor, "Workmen and Their Management," unpublished lecture manuscript, 1869, Harvard Graduate School of Business Administration, Boston, Massachusetts, p. 7.

17. *Ibid.*, p. 6.

18. Leon Grinberg. "The Relationship Between Obsessive Mechanisms and a State of Self-Disturbance: Depersonalization," *International Journal of Psychoanalysis*, 47 (1966): 178. Grinberg terms this more mature form of obsessional control "adaptational control."

19. Taylor's testimony before the Industrial Relations Commission, cited in Copley, *Frederick W. Taylor*, Vol. 1, p. 216.

20. *Hearings*, Vol. 3, pp. 1414 ff.

21. See Walter Heinrich, "Die Gesellschaftliche Funktionen des Gewerbes," *Probleme des Klein-und Mittelbetriebes in Handwerk und Gewerbe*, Münster-Westfalen, 1964, p. 28. See further by the same author, "Das Handwerk in Europa," *Europa*, Jg. 1950, Heft II.

22. American Society of Mechanical Engineers, "The Present State of the Art of Industrial Management," and Taylor's discussion of the paper, 1912, Taylor Collection.

23. *Ibid.* Taylor's italics.

24. *Ibid.*

25. Quoted in Daniel Bell, *Work and Its Discontents* (Boston: Beacon Press, 1956), p. 20.

26. *Ibid.*

27. *Ibid.*, p. 14.

28. *Hearings*, Vol. 3, p. 1450.

CHAPTER 5

1. Quoted in Erik H. Erikson, *Childhood and Society*, 2nd ed. (New York: Norton, 1963), p. 265.

2. The historical discusson of work is based on Adriano Tilgher, *Homo Faber* (Chicago: Regnery, 1968), Chapters 1–3; and Hannah Arendt, *Vita Activa oder vom tätigen leben* (Stuttgart: Kohlhammer, 1960). See further Otto Lippman, *Lehrbuch der Arbeitswissenschaft* (Jena 1932).

3. Tilgher, *Homo Faber*, p. 8.

4. Zaleznik, *Human Dilemmas of Leadership* (New York: Harper & Row, 1966), p. 12.

5. Erikson, *Childhood and Society*, p. 222.

6. Quoted in Georges Friedmann, *The Anatomy of Work* (New York: Free Press, 1964), frontispiece.

7. Arendt, *Vita Activa*, pp. 77ff.

8. Karl Marx, *Economic and Philosophical Manuscripts*, in Erich Fromm, *Marx's Concept of Man* (New York: Ungar, 1964), p. 101.

9. *Ibid.*, p. 102.

10. Tilgher, *Homo Faber*, p. 5.

11. Mohandas K. Gandhi, *Bread Labour: The Gospel of Work* (Ahmedabad: Navajivan, c. 1960), p. 8.

12. Joseph Conrad, *Heart of Darkness* (Englewood Cliffs, N.J.: Prentice-Hall, 1960), pp. 23–24.

13. Solomon Ginsburg, *The Role of Work*, in *A Psychiatrist's Views on Social Issues* (New York: Columbia University Press, 1963). See further A. Winterstein, "Zur Psychologie der Arbeit," *Imago*, II (1932): 137 ff.

14. Ives Hendrick, "Work and Pleasure Principle," *Psychoanalytic Quarterly*, 12 (1943): 311–329.

15. B. Lantos, "Metapsychological Considerations in the Concept of Work." *International Journal of Psychoanalysis*, 33 (1952): 439 ff.

16. For Robert White's views, see "Motivation Reconsidered: The Concept of Competence," *Psychological Review*, 66 (1959); and further "Ego and Reality in Psychoanalytic Theory," *Psychological Issues*, Vol. 3, No. 3 (New York: International Universities Press, 1963).

17. White, "Motivation Reconsidered," p. 297.

18. White, "Ego and Reality in Psychoanalytic Theory," p. 35.

19. *Ibid.*, p. 41.

20. Erikson, *Childhood and Society*, Chapter 8.

21. Erikson, "The Problem of Ego Identity" in *"Identity and the Life Cycle," Psychological Issues*, Vol. 1, No. 1 (New York: International Universities Press, 1959), p. 128.

22. Erikson, *Insight and Responsibility* (New York: Norton, 1964), p. 128.

23. See "Work and Its Satisfactions," in Ginsburg, *The Role of Work*, see further Eli Ginzberg *et al., The Unemployed* (New York: Harper and Bros., 1943).

24. Emile Durkheim, *The Division of Labor in Society* (Glencoe, Ill.: Free Press, 1947), p. 40.

25. Elton Mayo, *The Social Problems of an Industrial Civilization* (Boston: Harvard University Graduate School of Business Administration, Division of Research, 1945). A short discussion of the theories of worker motivation, especially from the social aspect, is given in Abraham Zaleznik *et al., The Motivation, Productivity and Satisfaction of Workers* (Boston: Harvard University Graduate School of Business Administration, Division of Research, 1958), Chapter 2.

26. Abraham Maslow, *Motivation and Personality* (New York: Harper & Row, 1954). See further, Douglas McGregor, *The Human Side of Enterprise* (New York: McGraw-Hill, 1960), pp. 36–39.

27. Daniel Bell, *Work and Its Discontents* (Boston: Beacon Press, 1956), p. 6.

28. Letter to Birge Harrison, March 2, 1915, Taylor Collection, Stevens Institute of Technology, Hoboken, New Jersey.

29. William Fannon, *Recollections,* Taylor Collection.

30. See the *Recollections* of Carl A. Barth and Henry Gantt, Taylor Collection.

31. Gantt, *Recollections,* Taylor Collection.

32. Donald Roy, "Quota Restriction and Gold-bricking in a Machine Shop," *The American Journal of Sociology,* 57 (March 1962): 427–442.

33. Max Weber, "Zur Psychophysik der industriellen Arbeit (1908–1909)," in *Gesammelte Aufsätze zur Soziologie und Sozialpolitik* (Mohr: Tübingen, 1924), pp. 155ff, author's translation.

34. *Ibid.*, p. 155.

35. *Ibid.*, p. 158.

36. Elton Mayo, *The Human Problems of an Industrial Civilization,* Compass Books edition (New York: Viking Press, 1966), p. 158.

37. *Ibid.*, p. 174.

38. *Ibid.*, p. 177.

39. Sigmund Freud, *Group Psychology and the Analysis of the Ego,* in *Collected Works,* Vol. 18 (London: Hogarth Press, 1962), p. 134.

40. Frederick W. Taylor, *The Principles of Scientific Management* (New York: Harper, 1911), pp. 19ff.

41. Roy, "Quota Restriction," p. 430.

42. Helmut Schelsky, *Arbeiterjugend, Gestern und Heute* (1955), cited in Arendt, *Vita Activa*, p. 344.

43. Taylor, *The Principles of Scientific Management*, p. 39.

44. *Ibid.*, p. 120.

45. *Ibid.*, p. 125.

46. Charles Shartle, *Recollections*, Taylor Collection.

47. Taylor, *The Principles of Scientific Management*, p. 73.

CHAPTER 6

1. Frank B. Copley, *Frederick W. Taylor, Father of Scientific Management*, 2 vols. (New York: Harper and Bros., 1923), Vol. 1, p. 334.

2. Frederick W. Taylor, "On the Art of Cutting Metals" (New York: A.S.M.E., 1907), p. 4.

3. *Ibid.*

4. *Ibid.*, p. 7.

5. *Ibid.*, pp. 9ff.

6. Cited in Copley, *Frederick W. Taylor*, Vol. 1, p. xv.

7. Taylor, "On the Art of Cutting Metals," p. 11.

8. Lyndall Urwick, *The Making of Scientific Management*, 2 vols. (London: Management Publications Trust, 1949), Vol. 2, p. 94.

9. Taylor, "On the Art of Cutting Metals," p. 11, italics added.

10. *Ibid.*, p. 55.

11. United States Congress, House, Special Committee, *Hearings to Investigate the Taylor and Other Systems of Shop Management*, 3 vols. (Washington, D.C.: Government Printing Office, 1912), Vol. 1, p. 333.

12. Hugh G.J. Aitken, *Taylorism at Watertown Arsenal* (Cambridge, Mass.: Harvard University Press, 1960), p. 29.

13. The description of the methods of management before and after the introduction of Taylorism are contained in the first two volumes of the *Hearings*, especially in the testimony of General Crozier, Vol. 2, p. 1112ff.; Col. Wheeler, Vol. 1, p. 41ff.; and Major Williams, Vol. 1, p. 457ff. See further, Aitken, *Taylorism*.

14. Aitken, *Taylorism*, p. 85.

15. *Hearings*, Crozier testimony, Vol. 2, p. 1112.

16. *Hearings*, Wheeler testimony, Vol. 1, p. 83.

17. *Ibid.*, p. 118.

18. *Ibid.*, p. 76.

19. H. Dubreuil, *Robots or Man? A French Workman's Experience in*

American Industry, translated by the author (New York: Harper and Bros., 1930), pp. 15ff.

20. The description of the Taylor System in operation at the arsenal is taken from Williams' testimony, *Hearings,* Vol. 1, p. 460ff., and Aitken, *Taylorism,* p. 126ff.

21. Aitken, *Taylorism,* p. 127.

22. Henry Gantt, *Recollections,* Taylor Collection, Stevens Institute of Technology, Hoboken, New Jersey.

23. Taylor, Lecture on "Success," Taylor Collection.

24. L. Urwick, *Making of Scientific Management,* Vol. 1, p. 17.

25. Homer G. Barnett, *Innovation: The Basis of Cultural Change* (New York: McGraw-Hill, 1953), p. 7.

26. See Fritz Redlich, "Die Rolle der Neuerung in einer quasistatischen Welt: Francis Bacon und seine Nachfolger," *Der Unternehmer* (Göttingen: Vandenhoeck & Ruprecht, 1964), p. 238.

27. See H. A. Hopf, *Historical Perspectives in Management* (New York: Hopf Institute of Management, 1947), p. 11.

28. *Ibid.,* p. 13. See further, W. H. G. Armytage, *The Rise of the Technocrats* (London: Routledge and Kegan Paul, 1965), Parts 2 and 3.

29. See Barnett, *Innovation,* Chapter II. Many of the following observations on the theory of innovative process use Barnett's terminology and concepts.

30. Redlich, "Die Rolle der Neuerung," p. 237.

31. *Ibid.,* p. 235.

32. Barnett, *Innovation,* p. 185.

33. William James, *Principles of Psychology* (New York: Henry Holt and Company, 1890), Vol. 1, p. 251–252. Quoted in Barnett, *Innovation,* p. 256.

34. *Hearings,* Vol. 3, p. 1494.

CHAPTER 7

1. The details of Taylor's employment at the Manufacturing Investment Company are taken mainly from William Fannon, *Recollections,* Taylor Collection, Stevens Institute of Technology, Hoboken, New Jersey.

2. *Ibid.*

3. Frank B. Copley, *Frederick W. Taylor, Father of Scientific Management,* 2 vols. (New York: Harper and Bros., 1923), Vol. 1, p. 383.

4. Taylor to Hammond, June 14, 1893, Taylor Collection.

5. Letter from Taylor, cited in Copley, *Frederick W. Taylor,* Vol. 1, p. 388.

6. Scudder Klyce, *Recollections,* Taylor Collection.

7. See Thorsten Veblen, *The Theory of the Leisure Class* (New York: Macmillan, 1899); and *The Theory of Business Enterprise* (New York: Charles Scribner, 1904).

8. The status, views, and aspirations of the engineers of that period have been analyzed by D. Horowitz, "Insight into Industrialization: American Concepts of Economic Development and Mechanization, 1865–1910," Ph.D. dissertation, Harvard University, 1966. The above observations have been based especially on Chapter 9, "Engineers and Economic Development: A Self Portrait."

9. Robert L. Heilbroner, *The Worldly Philosophers* (New York: Simon and Schuster, 1966), p. 204.

10. Taylor to Griffith, June 28, 1893, Taylor Collection.

11. Copley, *Frederick W. Taylor,* Vol. 1, p. 387.

12. Taylor to Hammond, May 18, 1893, Taylor Collection.

13. Fannon, *Recollections,* Taylor Collection.

14. Taylor to Klyce, December 22, 1911, Taylor Collection.

15. Copley, *Frederick W. Taylor,* Vol. 1, p. 429.

16. Taylor, *Shop Management,* p. 130, Taylor Collection.

17. Copley, *Frederick W. Taylor,* Vol. 1, p. 443.

18. United States Congress, House, Special Committee, *Hearings to Investigate the Taylor and Other Systems of Shop Management,* 3 vols. (Washington, D.C.: Government Printing Office, 1912), Vol. 3, p. 1432, italics added.

19. Taylor to Steele, June 26, 1896, Taylor Collection.

20. Taylor to Couder, November 22, 1897, Taylor Collection.

21. Copley, *Frederick W. Taylor,* Vol. 1, p. 454.

22. Taylor to A. Jones, June 27, 1898, Taylor Collection.

23. Davenport to Taylor, November 22, 1897, Taylor Collection.

24. The history and details of the Bethlehem Company are based on Copley, *Frederick W. Taylor,* Vol. 2, Chapter 1.

25. Taylor to Davenport, January 4, 1898, Taylor Collection.

26. Taylor to Linderman, January 4, 1898, Taylor Collection.

27. Taylor to Wharton, March 20, 1899, Taylor Collection.

28. Taylor to Linderman, Recommendation No. 3, June 21, 1898, Taylor Collection.

29. Frederick W. Taylor, *Principles of Scientific Management* (New York: Harper, 1911), pp. 41 ff.

30. Taylor to Linderman, Recommendation No. 1, May 27, 1898, Taylor Collection.

31. Frederick W. Taylor, "On the Art of Cutting Metals" (New York: A.S.M.E., 1907), p. 53.

32. Copley, *Frederick W. Taylor,* Vol. 2, pp. 136–137.

33. Sellers to Taylor, January 18, 1900, Taylor Collection.

34. Copley, *Frederick W. Taylor*, Vol. 2, p. 114.

35. Taylor in informal conversation, cited in Copley, *Frederick W. Taylor*, Vol. 2, p. 46.

36. *Ibid.*, p. 47.

37. Taylor to Linderman, October 5, 1899, Taylor Collection.

38. Taylor to Linderman, March 15, 1899, Taylor Collection.

39. Taylor to Linderman, March, 1901, Taylor Collection.

40. Copley, *Frederick W. Taylor*, Vol. 2, p. 150.

41. Griffith to Taylor, April 4, 1901; and Taylor to Griffith, April 8, 1901, and November 16, 1901, Taylor Collection.

42. Taylor to Steele, March 11, 1901, Taylor Collection.

43. Taylor to Linderman, April 4, 1901, Taylor Collection.

44. Gantt to Taylor, April 23, 1901, Taylor Collection.

45. Linderman to Taylor, April 17, 1901, Taylor Collection.

CHAPTER 8

1. The psychological literature, clinical or theoretical, on failure and disappointment in career is scant. See, however, Abraham Zaleznik, "The Management of Disappointment," *Harvard Business Review*, Vol. 46 (November–December, 1967); and G. Rochlin, "The Psychology of Failure," in *Griefs and Discontents* (London: Churchill, 1965).

2. Sigmund Freud, *On Narcissism: An Introduction,* in *Collected Works,* Vol. 14, p. 85.

3. Rochlin, "Psychology of Failure," p. 310.

4. Oscar Wilde to Lord Alfred Douglas, January–March, 1897, in *The Letters of Oscar Wilde,* Rupert Hart-Davis, ed. (London, 1962), p. 466. This is part of the letter later published separately, in abridged version, as *De Profundis.*

5. See Paul Schilder, "Success and Failure," *Psychoanalytic Review,* 29 (October 1942).

6. *The Letters of Oscar Wilde,* p. 466, italics added.

7. *Ibid.*, p. 554.

8. Nietzsche to his sister, August 1883, in *Selected Letters of Friedrich Nietzsche,* O. Levy, ed. (London: Heinemann, 1921), pp. 166–167.

9. Taylor to Steele, November 19, 1901, Taylor Collection, Stevens Institute of Technology, Hoboken, New Jersey.

10. Zaleznik, "The Management of Disappointment," p. 69.

11. Theodor Reik, *Of Love and Lust* (New York: Farrar, Straus & Giroux, 1941), p. 110.

12. Dostoevsky to his brother Michael, July 18, 1869, in *Letters of Fyo-*

dor Michailovitch Dostoevsky, E. C. Mayne, trans. (New York: Horizon, 1961), p. 47.

13. Nietzsche to Herr Ob. Reg. R. Krug, November 16, 1880, *Selected Letters,* p. 132.

14. See Arnold A. Rogow, *James Forrestal: A Study of Personality, Politics and Policies* (New York: Macmillan, 1963).

15. Nietzsche to Peter Gast, August 20, 1880, *Selected Letters,* pp. 130–131.

16. The role played by Taylor's wife in this process is unclear. A distinguished management expert, who often met the couple during the last years of Taylor's life, has described her in a private letter as a "vain and shallow woman" who was of no help to him. We have, however, no further evidence on Taylor's wife which would either confirm or reject this opinion.

17. Frank B. Copley, *Frederick W. Taylor, Father of Scientific Management,* 2 vols. (New York: Harper and Bros., 1923), Vol. 2, p. 168.

18. *The Confessions of Jean-Jacques Rousseau,* J. M. Cohne, trans. (London: Penguin Edition, 1960), p. 460.

19. Nietzsche, *Selected Letters,* pp. 153, 154, 165.

20. *The Letters of Oscar Wilde,* p. 471.

CHAPTER 9

1. See Erik H. Erikson, "Identity and the Life Cycle," *Psychological Issues,* Vol. 1 (New York: International Universities Press, 1959), p. 116.

2. Eliot Jacques, "Death and the Mid-Life Crisis," *International Journal of Psychoanalysis,* 46 (October 1965): 502 ff.

3. Sigmund Freud, "Thoughts on War and Death," *Collected Papers* (London: Hogarth Press, 1924), Vol. 4, pp. 304–305.

4. Dante, *The Divine Comedy,* cited in Jacques, "Death and the Mid-Life Crisis," p. 505.

5. Frank B. Copley, *Frederick W. Taylor, Father of Scientific Management,* 2 vols. (New York: Harper and Bros., 1923), Vol. 1, p. 39.

6. Erik H. Erikson, *Childhood and Society,* 2nd ed. (New York: Norton, 1963), p. 267.

7. Copley, *Frederick W. Taylor,* Vol. 2, p. 239. See further Carl Barth's contribution in *Frederick W. Taylor, A Memorial,* Taylor Collection, Stevens Institute of Technology, Hoboken, New Jersey.

8. Copley, *Frederick W. Taylor,* Vol. 2, p. 224.

9. Kempton Taylor, *Recollections,* Taylor Collection.

10. *Ibid.*

11. Cited in Copley, *Frederick W. Taylor,* Vol. 2, p. 220.

12. *Ibid.,* p. 256.

13. *Ibid.,* p. 281.

14. Taylor to J. Sellers Bancroft, June 26, 1908, Taylor Collection.

15. Crozier to Taylor, December 14, 1906, Taylor Collection.

16. Hugh G. J. Aitken, *Taylorism at Watertown Arsenal* (Cambridge, Mass.: Harvard University Press, 1960); Chapter 2 gives the history of Taylorism at the arsenals.

17. See Copley, *Frederick W. Taylor*, Vol. 2, Chapter 10.

18. Letter of Brandeis, cited in Copley, *Frederick W. Taylor*, Vol. 2, p. 371.

19. Evidence Taken by the Interstate Commerce Commission in the Matter of Proposed Advances in Freight Rates by Carriers, August to December, 1910, Senate Document 725, 61st Congress, 3rd Session (Washington: Government Printing Office, 1911), IV, 2617.

20. Taylor to Goodrich, January 1911, Taylor Collection.

21. Biographical notes, Taylor Collection.

22. Letter to Johnson, the editor of *Century Magazine*, March 2, 1911, Taylor Collection.

23. Lucke to Johnson, April 12, 1911, Taylor Collection.

24. Gilbreth to Taylor, February 6, 1908, Taylor Collection.

25. Gilbreth to Taylor, May 20, 1909, Taylor Collection.

26. Gilbreth to Thompson, May 1, 1908, Taylor Collection.

27. Emerson to Taylor, November 17, 1905, Taylor Collection. See also Dodge to Taylor, May 28, 1906.

28. Taylor to Barth, October 29, 1909, Taylor Collection.

29. Taylor to Copley, August 19, 1912, Taylor Collection.

30. Taylor to Gilbreth, November 9, 1909, Taylor Collection.

31. Barth to Taylor, January 3, 1910, Taylor Collection.

32. The remarks on the union struggles against Taylorism are based on the standard work on the subject, Milton J. Nadworny, *Scientific Management and the Unions* (Cambridge, Mass.: Harvard University Press, 1955), Chapter 4.

33. *Ibid.*, p. 51.

34. *Ibid.*, p. 56.

35. Taylor to Portenar, June 10, 1916, Taylor Collection.

36. Taylor to C. B. Thompson, December 30, 1916, Taylor Collection.

37. Lyndall Urwick, "The Life and Work of Frederick Winslow Taylor," paper delivered before the XIth International Management Congress, in Paris on June 24th, 1957, p. 4; and Copley, *Frederick W. Taylor*, Vol. 2, Chapter 7.

38. Taylor to Barth, November 25, 1910, Taylor Collection.

39. Taylor to Gilbreth, October 29, 1912, Taylor Collection.

40. Taylor to Birge Harrison, May 26, 1913, Taylor Collection.

41. Copley, *Frederick W. Taylor,* Vol. 2, p. 438.

42. Letter to Birge Harrison, March 2, 1915, Taylor Collection.

43. Copley, *Frederick W. Taylor,* Vol. 2, p. 440.

CHAPTER 10

1. Alfred North Whitehead, *Science and the Modern World* (New York: Macmillan, 1925), p. 137.

2. The bulk of nineteenth-century German scholarship is a case in point.

3. See G. B. Baldwin and G. P. Schultz, "Automation: A New Dimension to Old Problems," Industrial Relations Research Association, Proceedings of the Seventh Annual Meeting (December 28–30, 1959): 124–125.

4. See Alain Touraine, "L'Evolution du travail ouvrier aux usines Renault," excerpted in Charles R. Walker, ed., *Modern Technology and Civilization* (New York: McGraw-Hill, 1962), pp. 425–443.

5. J. R. Gass, "Money and Motivation in the Automatic Factory," in Walker, *Modern Technology and Civilization,* p. 267.

6. *Ibid.*

7. See *International Encyclopedia of the Social Sciences,* 17 vols. (Chicago: Macmillan and Free Press, 1968), Vol. 3, p. 437.

8. Kurt R. Eissler, "Psychopathology and Creativity," *American Imago,* 24 (Spring–Summer 1967): 37.

9. See the various contributions in *American Imago,* Vol. 24.

10. See Phyllis Greenacre, "The Childhood of the Artist," *The Psychoanalytic Study of the Child,* 12 (1957): 47–72; and Ernst Kris, *Psychoanalytic Explorations in Art* (New York: International Universities Press, 1952).

11. Quoted in Harry Slochower, "Genius, Psychopathology and Creativity," *American Imago,* 24 (Spring–Summer 1967): 5.

12. Greenacre, "Childhood of the Artist."

13. Eissler, "Psychopathology and Creativity," pp. 52ff.

ASME, *see* American Society of Mechanical Engineers
Accounting, 3, 106, 131–132, 150
Adolescence, 24, 25, 27, 163
Agricultural machinery, 30
Aitken, Hugh, G. J., 107
American Federation of Labor, attack on premium bonus system, 182–183
American Society of Mechanical Engineers, 87, 104, 127, 133, 169
Amontons, Guillaume, precursor of Taylor, on work, 115
Appleton Mill, Wisconsin, 125
Apprenticeship system, 33, 36–42
choice of Midvale Steel Works as arena for reform, 43
identification with workers, 36–38
influencing personalities; *see* Davenport, Russel; Sellers, William
at University of Pennsylvania, 33
value of, according to Taylor, 38, 40
Arendt, Hannah, 78–79
Arsenal, Watertown, 107, 111
Associational aspect of work, 83
Automation, 4–5, 98, 191

Babbage, Charles, precursor of Taylor, 115
Economy of Machinery and Manufacture, 70
Baker, Ray Stannard, 176
Barnett, Homer G., on innovation, 114
Barth, Carl, 52, 130, 140, 146, 151, 161, 169–171, 173, 175, 178, 186
Belidor, Bernard Forest de, *The Science of Engineering in Fortifications and Civil Architecture,* 116
Bell, Daniel, 72, 85
Bergson, Henri, 76, 164
Bethlehem Steel Company, 9, 54, 99, 123, 137–151, 153, 154, 156–157, 169
"Braking" of work; see Strikes and lockouts
Brandeis, Louis D., 2, 174–175
Eastern Railroad case, 174
on scientific management, 175–176
Brinley, Charles, 45–46, 52, 62, 66, 157
British Institutions of Mechanical Engineers, 104
Brooklyn Navy Yard, 173
Business Cycles; see Depression

Camus, Albert, 78
Capital, 4
Capitalism, 3, 79
Career aspect of work, 80–83
Change, Technological; see Technological innovations
Child rearing in Taylor's time, 16–18, 23
Cicero, on work, 76
Civil War, American, 20, 42, 122
Clark, E.W., 41–42
Clemenceau, Georges, on the Taylor system, 2
Collective bargaining, 185
Colper, Jean Baptiste, precursor of Taylor, 115
Communism, 80
Comte, Auguste, 40, 189
Conflict
Taylor's inner, 9, 62, 66, 75, 83, 92, 121–122
Taylor's neurotic, 85, 194
Conrad, Joseph
on associational aspect of work, 84
Heart of Darkness, 80
Control
of work, 3, 5, 55
of labor, 62, 65–66, 93
Cooke, Morris W., 170, 175
Copley, Frank B., 14, 16, 20, 22, 37, 43, 49, 52–53, 131, 136, 149, 165–166, 179, 187

214

Failures (*continued*)
self-reproach versus outward-directed reproach, 155–157
Fannon, William, 124, 125, 130
Fayol, Henry, 114
Ferrell, 28
Ferrell and Muckle, 28
Ford, Henry, 128
Forrestal, James, biography, 160
Frémont, precursor of Taylor, 117
French Academy of Sciences, 115
Freud, Anna, on adolescence, 24
Freud, Sigmund, 82–83, 91, 152, 163–164
on group psychology, 91–93
"love and work" concept, 75, 106
Fritz, John, 137–138

Gandhi, M. K., 80
Gantt, Henry, 86, 140, 150–151, 170, 175, 177–178
Gay, Edwin F., interest in scientific management, 1, 174
Generativity, crisis of, 165, 168
German Society of Engineers, 101
Germantown, 100, 124, 161–162, 169
Academy, 23
Germany, 8
Gilbreth, Frank, 1
devotion to spread of Taylor system, 178
Gillespie, James, on motion study, 71–72
Gompers, Samuel, 183
Goodrich (Admiral), 125, 175
Groups, psychology of, 91–92
Grozier, Brigadier General, 172

Harrah, Charles, 52, 123
Harrison, Birge, on Taylor's boyhood, 18–20
Harvard
Engineering School, 171
School of Technology, 28
University, Boston, 1, 10, 28, 38, 131

Hathway, Horace, 170, 173, 175
Hendrick, Ives, on work principle, 81

Illinois, University of, College of Engineering, 46
Immigrant labor, 30, 34, 68, 86
Income, 31
Industrial engineering, 189
Industrial expansion in the nineteenth century, 29–30
and engineers versus financiers, 126–129
personal management, 31
social upheavals and unrest, 31–32
Industrial management, 3, 8, 40, 97, 99, 106, 124, 188
Industrial organization, 4, 31, 91, 106–107, 115, 134, 138, 185
Industrial relations, 20, 90, 172, 178, 184
Industrial revolution, 5, 29, 87, 90, 107
Industrialization, 4, 34, 75, 80, 128
Innovation
analysis plus recombination, 118
catalysts for, 117, 118
definition of, 192–193
impact of, on levels of history, 188
importance of social support for, 117
relation of, to personality, 193
and search for prototypes, 119, 121
see also Innovations by Taylor; Technological innovations
Innovations by Taylor, 157, 178, 188
assessment of, 113–115
chronological list of, 102–103
engineering achievements, 104, 113
geared to concrete solutions, 100
hindrances to total job control, 105

Wilde, Oscar, and breakdown of ego ideal, 154–155
William Deering & Company, 132
William Sellers and Company, 49; *see also* Sellers, William
Winslow, Emily, mother, 14–15
  relation with Frederick, factor in failures and disappointments, 153–154
  views on child rearing, 16–17
Wordsworth, William, 155
Work, 3, 5, 7–9, 48, 67, 89, 91, 93, 95, 98, 122, 191
  for acting out neurotic conflicts, 85
  Bhagavad Gita concept of, 77
  in Christian Socialism, 77
  coordination of, 62, 108, 150
  as a craft, 68–69
  as a curse to the Greeks, 75–76
  effectance motivation of, 87
  ego aspect of, 80–83
  Hebrew view of, 76
  hierarchical ordering of, 84
  labor aspects of, 78–80
  measurement of, *see* Work measurement
  methods of, 2, 3, 68, 71, 73, 89, 112–113, 115, 147
  modern views of, 77–78
  morality of, 47, 75–77, 80
  primacy in individual life, 75
  in Puritanism and Calvinism, 76–77, 85
  rationalization of, 69, 89
  religious views of, 76
  restriction of, 9, 87, 91, 93
  Roman concept of, 76
  Taylor's attitudes toward, 85–87
  as total experience, 68
  in Western culture, 76
  Yoga concept of, 77
  see also Maslow, Abraham, on need categories in work; Mayo, Elton
Work measurement, 53, 55–56, 67, 70–73, 94, 98–99, 105, 107, 112–113, 115–117, 120–121, 142, 146–147, 168, 192
  definition of, 70
Workers
  dismissals of, 61, 90
  selection of, 142
  social status of, 68
  training of, 57
  unrest of, 31–32
World War I, 104

Yale and Towne, 171

Zaleznik, Abraham, 158

ELEVEN

Emma wrenched at the window-sash but the latch held fast. French doors opened from Kitty's room onto the balcony – she had almost reached them when she realized that the moonlight that shone so brightly on the tumble of sheets on the bed outlined a woman's hand and wrist. Hand and wrist and tousle of black curls among the pillow-lace.

She stood for a moment, then stepped close to the bed.

That was Kitty, all right. Sleeping like an innocent child, her other arm curved around Buttercreme, whose little round head rested in the hollow of her shoulder.

Quietly, Emma walked to the French doors, and looked out.

The dark-haired woman and the man in evening dress were still embracing, with a theatrical abandon that looked like progressing on to the honeymoon stage right there in the moonlight between the steep slope of the road-bank and the house.

It's Kitty's own house. Why fornicate in the front yard when there's a perfectly good bed . . .

The dress the dark-haired woman was wearing was the one Kitty had had on Wednesday night at the police station.

The one she got from the wardrobe department.

Which has at least three duplicates . . .

Ire smote her. Not anger or rage . . . simple vexation, as [s]he understood what she was looking at.

OH!!!

She would have stamped her foot, had she not feared to wake [Ki]tty – the genuine Kitty – sound asleep in her own bed . . .

[E]mma yanked the belt of her robe tight, ghosted back into [her] own room long enough to get her slippers, then ran lightly [dow]n the stairs, through the kitchen – catching up the house-[key] from the counter and locking the back door behind her [and] down the back steps. The inky shadow of the hill blan[keted] the driveway itself – concealing the rather seedy little

of Oxford. Oxford before the War, when she'd glide like a bird on her bicycle along Longwall Street, to The Misses Gibbs' Select Academy where she had been a day pupil, or to Mrs Willis's out along the Botley Road for her piano lessons. Walking with her mother early in the cool of May morning, to hear the choir singing in the Magdalen Tower. Seeing the undergraduates who looked so grown-up in their gowns when she was sixteen, that heartbreakingly beautiful summer before the War. Who looked so terribly young three years later, when she'd drive the ambulances from the train station to bring the wounded to hospital at Bicester. Sometimes, on warm nights in Michaelmas term, she had heard them strolling, late, along the Parks Road, singing. Those beautiful tenors and baritones, harmonizing in the dark.

In her dream she crossed the Magdalen Bridge, and quickened her step along Longwall Street. She thought, *I've missed them so. It will be good to see them again: Mother, Papa, Miles.* She had two of her father's books under her arm, and knew she'd taken them along to read when she'd been . . . wherever she'd been. Macaulay's *The Lays of Ancient Rome*, and a pocket copy of *Much Ado About Nothing*, always entertaining for a train ride . . . Her father would have acquired a catalog of the newest finds at the necropolis at Arrentium, he'd need help codifying the dates . . .

She glimpsed Miles, walking ahead of her. Miles jaunty and healthy, half-turning as if he'd wait for her, as he'd done ever since they were children, to go up the steps together.

But the house wasn't there. The place where it had stood on Holywell Street was only a thicket of trees, a tangle of overgrown rose bushes: albas, her mother's favorite, with petals fluffy as the skirts of Spanish dancers. The three shallow stone steps that had led up from the street to the door ended in nothing.

Miles was gone.

Emma cried, 'What happened?' and the effort to produce sound from her throat woke her.

For a moment she lay in the darkness, looking at the three tall, barely-seen rectangles of window opposite the foot of her bed and wondering, *What room am I in?*

The bow window of her bedroom at The Myrtles should have been there. The night-light (*That's not MY night-light . . . What happened to my little gold-glass night-light?*) showed her a low, square, boxy bureau, an unfamiliar chair.

And she remembered. Not one single thing from her bedroom had been saved, when they'd cleared out the house to sell. Someone from the hospital had gone in and gotten the clothes they'd thought she'd need, to go down to that dreary lodging in Headington, for the week she'd stayed, recuperating, before taking the train to Manchester and Mrs Pendergast's. Everything was gone.

All Father's notes had simply gone into the rubbish.

She'd never found out what had happened to Daphne, Mother's fat, white cat.

This wasn't the first time she'd waked like this, for one second puzzled that she wasn't in her own bedroom. It had happened every few weeks, during the horrible years she'd spent at Mrs Pendergast's.

It just felt like the first time.

It always felt like the first time.

It was Chang Ming barking.

Not the furious, defensive intruder-bark of last night, but the wary 'whuff' of suspicion.

Doggy toe-nails clattered in the hall outside her room. Black Jasmine gave a short yap as well, like a little quack.

Not enough to wake Kitty, Emma didn't think. After dinner her sister-in-law had had her usual round of telephone calls to Peggy Donovan ('*Did* I do anything really frightful last night, darling?'), Marie Prevost over at Warners (who was one of her main competitors for the title of the Silver Screen Goddess), and Blanche Sweet, one of the longtime reigning queens of Hollywood. But at nine fifteen Emma had come into Kitty's room and found her sleeping like a dead woman, the softly-complaining telephone under her nerveless hand.

It was now – she glanced at the clock on the nightstand – a quarter past one in the morning.

Headlights briefly swept Emma's window, then quickly died.

Cornero.

The glint of starlight on gun barrels leaped to her mind.

A deep voice saying, *Don't try it.* And then, *Where's Miss de la Rose?*

Emma swept her robe from the foot of her bed, wrapped it around her as she went to the window in the hall that looked out over the silly pseudo-balcony above the porch, and so down into the scrubby vale that was the front yard.

Kitty stood there, a darkly shimmering figure in the moonlight. From the shadows of the eucalyptus tree a man emerged, little more than a tall silhouette, and the white V-shaped gleam of a shirt-front. Dark hair, and the glisten of brilliantine – Emma thought, *Drat it!* as he approached, and Kitty, shaking back the dark cascade of her tousled hair, stretched out her arms to him.

Then movement at the top of the bank above them caught Emma's eye, and the drench of moonlight – only a day or two from full – showed her a man standing on the edge of the road, and the glint of something metal in his hands.

car parked there – and Emma kept to the drive's verge as she climbed towards the road. She reflected that the couple in front of the house were putting on a sufficiently interesting scene that there was little likelihood that the man up on the road – *Is that a telescope he has in his hand? Binoculars?* – would hear approaching footfalls.

And as she climbed she recalled the glimpse she'd had through the doors of the empress's garden last night, of Darlene Golden in her exiguous rags, talking earnestly with an extremely handsome young extra – in evening dress – from the *Scandalous Lady* set.

Ginny Field had been in the garden, too, she recalled. Kitty's stand-in. Her height, her build, with her same dark hair.

OH!!!

It was a scene straight out of *Much Ado About Nothing*, although Emma doubted Darlene knew its provenance. She paused beside the car at the top of the drive, long enough to write down its license-plate number before walking around it to the shape of the man, crouched low beside the road bank, above that long slope of shadow. Binoculars in hand. She said, very softly, 'Mr Madison?' and he swiveled on his heels, jerked to his feet.

Before he could say a word she stepped onto the top of the little road bank, called down into the darkness in her gruffest voice, 'You there! This is the police!' And taking Madison's hand – because it was indeed Colt Madison, speechless for once – pulled him to the brink and down the slope of rocks and weeds towards the couple, the yard, and the house.

'You see they're not making for the house,' she said, holding herself steady on the man's arm. 'They know the front door will be locked. Drat these plants . . .'

'Mrs Blackstone—' he began, his attention diverted between her and the fleeing lovers, who could be seen dimly in the moonlight, scrambling up the shallower slope where the road curved around the lot immediately to the south.

'Did Miss Golden hire you?' she asked, drawing him firmly after her up the tiled front steps. 'Or Mr Pugh?'

'I'm not at liberty to—'

'Naturally not.' Emma cut him off. 'Do you like Shakespeare, Mr Madison? He could get away with some amazingly hackneyed plots on sheer good writing. But ordinarily I'm annoyed by those plays in which the entire problem could be resolved in five minutes by one character asking another, "What were you actually doing?"' She had guided him across the living room and up the stairs – trailed by Chang Ming, the only one of the Pekes who could get up and down the stairs unaided – and stopped outside Kitty's door.

'I would really rather not waken Miss de la Rose at this hour,' she continued softly, 'considering how early she must get up to be on the set tomorrow. But do please look and make sure that that *is* Miss de la Rose – and please take my word for it that she has been in bed, and asleep, since nine thirty.'

The detective stood in the doorway of the room, looking at the woman sleeping in the moonlight, her tiny dog snoring audibly in the curve of her arm. Then he backed away, and with Emma beside him, retreated to the head of the stairs. 'I suppose you were asleep yourself, m'am.' In the dark of the upstairs hall, little was visible of the young man but the outline of moonlight on his handsome profile, and the pale blur of his topcoat.

'I was,' returned Emma. 'But do you imagine that Kitty – startled in the midst of her . . . er . . . *transports* – would have fled into the next lot and up the bank to the road, instead of back into her own house? Do you think that she could have circled back to come into this house through the back door . . .? Drat it,' she added, as the faint growl of a car starting in the drive reached them, 'there goes Romeo . . . Do you think that she could have circled back into this house and gotten undressed and settled down in bed in the time that it took yourself and me to come in and up here? And gotten her *dog* to fall asleep? I wonder if they came together or if she's left a car somewhere also.'

Taking his elbow, she led him down the dark stair to the living room again. 'Did you see her come out of the house, by the way?'

'I saw her come down out of the shadows of the porch.'

Profoundly flustered, Madison seemed to have lost all his cockiness and seemed a bit adrift without it.

Emma glanced through the long windows that flanked the front door, though she'd noticed already that the porch-light had been yet again quenched – almost certainly robbed once more of its bulb. Quietly, she finished, 'Would you like me to waken Miss de la Rose so that you can look at her in good light and ascertain that yes, she has just actually awakened from a sound sleep?'

Colt Madison was quiet for a time, his expression hidden by the stygian shadow of his hat. But she did see his lips, and they were tightly pressed. 'No,' he said, at length. 'That'll be fine.'

Which, Emma felt, told its own tale.

She led him out onto the porch, and closed the front door behind them. 'I believe the woman you saw was Miss Field, Miss de la Rose's stand-in,' she said after a moment. 'Though there is no way to prove this, if she denies it, as I'm sure she will. Are you prepared to believe that any of the extras on the Foremost lot – or in fact any extra in Hollywood – would be capable of accepting payment to enact a love scene such as you were told would be taking place here tonight, no questions asked?'

'Oh, hell, yeah,' said Madison at once. 'For twenty-five dollars and rental on the tux, *I'd* do the scene.' He was silent for a moment, fishing a pack of cigarettes from his pocket. 'So you figure somebody's trying to make Pugh jealous? Get him to dump Camille?'

'Or get him to withdraw his support – studio support from her before the hearing.'

'And using me as a chump.'

'And using you as a chump,' Emma affirmed.

Flame illuminated his narrowed eyes, his lips hardened now in anger.

'You can't pick your clients,' she went on after a pause. 'And of course I'm sure that the reason your client chose you for this task was because Mr Pugh trusts your observations. Perhaps you could tell your client that you could observe nothing because the police were called?'

'I'll tell her that and I'll tell her to stick her damn job.'
He expelled a line of smoke from one corner of his mouth.
'Make a monkey out of *me* . . .'

He slapped her on the shoulder, man-wise. 'You're a square
broad, Duchess.' He started to turn towards the steps, then
added, frowning, 'Can I ask you to keep this on the QT? I
told Pugh I was out workin' a lead about Marion Davies – and
I was, earlier tonight . . . and she's clean . . . But seeing as
this was just a peep show tonight, I'd just as soon keep separate
things separate.'

'It isn't my business,' said Emma. 'Unless of course for
some reason it becomes Miss de la Rose's business.'

He nodded, and blew another line of smoke. 'Understood.'
He shook hands vigorously with her, and descended the
steps.

A moment later, Emma heard his shoes scrunch the gravel
of the drive. *Am I EVER going to get a complete night's sleep
in this place?*

The headlights of his car went up. A moment later, the dark
bulk of the vehicle slipped away down Ivarene Street.

Emma sighed, and looking down, saw Chang Ming sitting
alertly on the threshold of the door, waiting to go in. It was
probably, Emma guessed, after two . . .

Movement on the road made her turn her head. Moonlight
gleamed on a second car, driving without lights, as it pulled
out of the driveway of the darkened house just up the road
from where she stood, and followed Madison's car away in
the direction of Franklin Avenue.

Kitty said, '*OH!!!*' when Emma told her – some three hours
later – of the night's events, in the cold electric whiteness of
the tiled kitchen as she made coffee. 'It's that *bitch* Darlene!
It *has* to be!'

'That would be my guess,' agreed Emma, and poured
steaming water into the coffee-press first, then the fat brown
teapot for herself. More water bubbled gently around the eggs
on the stove. Chang Ming and Black Jasmine, having devoured
their own breakfasts, stared at Buttercreme's dish in passionate
agony as the little moonlight dog picked at a fragment or two

of chicken liver, then sat back thoughtfully and contemplated the uneaten remains.

'So *that's* why Frank was acting so strangely yesterday! I will *fire* that *nasty* little slut Ginny—'

'You'll have to explain why,' pointed out Emma. 'And you know she'll deny it. As will Darlene.' She bore the coffee, and a small glass of orange juice, over to the table, all the sustenance Kitty could endure early in the morning. Awake since four, her sister-in-law had already bathed and donned full make-up – which would be changed to camera make-up the moment they arrived on the Foremost lot – and looked as exquisite as a jeweled doll. 'I doubt Mr Pugh will appreciate having to find another stand-in for you at short notice.'

Kitty sipped her coffee, and lit her third cigarette of the day. 'Do you think you could talk Zal into having trouble with his camera settings so we could make Ginny stand under the lights for two hours while he fixes them?' she asked.

They needn't have worried. Ginny Field did not show up for work that morning, so the start of scene sixty-three was delayed while Madge stormed across to Belle Delaney's little cubicle and ordered up another extra of approximately Kitty's height, build, and coloring like a sandwich. While waiting for this young lady – Ruby Saks was her name – to be dressed and made up and acquainted with her duties, Kitty leafed through the morning papers in her dressing room, looking for accounts of how her rivals in the Silver Screen Goddess sweepstakes had sought to prove their glamorous outrageousness on the previous night.

'Oh, Colleen Moore turned up at the Café New York with Ronnie Coleman, wearing a necklace that cost *three thousand dollars*! And they ordered a bottle of champagne that cost *one hundred* dollars! I'll have to tell Ambrose about that – he thinks *nothing* of paying that for a bottle of wine . . .'

'A *hundred dollars*?' Emma calculated what that was in pounds, and was – even after six months in Hollywood – scandalized.

'Oh, darling, that's *nothing*!' Kitty looked up from her paper in childlike surprise. 'Gloria Swanson has a solid gold bathtub. They almost couldn't get it into her house, it weighs so much!

John Barrymore paid I don't know how much – sixteen thousand dollars, I think – for his dining-room chandelier. Peggy's new car has real leopard-skin upholstery and solid gold door-handles. And Ambrose had an *entire Italian villa* taken apart in Italy . . . He's having it reassembled in the hills about two hours north of here . . . Villa Something-Or-Other. It belonged to some *tremendously* famous Italian a long time ago . . . Caruso? The opera singer? Robinson Caruso? Or was it somebody else? You'd probably know . . .'

She turned over a page. 'Oh, and Peggy told me that Anita Tempest over at Enterprise challenged Clara Bow to a chariot race! Not that Anita's ever sober enough to drive, and Peggy says Mr DeMille refused to lend either of them any chariots.'

'Good for Mr DeMille.' Emma wondered whether any of the leading contenders for the title of Goddess of the Silver Screen would manage to get herself accused of a still-more-glamorous, mysterious crime before the fan votes were cast on the twenty-fifth.

'And if she did,' she added, when she encountered Zal later in the morning in the Imperial Box at the Coliseum, 'would the Pettingers try to have Kitty arrested as Accessory Before the Fact? Or just suffer an apoplexy from sheer outrage?'

Zal considered the matter for a moment. 'Myself,' he said at last, 'I'd vote for Clara, or Anita, getting kidnapped and taken out to some mysterious shack in the desert, and rescued by Ramon Navarro. Or Ford Sterling, if Navarro's too expensive.'

'You can have Colt Madison for twenty-five dollars and the rental of a tuxedo,' Emma informed him helpfully. 'Personally, I fully expect to see one of them fly an aeroplane to Cuba, to reunite with a lost love.'

'That's not bad.' He craned to look over the carven balustrade to where the Christians were assembling below. 'And if the girls don't think of it, I bet you can sell that to Frank as the scenario of Kitty's next picture.'

The emperor's box overlooking the floor of the Coliseum for scene sixty-three was truly an impressive construction. A flight of thirty steps, of gold-latticed marble, led from the sand up to the terrace itself ('Won't the lions climb up them to eat the emperor?' inquired Emma), and the throne at the top was, a little to Emma's surprise, a handsome marble copy of an actual curule chair – ersatz marble, but still more or less Roman. While Doc Larousse and his minions shifted reflectors, Madge walked Kitty through her entrance through the great double doors at the top, slave-boys and priests following her and among them, head bowed in chains, poor (and still very scantly clad) Elmore Perkins, humbled and enslaved.

A little shyly, Emma went on, 'Thank you for staying Thursday night.'

'My pleasure. I'm only sorry I missed last night's show. You all right?'

She nodded, and their hands briefly touched.

'Duchess!' yelled Madge. 'You hear that? I'm gonna need a scene before this one, of Elmore in the dungeon with his mom. Get down here . . .'

His glance was like a smiling kiss, and her eyes received it like one, before she hurried down the thirty marble steps to the 2000 square feet of laboriously imported sand.

Frank visited the set just before lunch. Darlene Golden, in a flutter of discreetly placed rags, halted on the bottom step of the flight (up which it was her task run, to throw herself at Kitty's feet) and instead flew to the producer's side. As Madge's exasperated 'Cut!' rent the air, Kitty turned her head and met Frank's eyes with what novelists generally called a 'speaking glance': *I adore you but I will not delay the filming . . . unlike SOME people I could name . . .*

Frank evidently understood. He was noticeably short with Darlene and, when the blonde actress returned, a little chagrined, to the gaggle of nervous Christians in front of the lion cage ('You're not really going to let those lions out of the cage while we're down here, are you, m'am?' inquired one of the younger girls timidly), clearly had eyes for no one but the empress.

When at about four o'clock Madge finally yelled, 'Print that one!' and Mr Torley emerged from the lions' cage to retrieve his food-stuffed and opium-drowsy pets, Darlene turned again to the producer, with some manufactured query. Pugh answered her, but his eye was on Kitty, descending the marble stair like an empress indeed, peacock cloak making iridescent wings around her and jewels glittering in the California sunlight. Emma could not keep from smiling at Darlene's expression as Pugh strode to meet Kitty, hands outstretched.

'You don't really think Darlene actually had anything to do with Mr Festraw's death, do you?' Emma asked, as the lights crew began to dismantle set-ups and shift reflectors.

'The stakes for her are pretty high.' Zal polished his glasses with one of his clean handkerchiefs, following her gaze. 'Darlene claims twenty-five but she's closer to thirty-five. She worked for Christie Studios just before the War, and before that was doing one-reelers for Polyscope in '09. She called herself Mary Freedom back then and her hair was brown. If she doesn't hit it big this year or next it's gonna start to show.'

Down below, Madge was herding Christians into position for what would be – until sundown and probably far beyond – a succession of close-ups and reaction shots. 'Zal!' she shouted. 'You think we can get scene sixty tonight, while we got all the Christians here? It'll save us half a day tomorrow—'

He raised his hand in assent, turned back to Emma. 'Is that worth killing a man for?' he asked quietly. 'You tell me.'

'You tell *me* if she makes enough to hire someone to do the shooting,' said Emma slowly. 'She'd certainly have had access to Kitty's dressing room, to get the gun and the stationery. Although . . .' She hesitated, not sure how to express her thought that something, somewhere didn't fit. 'In a way,' she added, 'it would make things simpler if she *was* behind it.'

'*Zally!*' yelled Madge again, as Elmore's unfortunate mother and sisters took their places amid the reset reflectors which would immortalize their terror and agony in close-up.

Zal raised his eyebrows. 'You mean, now at least we know which way to look?'

Emma drew breath to say, *Maybe*, and then let it out. For the third or fourth time that morning, she wondered if she had indeed seen a second car, gliding without lights down Ivarene

Street in the moonlight last night. And if so, if it had meant anything . . .

Prior to her tender encounter with Mr Pugh at the foot of the marble staircase, Kitty had spoken of exhaustion and looking forward to another night of sleep. But Emma wasn't in the least surprised when, at five – the Christians being disposed of – Kitty scampered to her dressing room and reemerged made-up, hair dressed, and exquisite in a black-and-emerald street frock just as Frank Pugh had his long black Pierce-Arrow brought up to the Hacienda's front door.

'I'll be home before ten, I *promise!*' Kitty squeezed Emma's hands, and Mr Pugh smiled benignly. 'I'm absolutely *ruined* . . . but I *can't* pass up steak at the Brass Rail!' She turned her head, raised eyes brimming with adoration upon her escort.

Personally, Emma doubted she'd see her errant sister-in-law much before midnight. She packed up dogs, astrology magazines, make-up, kimonos, and stray earrings in the grateful expectation of (*at last!*) a quiet evening, and was indeed able to complete scene sixty-five A (the saintly Demetrius whispering words of comfort to his mother and sisters in the dungeon) before Kitty returned at ten.

'Honestly, it's Darlene I'm going to murder one of these days, not Rex.' Kitty unpinned her hat, shook out the storm cloud of her dark hair. 'Filling Frank's head with lies about me – after he let Darlene positively *hang* on him this afternoon, too! *So* unfair . . . Yes, darling, Mama's home!' She stooped to cuddle Black Jasmine, standing on his shaky little hind legs to gaze up in adoration into her face. 'And did you see that *gorgeous* boy they've got working Wardrobe now? He must have eyelashes an inch long . . .'

After Kitty went up to bed, Emma stepped out onto the porch – for the third time that evening – thinking she had heard some sound in the street. Nothing stirred in the velvety darkness. In the leaves of the eucalyptus tree, the reflection of Kitty's bedroom light went out. Silvery above the hills, the moon cast the street, and the yard, in blackest shadow. An army of bootleggers – or disgruntled cinema goddesses – could be hiding near the house . . .

Except, of course, the dogs would bark.

Emma smiled at the thought of them. *Faithful little guardians . . .*

She still checked every door and window three times, before she went to bed herself.

Lying in the darkness, she could not put from her mind the image of Rex Festraw's body, lying on the dressing-room floor with rose petals strewn about him.

It's no accident, she thought. *No random event.*

A man was killed, and killed for a reason. Brought out here from New York – specifically – and killed . . .

And Kitty knows more than she's saying. Unless she really WAS with that saxophone player from the Grove . . .

But why not say so? Not to Mr Pugh or Mr Fishbein, of course, but . . .

A door creaked in the hall and she nearly startled out of her skin.

The soft tread of stockinged feet. A faint clatter of doggy toe-nails. Kitty's whisper, 'No, darlings, you can't come with me – be good little cream cakes for Mama . . .'

Emma looked at her clock. Twelve thirty.

Moving soundlessly to the door, Emma saw her in the moonlight, in slip, stockings, and a softly-gleaming kimono. She almost stepped into the hall herself – *What on EARTH are you doing up at this hour?*

And the next second: *She'll lie.*

And if she knows I know she'll take more care next time . . .

Kitty tiptoed back into her room, carrying the lipstick and powder-box which she must have left in the smaller bathroom at the top of the stairs.

Emma swept her robe from across the foot of her bed, slipped it over her nightdress and padded in swift silence down the stairs to the telephone-niche in the lower hall.

She's meeting him again. Whoever he is.

And if I can catch them, at least I'll be able to make sure that she isn't convicted of shooting Mr Festraw. And maybe I'll learn something of who she's screening. And why.

Kitty's bedroom door had been left ajar, and by the faint trickle of light she could see to dial. Zal's voice was sleepy but unsurprised. Presumably he got calls at this hour from the studio as well. 'Yeah?'

'Zal, it's Emma,' she whispered. 'I'm so sorry to wake you, but . . . Kitty's going out. Secretly, without waking me. She came home early and pretended to go to sleep. I suspect she's going to meet whoever it was she met Wednesday. She's putting on her make-up now.'

'The woman never disappoints me.' The drowsiness vanished from Zal's voice at once. 'Don't stop her. I'll be there in twenty minutes.'

It was a good fifteen miles to Venice, where Zal lived, and in the daytimes, with automobile traffic and streetcars impeding one another at every intersection, Emma knew it could take upwards of twice that in Zal's rickety Model-T.

But even before Kitty crept downstairs, shoes in hand, oblivious to her hastily-dressed sister-in-law sitting in the dark of the living room, Emma saw the flicker of headlights on Ivarene Street. A moment later she glimpsed the dark gleam as the Model-T turned itself around at the top of the drive: carefully. Ivarene was a narrow street, and without headlights it was little more than a slot of darkness between the close-crowding hills. A moment later she heard the slight rustle of silk and drew back further into the darkness of the curtains, as Kitty passed through the hall and into the kitchen, dressed again in emerald and black, diamonds winking on her heels.

The door of the kitchen clicked very softly. Emma at the same moment slipped through the front door, and made haste to cross the scruffy grass patch which Californians considered a lawn – though she knew it would take Kitty several minutes to get the garage open, and more if Mr Shang heard her and came out to inquire. Zal met her halfway down the rough, pebbly slope that led up to the road, and helped her up with surprising strength.

In the stillness, the sound of the Packard starting up sounded like a salvo of cannon-fire.

'Thank you,' she whispered as he opened the Tin Lizzie's door for her in the darkness of a neighboring drive.

'Don't thank me, I'm dying to find out what the hell she's

really up to. If we can track down the forged notes, that's the only thing Meyer really has on her, you know.'

'I know,' Emma whispered. 'And it's one of the things that keeps me from thinking this is all just some plot of Miss Golden's, you know. Not that she was lured away – but that she won't say where she was. You don't think she could be mixed up in something like . . . like smuggling, do you? Trafficking in opium or something?'

'If I was running dope I wouldn't trust Kitty to hang onto so much as a reefer. She'd either lose it in her handbag, or give it away to one of her mah jong buddies. Besides, this is Los Angeles. Meyer himself may be bringing in hop by the wheelbarrow load. There she goes.' He let in the clutch, but didn't turn on the lights. It was a half-mile down Ivarene Street to Vine, the moon sufficiently bright (Emma hoped) to keep Zal from driving over the steep side of the road. The streets were deserted at this hour, and the big yellow Packard was easy to follow, up through the rough-pelted dark bulk of the hills, then along Ventura Boulevard past small shops and a golf course, the indigo emptiness of the orchards and bean fields and the far-off glitter of lights where a housing development huddled in the darkness.

Then hills again, and deeper dark. Kitty put her car full-pelt up swooping curves of backbone ridges, heading towards the sea. Now and then the headlights of another car flashed in the Ford's rear-vision mirror, or glared yellow coming toward them – traveling every bit as fast as Kitty was, Emma thought – and then roaring past them and zooming away to the east.

It was faster than she'd ever traveled in a car before – and felt faster still with the lights off. But the full moon was bright, and she felt no fear. Zal was a good driver – better than she'd known, having only ridden with him in the streets of Hollywood and Los Angeles. And the moonlight on the hills, silver where it stippled the chaparral and cosmos-deep Prussian blue before it graded into the velvet of shadow in the gullies, had a magic for her, a sort of heart-shaking amazement that such a place, such a rolling wildness, existed only a few miles from places like Frannie's drugstore.

The silence was like the breath of the universe, overlaid

with the muted road noise of the tires. The red lights of Kitty's car ran before them, fugitive willy-wisps. The smell of the sage-brush was like song.

And then the sea. She'd seen it in daytime, never at night. Sapphire endlessness, threaded white where the moon was going over from zenith. Black islands floated in a blue-black world indescribable. Peace seized her heart and made her want to weep.

She looked north where the road wound to infinity along the ocean's hem and said, 'There . . .'

Gold lights, tiny with distance, following the road.

Zal said, 'Sycamore Canyon's a couple miles up. There's a roadhouse about a mile in. The City Hall Gang used to run it as a speakeasy, but it got flooded out last year – it's right on top of the wash there. Bet me that's where she's headed.' He slowed, and steered the little car carefully now down the twists of the road as it descended to the highway. 'Must be some *affaire*,' he added.

They passed one or two turn-offs into other canyons, moon-drenched for their first hundred yards and then black with shadow. Headlights overtook them, roared past and were gone. The world was an emptiness of hills and sea, waves running up to the drop just beyond the western edge of the road. A thread of starlight touched the side of Zal's glasses. It crossed Emma's mind to say, *Can we just keep driving? Kitty can find her own way home* . . . and she wondered where those words had come from, or where they might have gone, had they been uttered. Whoever Kitty was shielding – or *whatever* Kitty had been up to last Wednesday afternoon for two hours – unless that was cleared, there was no telling what a jury would think.

Particularly if members of the jury listened to the Pettingers' radio program on Friday evenings.

Or if Frank Pugh happened to have read that rumor-column in *Photo Play* last month . . .

Just before the road crossed the outlet of a stream on a white-painted wooden bridge, a dirt road turned off into a canyon. The stream didn't look like much – certainly not powerful enough to destroy a speakeasy, Emma thought – but her father had often spoken of how inconspicuous little watercourses like that one could swell unexpectedly to deadly torrents.

Moonlight glinted on flowing silk, smooth round stones. Zal guided the car with slow care over the unpaved surface. Pewter moonlight edged shadows deeper than death.

And there, sitting in the middle of the road, was the Packard. On the other side of the stream, where the shadows of the hills lay black, a broken sprawl of timbers spewed down the hillside into the stream, beside the remains of a rickety wooden stair.

At the top, in the cock-eyed remains of half a building, lantern-light gleamed.

TWELVE

When Zal helped Emma down the shallow bank to cross the stream, Emma could see, parked ahead of Kitty's yellow Packard, another car, sleek and new and flashy and black, nearly hidden by the shadows of the canyon and the trees. The stream ran noisily over a succession of small waterfalls to her right, where the canyon wound inland. Rocks ranging in size from that of an orange to that of a washtub cluttered the stream-bed, and by the moonlight Emma picked her way across more or less dry-shod, guided by Zal's steadying grip. With a hand on her waist as they approached the ruined house, he moved her gently to one side, so that she climbed the wooden steps close to the beam that supported them, almost in silence. They crossed the broken boards of what had been a sort of terrace above the stream – it still contained a couple of dilapidated tables and a kitchen chair, much the worse for weather – and she heard Kitty's sweet, almost childlike voice inside the house.

'This is all the money I could get together. I hope it's enough.'

As Zal was reaching for the handle of the twisted door a chair scraped sharply, and a man said, 'What's that?'

And Kitty: 'Oh, shit—'

Zal pushed open the door and stepped inside. And, Emma noticed, dodged quickly to the right . . .

One man had half-risen from the rustic table that was all that could be seen of the room in the yellow glow of a hurricane lamp that had been set on it. Emma had an impression of burly strength, like an overweight bear, and a long-chinned, slightly crooked face behind horn-rimmed glasses. Across the table from him stood Kitty, next to probably the most beautiful young man Emma had ever seen.

Between them on the table was Kitty's small, suede handbag, a paper sack, and a couple of crumpled packets of bills.

Kitty squeaked, 'Zal!' and caught the wrist of the beautiful young man as he would have made a move to dash back into the shadows of the broken room. 'It's all right,' she added to the young man. 'Zal's all right—'

'You're sure?' Panic showed in the gleam of white, all around those dark pupils. 'He's had me followed—'

'Oh, *utterly*, Eliot! I've known Zal for just *years* . . . Emma!' she exclaimed, catching sight of her sister-in-law, still in the doorway. 'What are *you* doing here?'

'Trying to learn what *you're* doing here,' Emma replied. 'I take it,' she added, looking across at Kitty's companion, 'that this is the gentleman with whom you actually spent the time when you were supposedly murdering Mr Festraw?'

'I *didn't*!' Kitty almost stamped her foot in vexation, and Zal stepped closer to the table, and held out his hand.

'Jordan,' he said to the young man. 'I'm Zal Rokatansky, one of the cameramen at Foremost. I think we worked together on *The Devil's Wedding*.'

After a moment's hesitation, Eliot Jordan came around the table and accepted his grip. In the lantern-light Emma read even more clearly the fear in that exquisitely-boned, painfully youthful face; the desperation that stiffened the Greek god shoulders. The burly man moved to stand beside the young actor, with a protectiveness that chimed in Emma's mind like a bell.

'Eliot was just telling me,' said Kitty, 'that he *never* sent me that note! And I waited for him in the filmstock room for nearly two hours—'

'Was that where you were?' asked Emma.

Kitty nodded. 'I have a key. Pretty much everybody on the lot has keys.'

Including Taffy the Bootlegger, I suppose . . .

'I never sent a note, Mrs Blackstone.' Jordan's voice was a youthful, rather scratchy tenor. No older than some of the boys she'd taken to hospital from the train station, she thought. *He should still be in school!*

'I was just telling Kitty. And I wouldn't have done it anyway. I know better than to go anywhere near Foremost these days. Mr Jesperson would have my head. He's got me under a personal services contract . . .'

'But I got a note from Eliot – or supposedly from Eliot,' Kitty amended, 'Wednesday morning, saying he just *had* to see me, that it was urgent. Well, we'd talked about him leaving Hollywood – why he has to leave Hollywood – and I thought it was about that. I *hoped* I was mistaken,' she added, with a sidelong glance of mischief at the youth's face in the lantern-light, 'and that he'd been suddenly *overwhelmed* with the desire to make passionate love to me . . .'

Eliot ducked his head and laughed as if in spite of himself, and his bulky companion's grimness melted, suddenly, into a swift, disarmed – and surprisingly beautiful – grin.

'But I thought it was just about money.'

'It's all these movie stars ever want,' sighed the burly man, shaking his head. He held out his hand to Zal, said, 'Ricky Lyman.' He had a baritone as comforting as the scent of well-made coffee. 'I work in the accounting department at Enterprise.' He shook hands with Zal, then clasped Emma's fingers in a light, courtly grip, almost as if he'd bend to kiss them.

'This money?' Zal nodded at the bills on the table.

Eliot Jordan raised his chin a little, said, 'Kitty agreed to help us – me,' he corrected himself quickly. 'Help *me*. I have to get out of Hollywood – get out of California. I haven't done anything – anything *evil*,' he added. 'But I can't . . . Mr Jesperson, the owner of Enterprise, has . . . threatened me. And threatened me with legal action if I try to quit the studio. It's . . . not something I can take to court.'

Emma's glance went from the young actor's face to that of the overweight, bespectacled young accountant who stood at his elbow, who watched him with such anxious caring, the whole of his heart in his eyes. 'Eliot's most recent picture made three hundred thousand at the box office in three months,' Lyman said after a moment. 'If you've met Mr Jesperson, Mrs Blackstone – I know you have, Zal – I think you'll understand why Eliot would want to leave the studio. I've tried to talk him out of it – our employer may be the reincarnation of a rabid hyena but he's right when he says that Eliot will be the next Valentino. I don't think that's something he should throw away—'

Eliot said softly, '*I can't.*' He moved his hand back, without turning his head to look, and grasped Lyman's hand. The reassuring strength with which the pressure was returned confirmed Emma's conviction of what was going on – between these two young men, and the studio head who wanted to shape the publicity for Eliot Jordan's career. She wanted to ask, *Did he order you to marry one of his female stars?* but knew that wasn't a thing that could be spoken of.

What existed between these two men was against the law. Lou Jesperson going to the police with it would not only end his new leading man's career, it could easily result in both men being jailed.

Jordan said, 'We're going to Oregon. Ricky and I. I have some land up near Eugene, in the mountains . . .' He moved his hand, to silence something Lyman would have said. 'It was my grandpa's. But Jesperson's had a PI on my tail for a week now, ever since we finished shooting *Who's Her Man?* He's vindictive. He gave me an ultimatum.' He shook his head.

'And I got this note on Wednesday morning,' put in Kitty. 'Saying Eliot had to see me, right away, that it was urgent, and to meet him in the filmstock storeroom at two. I took Buttercreme with me because I *knew* Madge would give birth to a litter of kittens if I just disappeared. I waited nearly *two hours*, and when I tried to phone Eliot Thursday he couldn't answer. So I couldn't very well say anything, really, because it would all come out in the fan magazines, you know, and Jesperson, the old pig, would hear of it. I can't *imagine* how Peggy manages to sleep with him!'

'Kitty,' admonished Lyman gently, 'that's really a very unkind thing to say about pigs.'

'Do you have the note?' asked Emma.

'Oh, gosh, no! I tore it up and flushed it down the toilet behind the extras' dressing room. You never know who's lurking around in that studio. That's the kind of thing Thelma Turnbit, the nasty old shrew, would love to get her hands on, or that tattletale who writes the column in *Photo Play*. And I mean, if bootleggers or one of Rex's other ex-wives or Gloria Swanson or someone—'

'Gloria Swanson?' said Lyman, startled.

'If one of *them* could manage to sneak onto the lot and kill Rex in my dressing room, they'd *for sure* steal a love note from Eliot.'

'Why would Gloria Swanson want to murder your ex-husband, Kitty?'

'Did it look like his handwriting?' asked Zal.

Kitty frowned. 'I don't know. I don't think I've ever seen your handwriting, Eliot. It was on Enterprise Studios notepaper. But anyway,' she went on, 'Eliot met me at the Café Montmartre Thursday night when I was there with Frank – that was when I saw Gloria come in wearing those *gorgeous* earrings . . . Eliot slipped me a note by one of the waiters, and we met by the telephones at the back just for a second, and he said, he and Ricky had to leave, soon, tonight, and could I help them? Because he knows Jesperson is going to sue him and have him prosecuted for breach of contract if he leaves, so he can't really touch his bank account. But they have to get away before Mr Jesperson makes him marry that awful bitch Desiree Darrow . . . And I said I'd help them. And Jesperson's going to have a *stroke*,' she finished triumphantly, 'when he hears Eliot is gone. I'll clip out the obituary and send it to you,' she promised, with a dazzling smile.

Eliot smiled down at her – the top of her head barely reached his shoulder. 'Kitty, if you could cook,' he said softly, 'I'd marry you.'

Ricky Lyman took her hand, and pressed his lips to her fingers. 'And I'd marry you, too.'

'Don't even *talk* to me,' wailed Kitty, 'about marrying *anyone*—'

'It would solve your problem with Jesperson,' pointed out Zal, and Emma poked him in the ribs.

'Brute! I'm sorry,' she added, turning to the two lovers. 'I didn't mean to intrude on your personal affairs, but it's Kitty's refusal to say anything about where she was last Wednesday afternoon that has gotten her into trouble. I felt . . . Well, I'm afraid I felt that we had to at least find out a bit more of who she was screening, and why – though of course everything that has been said here tonight will go no farther.'

'Kitty,' began Eliot, reaching for her hand, and Emma shook her head.

'What you've told me tonight,' she said, 'has helped us, really. I mean, the police won't believe the faked note no matter who it was supposed to be from. But the fact that someone faked it tells us that . . . Well, that someone is going to a great deal of trouble to have Kitty accused of the murder, but that they're going about it very stupidly. Too stupidly for it to be a serious attempt.'

Eliot said, 'Hunh?' and Ricky Lyman nodded.

'You mean someone wants her accused real good, but not convicted.'

'Yes,' said Emma softly.

Zal cocked his head to one side. 'You mean it's a publicity stunt.'

'I . . .' She hesitated. 'To do murder – to kill a man—'

'We don't know,' pointed out Zal, 'whether Festraw hit up Pugh for money before Festraw even got onto the lot. We don't know what, exactly, Festraw *had* on Kitty.'

'I don't know what he *could* have had,' protested Kitty. 'Well, other than my birthdate . . .'

'Festraw might not even have been telling the truth,' said Zal. 'And if you don't think Frank Pugh is capable of murder . . . Think again.'

'And Darlene was just trying to make what she could of the situation last night,' said Kitty slowly. 'But . . . Frank doesn't know about me and Eliot. I mean, about me being passionately in love with Eliot—'

'Are you sure about that?' asked Emma thoughtfully. 'Might rumors of it have surfaced somewhere, like that *Photo Play* story about you and Mr Crain? Might this be an effort to punish you, for instance? And Miss Golden is certainly doing what she can to exacerbate his jealousy. Jealousy is the only thing I can think of, that would cause him to do something this stupid.'

There was silence, during which the silvery clucking of the stream outside sounded very loud.

'And it *is* stupid,' agreed Zal after a moment. 'It's always stupid, to bring the cops into anything, especially in LA. It's always stupid to bring anything to trial. Particularly now, with the Hays Office snorting brimstone all around the town and people like the Pettingers hollerin' about Sodom and Gomorrah. Roscoe Arbuckle was acquitted – *acquitted* – of raping that girl in San Francisco, and these days he can't even get work as an *extra* in this town. The fans may think you being accused of a crime of passion is glamorous and romantic, but any DA – any judge – in LA would just love to make headlines for convicting a movie star of anything, much less something spectacular like murdering her husband. Frank's too smart not to know that once something goes to trial, things can turn on a dime. He may think Kitty deserves a scare for making goo-goo eyes at you, Eliot . . . but I don't think he's stupid enough to risk a picture, or a big-name star, on it.'

'That just shows you've never talked to some of the men I've dated,' remarked Kitty. 'They get jealous, they start thinking with their little brain, not their big one. If they *have* a big one.'

She turned, and held out her hands to Eliot and his friend. 'Send me a letter when you get to Oregon,' she said, her smile sudden and dazzling. 'I'll write to you when we find out who's really behind this, though I'll just *bet* it's Frank . . . Or at least, I'm so terrible at writing, it'll probably be Emma who'll write first, but I will really write, too. Ricky . . .'

She stepped close, and the big man gathered her up in his arms, hugging her with such affection as to lift her off her feet. When he set her down she turned to Eliot, who asked her softly, 'Would you like a mad, passionate kiss, or a real one?'

Kitty's smile was suddenly soft. 'A real one,' she said.

He framed her face in gentle hands, and kissed her forehead. 'You're a good friend,' he said. 'Thank you. More than I can say.'

THIRTEEN

'You want to be careful getting out of here,' said Zal quietly, as they descended the steps and picked their way across the narrow stream. 'I thought a couple of times there might have been somebody following us.'

'Why would they follow you?' asked Ricky. 'I could understand Jesperson's dogs following *us* . . . How would they even know about you?'

'I don't know who knows what about who,' said Zal. 'I just . . . and I may be completely wrong. Depends on if this really is a publicity stunt. Or what Lou Jesperson might be up to.'

Ricky and Eliot stationed themselves on the rocks above the narrow stream, Eliot holding the hurricane-lantern high. By its light Zal backed his Ford around where the stream widened and shallowed below the old nightclub, and into a flat spot which Emma guessed had been used for a carpark in the building's livelier days. 'The thing we do not need,' he said, easing the little vehicle backwards up the gentle slope, 'is a puncture. I'm amazed we didn't get one on the way here, the way Kitty was driving—'

Under Ricky's guidance, Kitty maneuvered the Packard down through the stream after them, turning more sharply and pointing its long nose back down the canyon road to the highway, dimly glimpsed in the moonlight beyond. 'You want to ride with me back to Kitty's?' asked Zal, glasses flashing in the reflected headlamps as he cut the wheels around.

'If you live in Venice,' protested Emma, 'you can get home from the highway—'

'It's no bother,' he said.

He has to be on the set at six tomorrow morning . . . THIS morning . . .

He came only to help me. To help Kitty.

'Are you all right?' He waved to Kitty, and the Packard

roared away like the proverbial bat out of hell. 'I keep asking you that.'

As Zal, much more sedately, guided the Ford back onto the road Emma looked back, and saw Ricky put an arm around Eliot's shoulders as the two men walked into the shadows to Eliot's car.

A long drive in the sinking moonlight, she thought, *along that black-sapphire sea. North to Oregon, hundreds of miles, endless . . .*

'I have some land up near Eugene . . .'

She said, 'I'm not sure.'

'Anything I can help with? "No, I'd rather not talk about it", is a perfectly acceptable answer.'

'I don't think it's anything you can help with,' she said after a time. 'I got a letter Wednesday from my Aunt Estelle, the only one of my family to have survived the influenza. She'll be coming through Los Angeles on the thirtieth, on her way back from India – her husband is a senior clerk at the consulate in Delhi. Was, I should say. He's gotten a posting in England, and they're returning to Oxford. She's offered to take me back with them, and give me a home there.'

He was a dark shape in the dark car, the headlights two slanted cones on the pavement ahead. A silver glint on the corner of his glasses. 'You going to take her up on it?'

'I don't know.' It was enormous relief only to say it. To say it to *him*.

After a long time he said in a quieter voice, 'I know you miss it.'

'I miss the life I led there, yes,' she agreed softly. 'I miss the quiet . . .'

But this place – this stillness, driving along the moon-fringed sea – was quiet, a silence different, but just as deep as the mists on the Cherwell. Just as heart-healing.

She went on, a little hesitantly, 'I miss working at something I love. Having . . . a purpose in life, beyond looking after Kitty's dogs. Being around people who understand why I'd even want such a thing. People who understand the hunt for what really happened, the piecing-together of puzzles from manuscripts and old poems and bits of pots and tombs.'

Zal said, 'I know. I worked for three years in a paint factory, after my dad died, just so my mom and sister would have a roof over their heads. The whole time I felt like – I don't know, like I'd been shut into an iron maiden. Or like I'd been transported to another planet, where nobody understood about light, and texture, and how things look . . .' He shook his head, his eyes on the road unspooling before them. 'The worst of it was not knowing if I'd ever be able to get out. I used to have nightmares about that. About waking up old, and still being there.'

Stillness for a time, and the whisper of the tires on asphalt. The blue-black infinity of the sea.

She asked softly, 'Are you happy now?'

'I am.' She could hear the smile in his voice. 'Happy now in 1924, and happy now this minute.' And, quieter: 'Will you be able to go back to your studies there?'

'I think so. In Oxford, at least. I'd wanted to study in Paris, but Father needed me. So I read History at Somerville, which I could walk to from home. I loved the work, but . . . I did feel as if I'd been trapped. It was one reason I'd wanted to go to Paris. But of course it was for the best, because of the War. A lot of people had a hard time getting out, the Germans invaded so suddenly. And it was my father, who was training me to be an archaeologist. So when I married Jim I felt . . . Oh, like I was running away with the gypsies. He said we'd live in the United States – he'd been offered a job with an architect's firm in New York, so that's where we'd be living. He loved New York. I felt terrible, as if I were betraying my father, but Father said, "You must go, of course. Whatever will make you happy."'

'You were lucky.'

There was a note in his voice that made her glance quickly sidelong at him, but his gaze was on the road ahead. In time she went on, 'Working with Father – studying classics and Latin and Greek, and getting ready to go on a dig with him – it was odd for most girls, I suppose. But among the dons and scholars at Oxford it felt . . . well, very usual. Expected, in a way. On a dig, one would take camp-baths and clean linen and one's cook and a change of clothes to dress properly for

dinner. Some people took their valets. With Jim, I felt like
gates were opening up before me, into a new land, a new life,
something I'd never done before. Never dreamt, never even
thought about.'

With someone I loved . . .

Even now her hands ached for the light strength of his grip.

'And now you *have* run away with the gypsies,' said Zal,
his voice gentle. 'You think you'll be able to live with Aunt
Estelle?'

'Oh, yes. She's Mother's older sister, and I always found
her a little prudish and stuffy. But like Mother, she's a great
believer in letting people live their own lives. And her husband
is a dear. To look at him, you'd think he'd been mummified
in pipe tobacco for a hundred years, but he's kind, and always
trying to be helpful. He's deeply involved in the Church – I
think he's an advertisement for all that's best about Christianity.
And he collects all sorts of things from India, picture-scrolls
and ceremonial dishes and musical instruments. And I'm . . .
I'm *tired*,' she confessed. 'When I thought of New York, I
thought of being there with Jim. With someone to share things
with, someone I could go to, if there was a problem. I never
thought I'd be trying to make my own living in a foreign
country, on my own.'

'Are you happy here?'

Am I happy here?

The moon on the sea, where it frothed silver on the rocks,
forty feet below the road. The stillness of the dry hills they'd
come through. An alien planet, an alien land. The strength of
his arms the night he'd asked, *Do you want me to stay?*

Had the nymph Calypso asked Odysseus, *Are you happy?*
finding him alone on the cliffs of her island, looking towards
Ithaca?

She opened her lips to say, *Sometimes . . .* or maybe to say,
Yes . . . but suddenly there was a dark rushing shape and a
roar of tires and Zal yelled, 'Shit!' and swung the wheel as
a lightless car, bigger than the Ford and faster, whooshed up
beside them and cut hard into their side.

Zal hit the brake in the instant that the other car swerved
toward them, so that the impact was barely a clip on the left

side of the hood. Then he whipped the wheel around again, trying to swing past on the left. Their attacker gunned his engine, the bellow of far more power than the Ford could boast, and slammed them toward the cliff that rose on the land side of the highway. Emma grabbed the hand-strap beside the door, heart pounding as Zal braked again, shoved the car into reverse to pull clear, though she guessed there was no way they'd be able to escape the bigger vehicle. The Model-T lurched in a way that told her, tire puncture, tipped over into the ditch that separated highway from landward cliff and the next instant bashed diagonally into the cliff itself. The other car stopped and she saw the bulky shape of a man framed beside its driver-side door.

Saw the glint of steel in his hand.

Saw the glint of steel because headlights were roaring towards them from the south, at what Themistocles of Athens would have termed *ramming speed*. The man in the attacking car fired at the Model-T, and the glass of the window behind Emma's head exploded in a torrent of shards. The oncoming headlights swelled and the attacker ducked down and into his own vehicle. It pulled back and roared away north only feet in front of Kitty's yellow Packard, whose headlight-glare showed that it lacked a rear license-plate, and that its curved rump was dark-green with the black shape of a tire on it, and a boxy cabin beyond.

The Packard screeched to a stop and Kitty sprang out, stumbling in her diamanté heels as she ran towards them (*ONLY Kitty would wear shoes like that on an expedition to meet someone in a ruined roadhouse up a canyon . . .*).

'Darling!' she gasped. 'Darling, are you all right?'

Zal had already cut the engine. He scrambled out and was coming around to help Emma, should she need it, when she pulled herself out by the sides of the door. Her legs shook so badly she nearly fell. 'I'm all right,' she managed to say, as Zal caught her elbow. 'I'm not hurt . . .'

A few bits of glass clinked from the sleeve of her jumper. She felt something warm on her face near her ear and wiped at it, wincing as her fingers caught another splinter of glass. It was big, she pulled it free . . .

He shot at us. He was trying to kill us . . .

'Darling, what happened? Who *was* that?'

'Tell me and we'll both know,' said Zal grimly. His hand on Emma's arm was perfectly steady, but the next second he pulled her to him, clutched her hard against his body for an instant. His grip was like a gasped cry: *You're alive. You're alive . . .*

'I realized I could just as easily get back to Hollywood through Venice as I could over the Pass,' Kitty gabbled. 'I was going to let you catch up and ask Emma, did she want to leave you at your house and come back home with me. Then I saw this car try to hit you—'

'I thought somebody might have been following us.' Zal kept his steadying hold on Emma's arm as he led her back towards Kitty's car. 'But pretty much nobody ever drives out that way, not on a Saturday night. And who the hell would be following Kitty? Other than us.'

'This isn't just jealousy.' Emma sank into the velvety squabs of the Packard's upholstery, trembling now as if the mild spring night had turned arctic. Kitty produced a silver flask from her glovebox and Zal opened it, and passed it to Emma. It was very high-quality gin.

Courtesy of Mr Cornero, I suppose . . .

'And it isn't a publicity play . . .'

'He's insane,' said Kitty unsteadily. 'Frank. Oh, God . . .'

'If it is Frank.' Emma thought of his eyes, of the cold fury as he'd pulled out into traffic on Sunset Boulevard. Of Darlene's attempts to stir up just that emotion in him . . .

'Rex got that way, sometimes.' Kitty shivered. 'Really, literally crazy with jealousy. But he'd be cold in everything else, like Frank. He'd lie, and get very, very clever about his lies. You can't reason with them when they're like that, or expect them to be thinking reasonably.'

'You get a look at the car at all?' Zal handed the flask back to Kitty after taking another swig himself.

Kitty shook her head. 'I think it was a coupe . . .'

'Chrysler coupe,' he agreed. 'I didn't see the plates.'

'There weren't any,' said Emma. 'At least not on the back. But the car was dark green. And I'm pretty sure the driver was alone.'

'Why pretty sure?' Zal slid into the back seat; Kitty polished off the gin in the flask, lit a cigarette, and pressed the self-starter. The big engine rumbled into life like a dragon purring.

'It was the driver who shot at us. If there'd been anyone else in the car, I should imagine the driver would have stayed at the wheel, ready to escape. Thank you.' She turned her head, to Kitty's profile outlined against the reflection of the headlamp glow. 'You saved our lives.'

That's twice, she thought, *Kitty has saved my life. Once from violent death, once from a slow one . . .*

'I'm just sorry this bus isn't equipped with a Maxim gun.' Kitty's voice was suddenly hard as flint. 'And if that *was* Frank . . .'

'We have no idea who it was,' said Emma firmly. 'But I think it might be a good idea to speak to Mr Cornero again, and see what advice he has to give on the subject of murder.'

And then, between exhaustion and shock and not enough sleep the night before, she burst into tears.

FOURTEEN

The Bel Giardino Club stood a few blocks from Chaplin Studios, a two-and-a-half story building of brick with a stucco arcade nearly hidden behind a blazing wall of pink-and-turquoise neon. Helped from the back seat of Ambrose Crain's Hispano-Suiza, Emma had an impression of shop-windows behind the arcade on the ground floor. Dark now – it was nearly ten o'clock Sunday night – they seemed darker still against the vivid hell-mouth glow of the club's open doorway.

Emma wondered if bootleggers – even good Italian Catholic ones – respected the Fourth Commandment. Film producers, at least, did not, particularly film producers whose pictures were half a week behind schedule and required rental elephants. She hoped that Kitty – who had been at the studio since seven that morning – and Zal, who had been there since five – wouldn't have too grueling a night when rioting mobs stormed Nero's palace.

A doorman who resembled a tractor in a bellboy's uniform bowed as Mr Crain entered, with Emma on his arm. The wide hall just within was carpeted in crimson and ablaze with light-bulbs, and a doll-faced young woman behind a counter, wearing far too much eye-paint and far too little clothing, took the sable stole that Kitty had lent Emma for the occasion (*'Darling, you CAN'T go to a nightclub wearing that tweed thing of yours!'*). Mr Crain surrendered his very handsome vicuña topcoat and silk hat at the same time, and inclined his head approvingly at the sight of Emma's dress. (*'I had Mary Pickford pick it out for you, dearest,'* Kitty had explained, when the box was delivered to her dressing room that afternoon. *'She has the best taste of anyone I know!'*) The midnight blue silk, stitched with black and silver beading, had taken Emma's breath away.

It was the first evening dress she'd had in ten years. The

first new garment she'd had in seven. 'Kitty—!' she had
protested, and her sister-in-law – refreshing the pallid yellow
camera make-up and resplendent in yet another ensemble of
the exiguous gauze that seemed to be standard daywear for
ladies in Babylon – had waved her words aside.

'If Ambrose is taking you hunting bootleggers all around
the nightclubs tonight you can't go dressed like somebody's
maiden aunt.'

'Before I met Kitty,' confided Ambrose Crain, when arrangements had been confirmed over the telephone, 'it had been
quite twenty years since I'd gone to nightclubs. I shall feel
quite the dog, turning up at one with another woman!'

Will I turn up in Photo Play *now as well?* she had wondered.

Now, surveying her dress in the garish lobby, he murmured,
'Exquisite, Mrs Blackstone,' and once again offered her his
arm. 'A privilege as well as a joy to be seen with you.' He
led her up the stairs to the nightclub above.

In a well-fitting but elderly tuxedo, the old millionaire
looked almost dapper himself. With a tingling delight which
almost distracted her from her apprehension, Emma looked
around her. When she'd told Zal – over a hasty commissary
lunch – of the evening's plans, she'd answered his query, 'At
heart, I know nobody's going to try to murder me in a nightclub. Not when I'm with someone like Mr Crain. And if Tony
Cornero wanted to murder me he'd have done so the other
night, wouldn't he? I'll be quite all right.'

She almost believed this.

During that conversation, Madge had already been bellowing
for Kitty and the cameras, so Zal could only take Emma's
hands and kiss her quickly on the lips. 'Wish I was there tonight
instead of at Caesar's joint,' he'd said. Emma had gone to help
Kitty out of her kimono and to make notes of the changes
Madge had made in the preceding scene, which would involve
an alteration of tomorrow's dialog (altered twice already to
account for the disappearance of the Soothsayer).

She'd taken the dogs home by cab, fed them, bathed and
made herself up simply, and inserted half a paragraph and three
title-cards which explained the sudden reappearance of the
commander of Nero's bodyguard as well (last seen falling into

the lions' den in scene twenty-one). As she dressed, she felt obliquely glad to know that old Mr Shang and his wife were down in the cottage behind the house, even though that antediluvian couple would have been of no assistance whatsoever had the owner of the dark-green Chrysler turned up on the doorstep with a gun. Her heart beating swiftly, she'd had a few minutes to wait before the headlights of Mr Crain's Hispano-Suiza had zig-zagged down the drive, to reflect that this was the first time in six years that she'd 'put on the dog', as Jim had termed it. That she'd dressed up to go dancing.

The last time had been the sixth of May, 1918. Almost exactly, she thought, six years. It had been Jim's last night in London, before returning to the Front. The last time they'd danced together, joked together. The last time she'd gone to sleep with the soft smoothness of his skin beneath her cheek. The following morning, May seventh, just before dawn, had been the last time they'd made love.

Four weeks later, he was dead.

As she'd heard the car stop at the bottom of the drive, heard the chauffeur's door open and then the door of the back seat, she'd whispered, 'Oh, Jim. I'm sorry.'

But the echo of his voice that she'd heard in her heart had been light: *For God's sake, Em, don't be sorry!* He had had, in his way, a spirit as eager for enjoyment as his sister's. *Have some champagne for me!*

He knew, she thought, that she'd still be with him if she could.

So when the *maitre d'* took them to a table that bordered the dancefloor and Mr Crain asked, 'Would you like something to drink, Mrs Blackstone? I understand the drinks here are first-class,' she had said, 'Champagne, please.'

'Your best,' instructed the old millionaire quietly, and Emma smiled.

Jim had loved good champagne.

To the *maitre d'*, she'd murmured, 'Is Mr Cornero here this evening? My name is Mrs Blackstone; he said that I might be able to find him here.'

'Mrs Blackstone.' The man bowed, small and sleek in a Latin-lover way but exquisitely polite. He'd clearly heard her

name before. 'Mr Cornero should be here at about eleven,
m'am. Would you care to wait? Drinks are on the house.'

She glanced across at Mr Crain, who nodded. 'I've been
drinking bootleg cocktails for a year in Kitty's company,' he
whispered, as the *maitre d'* retreated in the direction of the bar.
'But this is the first time I shall make the acquaintance of a
gangster. I must say, I'm quite tickled – though of course,' he
added more seriously, 'I am shocked, and concerned, at the
circumstances. I've asked Mr Hwang' – that was his chauffeur
– 'to remain in the building after he's parked the car. He'll be
downstairs in the hall, in case of – well – *need.*'

And Emma smiled again, and told him what she'd said to
Zal that afternoon. 'I truly don't think what happened last
night has anything to do with Mr Cornero. If he'd wanted to
harm any of us, he had plenty of opportunity to do it Thursday
night. But *somebody* means us harm – Mr Rokatansky and
myself. And I can only assume it's because of whatever it is
that's going on with Kitty. Whatever it is.' She spread her
hands. 'You wouldn't have any idea – any thought of any
possibility . . .?'

'I have cudgeled my brains, Mrs Blackstone,' said the old
man, with a helpless gesture. 'And Kitty – well, she doesn't
often talk about herself, does she? It's as if she lets go of her
past, in her eagerness to run on ahead and see what the future
holds.'

'That's as good a description of her as I've ever heard, sir.'

His answering smile, and the movement of his fingers,
brushed the compliment aside. 'It's a quality I wish I shared,'
he said. 'Are you familiar with Cafavy's poem "Ithaca"? I
forget how it goes, exactly: That Ithaca will not make you
rich; it's the road that makes you rich.' His breath escaped
him in a little sigh. 'I think that's how Kitty sees life.

'I wish I could. Even now I find myself entangled in the
past, like my poor son, who hasn't ventured off Long Island
in fifteen years. He'll go into New York, but I doubt he's even
been as far afield as Connecticut. He has our money – my
money, actually – and he's going to stay home and cultivate
what's there like a potato-patch. My wife – my ex-wife,' he
corrected, a trifle stiffly, 'does not travel, and doesn't want

him to. Sometimes I think they both think it's still 1910. And I find myself preoccupied by things I did wrong, or should have done differently. Wanting to go back and make things be the way I think they should have been.'

His smile was rueful and a little sad. 'Do you do that, Mrs Blackstone? Want to go back as Kitty does on the filmset, and do a second "take" because she tripped or turned the wrong way, or because someone had left a coffee cup on the arm of the throne?'

'Sometimes,' said Emma softly. 'Do you think one can do it, sir? Go back and do another take?'

The kindly gray eyes rested on her for a moment, as if trying to see what lay behind the words. 'I should like to think one could,' he replied slowly, then nodded friendly thanks to the waitress who set two glasses on the table, a single-malt scotch, and her champagne, and slipped a dollar bill onto the woman's tray. 'But it's never exactly the same situation, is it? Faced with the identical situation, and given the same information with which to meet it as we had before, would we not make the same decision?'

For a moment she was back in that lingerie shop in Regent's Arcade, where a tall young man in an American uniform was looking around him in bemused bafflement. The street outside had been full of young men in American uniforms, tall and robust, healthy as the English, after a year and more of food shortages, had ceased to be. When his eyes had met hers, she'd smiled. It was her smile, she thought, as well as her VAD uniform, that had given him permission to come over to her, to ask, *Excuse me, miss, but could you help me pick something out for my sister . . .?*

Her mother, and the governess she'd had as a child, would both have cut off the exchange before the smile, let alone before she could say, 'Yes, of course . . .' She recalled she'd felt a little shocked at herself for speaking to the young man.

Had he met her eyes because she'd worn her blue-and-white uniform that afternoon? Would things have been different if she hadn't?

Where did these things start, anyway?

Or did it matter?

The memory made her glance aside from her companion, and across the dancefloor she saw, with a start of surprise, Colt Madison, his hair now tar-black and shining with brilliantine. He was in evening dress and wore the least-convincing Van Dyke and monocle this side of Millie Katz's Wardrobe counter . . .

Their eyes met for a startled moment. Then Emma saw the petite, delicate, and unmistakable figure of Gloria Swanson a few yards away, glittering like a jewel-crusted stiletto as her escort – a French nobleman whom Emma had encountered at Frank Pugh's Christmas Party the previous December – bowed her into her chair.

Good heavens, is he still sleuthing after the other women in that silly competition?

After last night the hypothesis seemed absurd – *Even if it WAS Gloria Swanson or Darlene Golden or Blanche Sweet, they'd have hired someone else to do the deed . . .*

But the thought that another star's studio would cover her transgressions, and pay Detective Meyer to 'lose' whatever evidence there was, returned like a queasy shadow on her thoughts, and she felt as if she'd reached into a dark cupboard and encountered half a century worth of cobwebs and spiders.

Hollywood . . .

You will have a home with us, Aunt Estelle had promised.

Well, far be it from me to 'blow' the poor man's 'cover', as I think they say in the espionage novels . . .

She sipped her champagne and replied to her companion's question with a half-smile. 'Nine times out of ten I think yes, we'd still take that left-hand path, sir. But do you sometimes want to just . . . go back to that place and that time? Not for any particular decision, but simply to smell the air there? To see the sunshine of that particular day again?'

'New York in the Eighties?' His answering smile was as gentle and as dry as the champagne. 'Struggling and maneuvering to make sure one is seen at the best houses? To make sure one meets the "best men of business"? What a long time ago it seems.' He almost chuckled.

'And speaking of the best houses,' said Emma, 'Kitty tells me you're building an Italian villa, one that used to belong to someone Italian and famous. She doesn't think it was Robinson Caruso the opera singer, or the Pope—'

Crain chuckled. 'No, nobody so famous. One of the lesser Medici, I was told. It's probably late-eighteenth-century. You'll see it,' he added, 'once Kitty is done with this picture. I plan to take her there for a rest, and I'm virtually certain she won't go without her dogs . . .'

'And her gramophone.' They both laughed, at the foibles of their friend.

'And her astrology magazines . . .'

'Excuse me – Mrs Blackstone. Mr Crain.' Colt Madison executed a very continental bow, to go with the generic European intonation of his words.

Mr Crain regarded him in some surprise, and Emma said to her companion, 'Would you excuse me for a moment, sir?' and got to her feet. Madison led her to the far end of the bar with the practiced grace of a gigolo, and touched his lips with a cautionary forefinger.

'You're very astute, Mrs Blackstone,' he murmured. 'I beg of you, not a word to me, or a sign that you know me. Too many people here would recognize my face.'

'Including Miss Swanson?'

He nodded slowly, as if approving her perspicacity. 'So far, so good,' he said. 'I've ruled out Barbara la Marr and Pola Negri – you can always find out from their maids what a movie queen has been up to – but the woman I talked with over at Paramount said Swanson sometimes meets with some fairly sketchy customers here. And that boyfriend of hers knows enough people in the City Hall Gang that he bears checking on, if you know what I mean. We'll find 'em,' he added, nodding wisely. 'We'll find 'em.'

He glanced across at Miss Swanson – whose necklace really did look as if it had cost $1,750, though, thank goodness, she'd left her cheetah back at the Paramount menagerie. Her companion helped the Paramount star to her feet, and they moved out onto the polished boards of the dancefloor. As all film stars did, Miss Swanson, in person, had a slightly fragile air within her sheathe of bugle-beads and sequins. The camera, Emma knew, made its subjects look about ten pounds heavier than they actually were, and every actress in Hollywood had a 'potato clause' in her contract, specifying immediate suspension if she gained too much weight.

No wonder so many of them take cocaine . . .

Or, in Miss Swanson's case, lived on health food . . .

'Your secret is safe with me,' whispered Emma. 'And honestly, I wouldn't have gone to speak to you, seeing that you were in disguise.'

Madison smiled, and patted her cheek. 'You're a good egg, Duchess.' And he wove his way back through the crowd to his table.

Turning back to her own table, Emma saw the sleek head and burly shape of Tony Cornero there. Both he and Mr Crain rose as she approached. 'Would you rather I left you together here, Mrs Blackstone?' Mr Crain asked. 'I realize your business may be confidential.'

Cornero raised his eyebrows, with a glance that referred the question to Emma. Emma said, 'Not . . . Not as such. If you don't mind, Mr Cornero . . .'

'Hey, I'm just a businessman trying to make a living.' The bootlegger spread his hands innocently, as he had done Thursday night. 'Just like Mr Crain – but on a much smaller scale, of course. I'm not the one who owns five hundred acres of Long Beach oil fields. Giovanni said you wanted a word with me, m'am?'

Crain held her chair for her as she sat, and took the seat beside her again. Briefly, Emma outlined what had taken place the previous night: that Miss de la Rose had gone out, late and secretly, to meet and help a friend who had to leave Los Angeles immediately and needed money. 'Nothing to do with Mr Festraw's death or the film industry,' she added, not quite truthfully. 'It was a personal matter, and a confidential one.'

Cornero made a very Italian grimace and gesture, to show he understood.

'Miss de la Rose drove back along the coast highway toward Santa Monica, and my friend Mr Rokatansky and I followed in his car. We were overtaken by another car which first tried to drive us off the highway – over the cliff there into the sea – and then shoved us into the cliff that comes down on the inland side of the road. The driver of that car – which was without lights – then stood up out of the car and fired a shot at us. But by that time Kitty had seen what was happening, turned around, and came back. The other driver got into his car again and fled. No one was hurt,' she concluded, 'but it was clearly an attempt on our lives. I don't know whether the other driver thought Miss de la Rose was in the car – whether he thought Mr Rokatansky was driving Miss de la Rose's car back to town. Mr Rokatansky said he thought we'd been followed from Hollywood and along Ventura Boulevard and through the hills. We'd left Miss de la Rose's house at about twelve thirty and there's very little traffic on the road, he said, at that time.'

'*Mannaggia*,' said Cornero quietly. 'You get a look at the car?'

'It was a dark-green Chrysler coupe. The license plate had been removed. If you know of – or know how to find out about – the owner of such a car . . . I understand that in your business as nightclub owner,' she added tactfully, 'you have the opportunity to hear things from people.'

'Yeah,' said Cornero. 'Yeah, I'll ask around. Thing is, there's a gumshoe named Sid Gross who drives a dark-green Chrysler coupe. Has offices downtown in the Bradbury Building. And he's the kind of guy, if I wanted some dirty work done, I might take it into my head to ask him if he knew anybody who might want to do something like that, if you know what I mean. You want I should ask the folks at his garage whether he's got any new scratches on his fenders this morning?'

'Thank you,' said Emma, from the bottom of her heart. 'If you can.'

Mr Crain spoke up. 'Will you need an advance of some kind to cover incidental expenses?' he asked, and reached for his wallet. 'In case, for instance, this Mr Gross has hidden his vehicle—'

'Thank you,' said Cornero. 'That's very kind of you, Mr Crain, and yes, we'll probably need some kind of grease. I don't need anything now. Can I let you know?'

'Of course. And do you have,' he went on, with the soft-voiced good breeding of a businessman inquiring about market shares, 'any recommendations for an investigator in New York, to follow up on this Stan Markham Mrs Blackstone told me booked rooms for Mr Festraw at the Winterdon? My son handles my firm's business matters in New York,' he added apologetically. 'But as I was telling Mrs Blackstone just now, he works mostly from our home in East Hampton. He has never really approved of me personally handling the California interests.'

He frowned, as if at the recollection of conversations that had ended in uncomfortable compromise. 'He thinks I should purchase some respectable property in Palm Beach – which in fact I have – and retire there myself instead of building a hotel. He is extraordinarily old for a man nearly forty, and I doubt he'd know the names of any investigator in the city.'

'I'll hook you up with one,' said the bootlegger. 'A good honest one, not some half-baked ambulance-chaser. Though who the hell,' he added, as Crain handed him a card from his silver case, 'would want to bring Rex Festraw clear out here, and put him up in a class joint like the Winterdon, just to bump him off? You could save your money and have him done in Jersey. Bad management.'

He shook his head. 'The guy wasn't connected back in New York – strictly small-time. Unless he was secretly romancing some wealthy widow and her family wanted to rub him out to keep her from disinheriting them, but frankly, the way that guy's shirt smelled – not to speak of his breath – that don't seem very likely to me. And I never heard of it. Not from the boys in New York.'

He frowned, puzzling over the inconsistency.

'It's one of the things I hope to learn from your investigator,' said Crain.

Emma turned back to them, having become momentarily distracted by the entrance of Kitty's friend Peggy Donovan, clearly intent on out-vamping both Miss Swanson and Kitty in a golden dress flashing with sequins and fringe and a necklace that made Miss Swanson's look like something picked out of a Christmas cracker. She was accompanied by two unbelievably handsome young men – Emma wondered whether she'd rented them for the occasion.

Now she said, 'But why drag Kitty – Miss de la Rose – into it, which it's quite obvious that the murderer has taken pains to do? Everything connected with Mr Festraw's death is the . . . the oddest mixture of what sounds like careful – and expensive – planning, and sheer clumsiness.'

'Perhaps they're simply out to obfuscate their own guilt,' suggested Crain, 'without seriously harming Miss de la Rose. They know she's the obvious suspect, if the man is murdered for some other reason . . .'

'That's what it looked like,' said Emma quietly, 'until they – whoever "they" are – made a very serious attempt to murder Mr Rokatansky and myself. And maybe Miss de la Rose as well, if they thought she was in Mr Rokatansky's car. What could be at stake that's worth that?'

There was an uncomfortable silence, into which Miss Swanson's voice could be heard saying, 'Peggy! *Darling!* That dress is *gorgeous* on you – *far* better than it looked on *me* in *Gilded Cage* . . .'

'And it makes me wonder,' concluded Emma quietly, 'what "they" – whoever "they" are – are going to try next.'

FIFTEEN

'**M**r Madison!'

At the sound of a feminine voice Colt Madison turned from the door of the studio guard-shack with his cocky, welcoming smile: *Hey, women call my name all day . . .!*

Past his shoulder Emma saw the guard's book open on the counter. Checking who'd come and gone last Wednesday – she wondered whether Rex Festraw had entered his name, or had simply slipped Floyd a couple of dollar bills, as she was fairly certain Mrs Turnbit had done. 'Hey, baby—'

She paused a few feet from him, and nodded toward the far corner of the little kiosk, out of range of a casual eavesdropper. And simply out of the way of passers-by: in the brightness of a Monday morning, with Christian martyrs scheduled to be thrown to the lions on Stage One and the studio's two resident comedians commencing an epic about a dance competition on Stage Three, the open dirt between the gate and the Hacienda fairly swarmed.

Madison followed her around the corner. His golden locks had none of the residual stain and deadness left by dye, so what he'd had on last night must have been a wig. The skin along his hairline showed traces of reddening, as well as that on his lip and chin, where the Van Dyke had been glued last night.

'Do you know a Mr Sid Gross?' she asked.

He stepped back a half-pace with a movement of his head that Madge Burdon – and Zal – would have described as a 'double take'. 'Hey, you're not getting mixed up with him, are you, Duchess?' His brows plunged down over the Praxiteles perfection of his nose. 'He's bad medicine, and crooked as a dog's back leg.'

'A gangster?' Emma widened her eyes.

Madison's lip curled. 'It takes' – he bit back Kitty's favorite items of anatomical synecdoche descriptive of courage, and substituted a less vulgar body part – 'guts to be a gangster, baby. Gross is a bagman for Charlie Crawford's Connection, to drop off payments to City Hall.'

'Is he dangerous?'

The detective thought about it for a moment. 'If he thinks he can get away with it,' he said at last, and shrugged. 'Give him enough money and he'll shoot somebody in the back, if that's what you mean. What're you askin' about him for, doll? Nobody in the Connection would trust a job to the guy; everybody downtown knows him too well by sight. No,' he went on, 'the guys they'd use would be Iron Man or maybe Teddy Knucks. I know 'em all by sight. Gross . . .' He shook his head. 'He's not one of that group. Personally, I'm surprised Crawford uses him. The guy's scum. Where'd you hear about him?'

'Oh.' Emma tried to sound taken aback. 'Oh, dear. Yesterday I found his card in the mailbox at Kitty's house, you see. I have no idea how long it had been sitting there. It's a deep box, and generally I just reach in and grab whatever's there.'

'Hunh.' Madison frowned again, and groped in his pocket for a cigarette. 'I wouldn't worry about it, hon. But let me know if the guy tries to get in touch.'

'I will. Thank you.' Emma looked as helpless and admiring as she could, not easy with a man only an inch or two taller than herself. 'What does he look like, by the way? Mr Gross?'

'Gross,' replied the detective, and laughed at his own pun. 'Big guy.' He measured something above his own six-foot height. 'Fat. Not Fatty Arbuckle fat, but big like a wrestler.' Emma recalled the tall bulk of the shape rising out of the driver's side of the dark-green Chrysler.

'Dimple in his chin, kind of thick mouth, squinty little eyes. Fat earlobes that sort of hang down.' He demonstrated with his thumbs. Emma felt a moment's surprise at this very technical description, but realized in the next second that this was Madison's job; to note things that couldn't be easily altered. 'Nose that comes down straight and then like a little potato at the tip; mole on his left nostril. No oil painting, that's for sure.' He chuckled again, just a trifle smugly, as if comparing the man with his own movie-star countenance.

'Say, I want to thank you for not blowin' me last night, Duchess,' he added. 'Far as I can tell, Swanson's out of it. And I got hold of Darlene's bankbook, and the dough she paid Ginny Field and Barney Grissom – that was lover boy the other night – seems to be the only outlay that doesn't look kosher. No big pay-outs, like you'd see if she was setting someone up for an underground hotel-room. So it's lookin' like I said.' He blew a line of smoke, and moved his head a little, to survey a couple of shapely young extras who stopped at Floyd's window, then hastened on towards Belle Delaney's open door at the corner of the Hacienda, slim ankles almost twinkling in the morning sun.

Et vera incessu patuit dea, reflected Emma. *As Virgil said of Venus. 'Her true godhead was obvious in her walk . . .'*

'Festraw's got to have been mixed up with the City Hall Gang. They're the only ones who'd be keepin' it this quiet. Which is good,' he added with a self-satisfied smile. 'Means it'll be easy to sort out. Couple thousand to Crawford, couple thousand to Cryer's re-election campaign fund . . . Kitty hasn't come clean about where she was, has she?' The blue eyes narrowed piercingly into hers. ''Cause that's what's holdin' up the show.'

Emma shook her head. 'I honestly think she was looking for that silly dog.'

'Well, if she was,' said Madison, 'nobody out there buildin' the sets saw her. And that red kimono she was wearing—'

He must have gotten that part of the description from Mr Fishbein—

'—would'a made her hard to miss.'

And anyone in the armor and helmet of the Praetorian Guard, Emma reflected – as she followed in the wake of the two goddesses now bound for Wardrobe – *or in a Ruritanian cavalry uniform, or fancy evening dress at two in the afternoon – even carrying a gun – would have passed completely unnoticed.*

There had been two hundred and fifty extras on the Foremost

lot on Wednesday afternoon. Emma had brought one of her blank copybooks with her, and Millie Katz in Wardrobe – skinny and brisk, like a reincarnated witch – was perfectly happy to turn over Wednesday's log to her, and give her a place to sit in her cubbyhole office, and a cup of coffee. Past the open door Emma watched them come through – men, women, and three or four children – and fill out wardrobe slips. Millie would then check the list of the day's costumes, write a size, and toss the slip into her basket. The names, outfits, and sizes would be transferred to the ledger once the rush was done and the sixty-five 'rags' extras had gone around first to Wardrobe, then to the extras' dressing room, where two of Herr Volmort's assistants waited with buckets of blood-paint and dirt. Madge would need them all in the Coliseum set just after lunch, looking suitably downtrodden, blood-streaked, and radiant with the glory of martyrdom.

On Wednesday, costumes had been needed for cavalry, peas-antry, Romans, slaves, aristocratic dinner guests, and Roman soldiers – not to speak of thirty horses from Chatsworth Livery, and Socrates the Elephant. The cavalry, Emma guessed, had been mostly the known 'riding extras' and set them aside for last. Three Roman soldiers, ten male peasants, four male slaves, and three dinner guests had needed 'extra large' costumes. She copied the names, and when Millie finished the most recent batch of martyrs and brought the slips in to the back office, Emma said, 'Mrs Katz—'

'Millie!' the woman corrected her with a wave. 'For God's sake, call me Millie. You call me Mrs Katz and I'll think you're talking to my mother-in-law, God forbid!' And she made three tiny spit-noises to avert so evil a possibility.

'Millie,' Emma corrected herself. 'And please, call me Emma . . . Bless you for letting me check this list! When you have a moment – and *only* when you have a moment, I see you're run off your feet here! – could you take a look at these names and let me know which ones are regulars? Are they people you knew by sight?'

The shrewd, dark eyes twinkled. 'Mr Gumshoe finally caught on that anybody could walk onto the lot claiming to be an extra, did he?' She took the list, pulled a pencil out of the tight, dark bun of her hair, and scratched off twelve names. 'Guy you're lookin' for white or black, honey?'

'White.' It hadn't occurred to Emma to ask Madison about this, but upon reflection she felt sure the man would have mentioned it, or Cornero would have, had Gross been a man of color.

Millie scratched out two more.

A Roman soldier, four peasants, and a slave were left.

The Empress Valerna stared down from the marble height of the Imperial Box at the Coliseum (which occupied most of what had been her garden the previous week), surveying with haughty scorn the 5,000 square feet of empty sand where the Christians would be standing in two hours. 'Come on!' Madge exhorted her. 'These are people who're always telling you what an evil slut you are! These are people who're getting what they deserve for being so fucken good all the time! Lemme see that contempt!'

Zal's assistant Herbie Carboy – like an undernourished scarecrow in a glaringly checkered vest – darted in front of Zal's camera with the leader board. This was take six. The camera itself hung in mid-air, mounted on a crane about two yards in front of the Imperial Box. Just out of the shot-line, the Rothstein Boys struck up Saint-Saëns' 'Rouet d'Omphale'. 'Camera!' yelled Madge. 'Action!'

Kitty bulged her eyes and bared her teeth. 'Well, fools,' she snarled. 'Where is your Redeemer now?'

'Cut! C'mon, Kitty, you're gonna watch 'em die, you're not gonna eat 'em!' Madge swept her arm in the direction of the imaginary martyrs. 'It's the Pettingers down there, an' they're beggin' you for mercy!'

Emma returned to the base camp just within the big doors, where Chang Ming and Black Jasmine rushed to the ends of their leashes, licking their noses in adoration, and stood up against her knees to be patted. The 'Rouet d'Omphale' revived like the curl of a breaking wave, and a moment later Madge shouted, 'Yeah! That's it! You'd spit on 'em if you weren't a lady!'

'Well, fools,' cried Kitty, 'where is your Redeemer now?'

It was another two hours – closer to tea-time than lunch,

though Emma unpacked her own sandwich and her thermos flask of tea at one thirty – before Kitty came down from her box, accompanied by Nicky Thaxter, in a golden wreath and the gold lamé toga which made Emma cringe. *No, no, even Mr Pugh should know they didn't have gold lamé in Rome!* 'What can I get you?' she asked, rising.

'Gin.' Kitty collapsed into her chair. 'And lots of it!'

'Make that two, darling.' Nicky hung his wreath over a corner of the magazine rack.

Emma unpacked the glasses from Kitty's picnic basket, set out the thermos, then went to the table by the stage door and brought them sandwiches. As she was loading up the plate Zal's voice asked at her elbow, 'What'd you find?'

'Six extra-large extras whom Millie Katz didn't know,' said Emma. 'A soldier and a slave in Rome, four peasants in Ruritania.'

'Shouldn't be hard to count.' Zal's face was beaded with sweat, despite the kerchief he'd tied around his head under his cap. Unlike Kitty and Nick, he hadn't had anyone from make-up fluttering over to him to touch up powder and Motion Picture Yellow between shots. 'We're gonna do the Christians long-shots this afternoon, and nothing scheduled for tonight, may wonders never cease. Can you be back here at eight? It's all indoors tomorrow. Nick gets to strangle Kitty and after thirteen takes to get the chariot scene right this morning I don't blame him one bit. God knows how long that'll take.'

'You're exhausted—' Emma began to protest, and Zal grinned.

'Hey, I've been waiting for weeks for a chance to take you to the movies. I just didn't think I was gonna have to run the projector myself.'

Emma chuckled, and started to shake her head again, but Zal's face turned quietly grave. 'After what happened Saturday night,' he said, 'I don't think we can wait.'

'No.' Emma touched the scab on her temple where the shot-in window-glass had cut it. 'No.'

For almost another hour Madge rehearsed the martyrs being brought into the Coliseum while Zal and Emma, Kitty and Nick, joked and flirted over gin, tea, and sandwiches. Most of the morning had been spent filming the lions as they'd snarled and paced behind the barred grate at the side of the arena. 'Come on, Madge,' Gren Torley had coaxed, 'the poor guys are starving!'

'Good,' retorted Madge. 'I want 'em to look starving! If they eat now they'll fall asleep on me, and we gotta have 'em lookin' mean in the background.'

Herr Volmort, more than ever resembling something that had crept out of a sepulcher in the middle of the night, descended on the base camp, to powder the Imperial couple and touch up their hair ('Does that spit-curl look the way it did this morning, darling?' inquired Nick anxiously), and Emma was left alone again, with Buttercreme and Black Jasmine on her lap and Chang Ming panting happily at her feet.

The lions glared at the tiny dogs. 'Yeah, I'm sorry, boys,' Torley apologized, and put his hand through the bars to scratch Big Joe's ear. The lion licked his hand disconsolately.

Among the extras, Darlene Golden seemed to shimmer like an orchid in a bed of geraniums – a portion of the morning, between lions, had been spent filming close-ups of her, reacting to the Evil Valerna's triumphant scorn. Zal checked the reflector dedicated to keeping a luminous aura on the beautiful slave-girl's face and hair, and gave Herbie a brief lesson in its more subtle effects. The Rothstein Boys left their pinochle game behind the dais, and now plunged into 'Onward, Christian Soldiers', as the Christians filed onto the bloodied sands of the arena to meet their destinies. At the top of the stairway, the Temptress of Babylon flung back her head with a victorious sneer. 'Well, fools,' she cried, for the two hundredth time that day, 'where is your Redeemer now?'

'You're crowding up back there!' roared Madge. 'What'd I tell you about crowding up? Anybody'd think you *wanted* to get chomped by those lions!'

The Christians retreated into the passageway.

Onward, Christian soldiers, marching as to war . . .

'Action!'

'Well, fools, where is your Redeemer now?'

'You frikkin' idiots, stop at the frikkin' tape! We're payin' for those cats, we gotta see 'em in the background!'

The Christians retreated into the passageway again.

'Action!'

'Well, fools, where is your Redeemer now?'

Among them, Darlene looked sulky whenever the camera wasn't actually rolling. Emma noticed that Frank Pugh did not put in an appearance on the set.

At four, she hooked up the leashes on all three dogs, and took them for a stroll around the Hacienda.

Returning, she met Kitty and Nick in the stage doorway, both resplendent in gaudy kimonos, his more vivid than hers. (*That gold lamé must be excruciating under the lights* . . .) Kitty flung out a hand, tossed her head, sneered at Emma and cried, 'Well, fool, where is your Redeemer now?'

'In the office,' returned Emma, curtseying deeply. 'Preparing the paperwork to send *you* to Hell, your Majesty. Do you need help getting changed?'

By the time Emma had gathered all Kitty's usual impedimenta and arranged with one of the guards to have it taken to the car, Kitty had changed clothes, cold-creamed the camera make-up from her face, and completely reapplied foundation, powder, rouge, and kohl, despite the fact that she was going straight home. She was just putting on her mascaro when Emma climbed the steps to the temporary dressing room – shivering a little, still, as she passed the door of the suite in which Rex Festraw had died.

'Peggy's going to meet us at the house, darling,' announced Kitty. 'I'm too absolutely *ruined* to do anything but play a little pinochle, but she's stopping at Lee Chang's, so we'll have a decent supper anyway . . . Did you find out anything last night?' she added, as they descended to the car. 'I'm sorry I was too *devastated* this morning to ask. We didn't finish filming until nearly midnight, and if I ran down that corridor once I ran down it *three hundred times* . . .' Beneath the flawless concealment of foundation and powder, Emma could see the smudges of exhaustion under the huge, brown eyes. 'Did you have a nice time? Isn't Ambrose a pet?'

'Mr Crain is a lovely gentleman.' Emma smiled. 'And a very nice dancer.'

'I must say I like a man with a little more oomph,' admitted

Kitty, slipping in behind the Packard's leather-upholstered wheel – which was, Emma reflected, putting it mildly. 'But at least he doesn't step on your feet, like Tor would – you remember Tor Westlake, darling? That absolutely *divine* looking creature at Monarch? I was *utterly* ready to fall *passionately* in love with Tor until he stepped on my feet dancing . . .'

'I felt a little sorry for him,' said Emma softly. 'Mr Crain, I mean. He sounded so wistful, when he spoke of . . . well, not *his* family, but *a* family.'

'I'd take almost *any* family,' declared Kitty, 'over that pack of ghouls he's told me about. I thought *I* was bad, asking for two hundred dollars a month in alimony even if Clayton *was* a lot fonder of his valet than he was of me – though I will admit Duke was *gorgeous*! But I didn't take away Clayton's home, which I probably could have, if we'd really gone to court over it . . .'

She shook her head, pushing aside the recollection of her most recent spell of matrimony. 'And anyway, I wouldn't have done that to his mother. Clayton's mother is the sweetest person . . .'

Emma tried to estimate when this interlude could have been, as Kitty went on, 'Did he tell you about his villa? It's in the National Forest. He showed me pictures – of the way it looked when it was in Italy, I mean, before they took it apart. You'll love it, dear! We'll leave the minute the picture is wrapped.'

'I'm sure it's beautiful.'

And I may not see it. I may be on a train heading east – heading home. Thinking . . . What? Thinking, 'Whew, that's over. I shattered the mirror and sailed down the river to Camelot and here I am, wet and bedraggled, going home at last to Shalott . . . Going home at last to Ithaca.'

Kitty swung the big car up Ivarene, and her red mouth, more generous than the fashionable Cupid-bow pout in which it was painted, tightened. 'I just hope . . . Well, that somebody finds out about what really happened. About who really sent me that note that was supposed to be from Eliot, and who brought Rex out here from New York, and why they wanted to shoot him in my dressing room. I mean, it's all very well to have everyone thinking what a *femme fatale* and woman of mystery I am . . . Oh, Emma, did I tell you? Desiree Darrow planned to fly a golden aeroplane over Venice Beach and toast everyone there in champagne, only she got Jackson White – the stuntman – to teach her how to fly and wrecked his plane before she even got it off the runway . . . and nobody even *mentioned* her, in letters to the editor or *anything*, and Jackson is just *furious. And* she got two black eyes out of it and California Studios has had to put back filming *Maiden of Paris* for a week . . .'

Her sparkling glee faded suddenly. 'But the thing is, I want to know, one way or the other. I *need* to know, because once someone starts doing crazy things because they're jealous, they only get worse. And I don't want to spend the next five years looking over my shoulder every time Frank starts to think I might be seeing someone like Ambrose. Or Dusty over at Fox. Or Kenny at Independent.' She sighed. 'Or whatever-his-name is, that *beautiful* waiter at the Townhouse . . .'

It was on Emma's lips to say, *I think Mr Crain loves you* . . . But she didn't. So far as she could tell, Kitty's abiding emotional love was reserved for her friends, and her dogs, not for the regiments of men she flirted with, danced with, slept with, and discarded like laddered stockings. *And why not?* she reflected. Kitty's extraordinary beauty, Jim had told her once, had made her little more than a commodity since the age of fourteen. *If she'd been plain*, he had said, a little sadly, *our parents wouldn't have cared much where she went, or with who. But because of how she looked, they treated her like she was a bitch in heat. They'd lock her in at night, pound her with every story in the Bible – Eve and Jezebel and Potiphar's trampy wife – every time she'd look at a boy in the street . . .*

No wonder she distrusted love.

And why, perhaps, she failed to recognize it in men.

Peggy Donovan – laden with cardboard cartons of Chinese food and blithering with news about the new picture she would be starting at Enterprise next week – was waiting for them on the porch. Emma shared a little egg fu yung with them, fed the dogs, and left the two actresses and three Pekinese together

as the sun was westering to walk the three-quarters of a mile
down to Vine again, to take the streetcar to the studio. The
last of the Christian martyrs were departing – traces of blood
and arena sand in the edges of their hair – but the gates were
still open. Arnie the night guard greeted her with a wave. Zal,
looking like ten sweaty miles of bad road, greeted her with a
grin and a kiss as she entered the little screening room at the
back of the Hacienda. 'Our girl all right?'

'The plan is for her to spend the evening playing two-handed
pinochle with Peggy Donovan and go to bed early.' Emma
followed the cameraman down to the three rows of seats that
occupied the center of a chamber which had clearly started
life as a dining room. 'Something I wouldn't mind doing
myself. I hope to goodness they don't have four gins apiece
and suddenly decide it's a good night to go to the Coconut
Grove.'

'You can't be her mother,' pointed out Zal.

'No.' Emma sighed, and relaxed. 'Nor would I want to be.'
She sank into the chair, glad of the room's quiet. Glad of the
stillness of the lot outside in the mild spring twilight, save for
the rumble of far-off traffic on Sunset Boulevard. 'And under
ordinary circumstances I wouldn't think twice. But . . .'

'Kitty Flint' – Zal used her legal name – the name of her
most recent husband – 'has a brain the size of a fingernail-
clipping, but she knows how to take care of herself. And I'm
pretty sure she knows how much use Peggy Donovan would
be to her in an emergency. Now sit down,' he added, 'and let's
see what we've got for last Wednesday.'

He retreated to the projection room, switching off the lights
as he went.

Emma had seen dailies before, the raw hanks of moving
imagery from which stories were later woven by the editors.
It was rather like watching the filming that afternoon: dozens
of nearly-identical scenes, of Dirk Silver and his cohort arriving
at the empress's garden, of Dirk (a.k.a. Marcus Maximus)
gathering Valerna in his arms while she fought against him
and against her own passions. Of Valerna in her garden, coming
upon the beautiful Philomela also (albeit unwillingly) in
Maximus's arms, slapping her and condemning her to die.

Over and over and over again. The beautiful Philomela flinched *before* she was slapped. The beautiful Philomela's hair got caught in one of the empress's bracelets. One of the Praetorians in the background scratched his armpit. There was a coffee cup on the plinth of the statue of David (Emma didn't know which was worse – the presence of the cup or the presence of a Renaissance statue in first-century Rome).

Two of the slaves were big men, well deserving of the appellation 'XLge'.

No Roman was nearly that size.

Then over an hour of watching the mob of peasants outside King Romberg's palace. They rattled scythes and cleavers and clubs, and shouted for the blood of the stinking aristocrats, until the cavalry charged in and scattered them. Larry Palmer was a much more laissez-faire director than Madge Burdon – or there was less precision required in the teeming mob – but he had two or three wide shots in which the camera panned the mob assembled in the courtyard. Emma easily spotted the three 'XLges'.

Someone – Emma checked her notebook when the lights went up, and identified the name of the missing Extra-Large Praetorian as Eddie Crump – had checked out cuirass, helmet, cloak, shield, and greaves, and had not reported for duty. He'd checked them back in at three forty-five, an hour and a half before any of the other Praetorian extras had.

'I saw him,' she said suddenly, as Zal appeared in the projection-room door. 'When we were looking for Kitty. He was over near Wardrobe with the peasants.'

Zal raised his brows.

'I thought at the time that Madge would thrash him with a vine-stalk, the way Centurions used to do with misbehaving troopers.'

'What time?'

She turned events over in her mind. 'It must have been two thirty or so. Not later than that, because when your friend Taffy looked at his watch, I looked at mine.'

'Sounds like they knew exactly when she'd be out of her dressing room, all right.'

'I wonder what Mr Crump told Millie?' She helped him

gather the film cans from the projection-room table, and carry them across the hall to Editing.

'Could have told her anything,' pointed out the cameraman. 'Migraine headache. Overdose of commissary food. Happens all the time. We can check Payroll but I'll bet you a fortune cookie nobody came in to pick up that money.'

SIXTEEN

B ut it was one thing to be reasonably certain that a 'gross' semi-crook named Gross had finagled his way onto the Foremost lot Wednesday afternoon disguised as an extra – and indeed, subsequent enquiry proved that a) 'Eddie Crump's' $3.50 pay envelope was still sitting in Payroll waiting to be picked up and b) nobody of that name had ever worked for the studio before or since – murdered Camille de la Rose's ex- (or current) husband, and left forged correspondence at the scene. Proving it was another matter.

'If the guy's connected with Crawford or the City Hall Gang,' pointed out Zal, over a very late donut and cup of tea at the Pacific Dining Car on Sixth Street that night, 'he's gonna have five guys swearing he was with them anyway. Or the cops will write down on their report that five guys named Smith, Smith, Smith, Smith, and Baskerville swore he was with them. And that doesn't really solve our problem.'

'No.' Emma turned from the glare of the street lamps and the wall of brick buildings across the street, to the soft yellow gleam of the Dining Car's lamps. The restaurant was nearly empty at this hour, the owners sitting at the only other occupied table in the room, adding up the day's take. She felt a pang of guilt – for keeping them up, and for leaving Kitty with no better protection than the empty-headed Peggy. But that egg fu yung had been many hours ago, and at the moment she felt a good deal of sympathy for poor Mr Torley's lions.

And it wasn't Kitty that Gross tried to kill Thursday night. Was it?

'And proving that he was on the lot – even proving that he pulled the trigger – still leaves us with the question of why?'

Zal sighed. 'Makes me long for the days when I was just photographing the pig races in Fresno.'

Zal drove her back to the house, in the late-model black Ford that Mr Crain had arranged for one of his employees to

sell to him ('I insist on paying – if something should happen
to Miss de la Rose I want to be sure you'll be able to pursue
the culprits . . .'). They found Peggy's car in the yard, the
front door unlocked, and old Mr Shang sitting on the front
steps with his wife, playing a long-necked Chinese lute. 'All
is well,' said the old man, setting the instrument aside. Starlight
shimmered white on the silk of his long hair as he rose to his
feet and bowed deeply. 'Yet knowing that there are those who
wish the lady ill, we came here to await your return. It is no
hardship for the beautiful Mrs Shang and this insignificant
servant to contemplate the stars.'

He helped his wife to her stubby little bound feet, and they
disappeared into the shadows around the side of the house,
like a crane and a tortoise, the lute slung on his back.

Peggy and Kitty slumbered on the living-room couches
amid a storm-wrack of cards, empty champagne glasses, and
snoring Pekinese. 'If you can drive the Ford to the studio in
the morning I can just take Sleeping Beauty here home without
waking her.' Zal gestured to Peggy.

'It's hardly fair to you.' Emma gathered up the red-haired
actress's coat and handbag and collected crumpled piles of
five- and ten-dollar bills that strewed the coffee table and the
carpet round about. She was tired now and her head ached,
and the thought that Mr Gross – whoever had hired him –
had been able to walk on and off the Foremost lot at will did
nothing for her unease about the darkness of the hills around
the house. 'They live like spoilt children – get drunk where
and when they please, seduce whoever comes in their path
regardless of consequences or previous marital arrangements
on either side, drive while intoxicated . . . and expect you to
pick up after them, like an unpaid nanny.'

'And feed their dogs,' added Zal with a grin, taking an
empty Veuve Cliquot bottle from beneath the table. 'And fetch
chilled slices of cucumber to put on their eyes when they wake
up after a bender – and it sure doesn't look like much of an
orgy went on here tonight.' He gently shook another bottle
which stood on a corner of the gramophone. The motor had
run down with the needle still resting at the end of the groove:
Baby of Mine, said the label. *Recorded in Chicago*.

Emma raised her eyes from Kitty, whom she had been regarding, she realized, with a combination of exasperation and tenderness. Zal went to the bar, and split the remains of the bottle between two clean glasses.

'And what do you expect?' He handed her a glass. 'From what Kitty's told me, the farm Peggy grew up on would make a Louisiana convict camp look like a weekend at the Ritz. Peggy told me once she ran away because she got tired of being raped by her cousins – and because one of them had started pimping her to his friends in the truck-stop in Tulsa. Rudy Valentino bussed tables and worked in dance halls when he came to this country; Barbara la Marr worked burlesque. Clara Bow's crazy father swore he'd knife her before he'd let her come to Hollywood. Tried it, too. These are people who have whatever that is, whatever that fire inside is called, that brings other people to warm themselves when they bring these stories to life . . . Like Mrs Glyn says, they have "It". But they've had no training for it. Or pretty much for anything else. La Marr's, what, twenty-eight? Rudy's the same . . . Clara isn't even twenty. They don't know they're not going to be beautiful forever. You give 'em a pile of money and a nice place to live and the whole world telling 'em they're God's gift, what do you think is going to happen?'

'And she didn't have to bring me out here.' Emma sighed again, and sipped her champagne, recalling with a smile her father's strictures on the beverage – delivered in flawless Latin, of course. And Kitty, she suspected, couldn't actually have told Veuve Cliquot from Miller High Life. 'Nor help poor Eliot Jordan. And you're right about Kitty. She can't act to save her life, but I see her on film and she makes every scene come alive.'

'That's what "It" is. They're kids.' Zal met her eyes over the rim of his glass, sipped the champagne. 'They'll get slapped with the hard side of this business soon enough. In a lot of ways they already have been. You be all right here tonight?'

Emma nodded, set her glass down on the mantelpiece, and after a long moment, Zal set his down also, took her in his arms, and kissed her. A little awkward, his beard tickling and the corner of his glasses brushing her cheekbone. But his arms around her were strong, as Jim's had been. The warmth of his hands was a comfort that went straight through her bones, to her heart. 'Whatever you decide to do about your aunt, and going back to Oxford . . . I want you to be happy, Em. Even if it's not with me. You let me know if there's anything I can do.'

He turned, scooped up Peggy in his arms – and he was right, she didn't stir – and carried her out the door and down the front steps, Emma following with an armful of velvet and monkey fur, sequined shoes and handbag full of cash.

Throughout the following day, and the next, Emma tried systematically to work out who, in Kitty's life, would want to have her accused of murder. Accused but not convicted – 'I can't believe anyone would actually think that that telephone call to her dressing room, much less those silly notes, would be accepted by a court,' she said to Zal, during a brief break in the filming of the strangling scene on Wednesday. 'But it's equally hard for me to believe that Mr Pugh – or Mr Fishbein – would go to the extent of . . . of actually *killing* someone . . .' She found she almost couldn't put into words the thought that had flickered into her mind half a dozen times since Rex Festraw's death.

And as she pronounced them, it struck her even more deeply how absurd was the idea. 'Much less bringing someone here specially from New York, and putting him up at a hotel . . .'

Not Mr Pugh . . .

Or the smiling, bespectacled Mr Fishbein . . .

'Don't you?' Zal's eyebrows tilted. 'You ever heard the details about the night Bill Taylor was murdered a couple of years ago? Before anybody even called the cops, his studio had a team over there cleaning up: burning love letters, trousering account books, tearing pages off his telephone pad, wiping up stains. I've seen tap dancers in vaudeville move slower than the press boys at Paramount trying to cover for wherever the hell Mary Minter had been the night before, not that I think poor Mary had the slightest thing to do with it . . . And I understand from men I've talked to on the force that about a week into the investigation they all

got word to lay off. Is covering up a fishy crime the same
as paying Sid Gross to go in and rub out an inconvenient
spouse? You tell me.'

He tapped the copy of *World of Film* that lay on Kitty's
make-up table, next to a thermos of gin and a bronze ashtray
upheld by three muscular nude atlantes. *The Goddess of the
Silver Screen*, flared the header of the article, accompanied by
a photo of Kitty looking mysterious and several much smaller
shots of the other contenders. 'This is coast-to-coast news.'
He glanced back at the magazine rack beside Kitty's camp-
chair. Another photo, equally sphinx-like, adorned the cover
of *Photo Play* under the headline of *The Secret Tragedy*. *Screen
World* bore a photograph of Kitty as the Empress Valerna,
beside the words, *Temptress of Babylon – The True Tale!* And
in less conspicuous letters, *The Triumphs and Passions of
Peggy Donovan*. 'You can't buy publicity like this . . . except
of course that they can.'

Commentary on Miss Swanson's cheetah and earrings at
the Café Montmartre ran a modest third.

'But . . . to bring Mr Festraw out here from New York – to
put him up in a hotel, not to speak of having those notes
forged . . .'

'Festraw could have phoned Pugh weeks ago,' pointed out
Zal. 'And Pugh could have read that *Photo Play* rumors column
about Kitty and Crain – and we won't even get into the studio
gossip about what's-his-name on the catwalk in Stage Three.
Free publicity and a way to show her she needs his protection
– what more could a guy want?'

'And killing us?' she asked softly.

Zal was silent. A few feet away, Kitty sat before her portable make-up table, while Zena Gosford delicately reshaped
the dark storm cloud of her hair.

'I talked to Benny Parr, by the way,' Emma went on after
a moment. 'Mr Pugh's driver, you know. He says Mr Pugh
got Mr Fishbein's call on Wednesday at a realtor's downtown,
and he seemed to be truly horrified and outraged. They had
to rush to the Merchants' Bank to get cash – which of course
is exactly what I'd do, if I wanted people to think I'd been
caught off-guard.'

'Well, he did used to be an actor,' said Zal. 'Way back, and not on Broadway. But he can put a show on if he needs to.'

Emma was silent, arranging and rearranging the notes she'd made on torn-out pages of her notebook, as she did when concocting scenes in a film.

Mr Pugh jealous. Stanislas Markham. Worked a job for Cornero Friday. Who could come onto the lot to get the gun and the stationery? (Dressed as extra . . .) Who phoned the dressing room?

Like Sam Wyatt's notes about sinister Chinamen and long-lost twins and the monkey's eyebrows . . .

What makes sense?

Or like trying to fit fragments of broken pottery into a design.

The probable impossible is to be preferred to the improbable possible . . .

'Do you really think he did it? Or had it done?'

'Kitty was right when she said some men go kind of crazy when they think somebody else is making nookie with their woman. When I was hiding out from the Draft Board in St Francisville, Louisiana, the whole parish was in an uproar because one of the most respectable men in town murdered a priest – a kindly, devout man, according to everyone in town that I talked to. Turned out Mr Respectable was "taking an interest in" – as they say – a girl at the local high school, and convinced himself the padre had evil designs on her. He spent thousands of dollars setting up a way to get the padre alone twenty miles outside of town and shot him, with evidence manufactured to convict some poor black sharecropper . . . and then left mud from the murder site on the floorboards of his car when he drove back to town. People do get crazy when they get jealous, Em. I don't understand it, but I know you can't tell by lookin' at 'em.'

Zal returned to his camera. The Two Neds wheeled troughs of crumpled newspapers into position between the set's windows and the backdrop of Rome, and more troughs behind the backdrop, to be ignited when the cameras rolled. Water-trucks were wheeled into position, just out of shot-line. Kitty and Nick Thaxter, make-up refreshed, took their places once again among the debris left by the ravening mob, for close-ups. Nick had spent the morning strangling Kitty for the master shot and it was now time for the interminable series of reaction shots.

'I cannot *tell* you,' sighed Kitty, when at seven o'clock that night she sat before her dressing-room mirror, repainting, 'how glad I'll be tomorrow when we finish burning Rome and I can be *done* with all this. Did I remember to tell you we're driving down the coast Saturday to San Diego, to stay at the Del? That *tiresome* man who was supposed to have the plumbing hooked up yesterday at Ambrose's villa never turned up – at least, that's what Ambrose told me – and now the place won't be ready for *weeks*! And by that time I'll be filming *Hot Potato*, and poor Ambrose will be tied up with Standard Oil. Did I tell you they struck oil on his Long Beach land? *Oceans* of it, darling – this was last month sometime – and he says Standard Oil has offered him a *fortune* for it . . . And of course the cook and the other servants he intended to hire for his villa for next week now won't be available until sometime in *July*! Oh, and I got him to write down what it's called . . . it's here somewhere . . . But the Del Coronado is *gorgeous*, darling, and you'll *love* it . . .'

'And what does Mr Pugh think you're doing over the weekend?'

'Oh, he thinks I'm going with him up to San Simeon ranch.' She licked the tip of her finest brush, and concentrated on edging her lashline with kohl. 'Mr Hearst – Marion's friend, the newspaperman, you know – invites people to go camping up there, but it's not really like camping . . . It's like what you were telling me about archaeologists bringing along table linen and portable bathtubs and their valets. Frank wants to get on Mr Hearst's good side to get financing for land to film Westerns on.'

Turning on her chair, she smiled sunnily upon Emma. 'You'll need to call him early Saturday morning, when he's just about to leave to pick me up, and tell him I'm sick and will join them Sunday if I feel better.'

As she followed Kitty down the stairs to where the car waited – Buttercreme's wicker carrier in one hand and Black

Jasmine tucked under her other arm – Emma wondered whether Kitty had some kind of back-up plan in case Mr Pugh offered to rush right over to Kitty's house with offers of hot toddies and chicken soup?

Although, she supposed, if the studio chief were willing to murder a man to generate publicity for his star he certainly wouldn't walk away from a weekend spent with William Randolph Hearst . . .

And though she tried to be flippant about that thought, it made her shiver.

And what, for that matter, would Detective Meyer have to say about the proposed vacation? The special hearing was scheduled for Monday.

And Kitty had nothing more to her defense than, *I didn't do it.*

She dreamed that night about Jim. About the endless warm twilight of early May, the sky still light at nine thirty but the trees of the Baliol meadows submerged in blue dusk. The last twitterings of the daytime birds, and the hoot of an owl somewhere. The smell of wet grass.

The bones of his big hand holding hers, the smoothness and texture of his palm. Six years later, she thought, she would still know the feel of his skin in the dark.

Still know his voice . . .

He said, 'If I should die . . .'

'Don't.'

'Hey.' She'd heard his grin, as much as seen it. He'd been quiet all evening, as if he could see the hours counting down on the clock. *Only forty-one to go* . . . 'Your dad goes digging around dead people all the time.' He finger-combed back the black swatch of hair that fell over his forehead. 'He's got about six skulls down in his study – those have to have belonged to somebody. From what he's told me,' he added in a softer voice, 'some of 'em a lot younger than me.'

She'd whispered again, 'Don't.'

'I just don't want you to turn into one of those crazy ladies in an old novel, Em. The ones who go around wearing black for the next fifty years.'

Smiling, she said, 'If it was good enough for Queen Victoria, I don't see why it shouldn't be good enough for me,' and he'd laughed, and with his arm around her shoulders hugged her tight. They'd turned into Holywell Street and she could see the lights of The Myrtles ahead of them in the darkness, the jaunty, eccentric roofline through the trees. Sleeping, she wondered why they'd come here – after the wedding they'd taken a room at the George, and he'd laughed at her, for feeling shy about lying with her husband under her parents' roof. (*'You think they don't know what we're up to?'*)

But here they were.

'I mean it,' he'd said softly. 'If I don't come back, I don't want to die thinking about you living the rest of your life alone.'

And he'd signed for her to walk ahead of him, to where the light glimmered. Halfway there she turned back to him.

But he was gone.

The following night, Rome burned.

Emma had been on the set that afternoon, while Madge was walking Kitty and the vengeful Praetorian Guards along the route and Zal set up his cameras. He'd spent the previous evening testing light settings and discussing angles with the director, and with Doc Larousse. Doc's reflectors and lighting trees surrounded the maze of unpainted pillars, cardboard statues, and cock-eyed architraves like H.G. Wells's Martians closing in for the kill. Emma herself had seen how wide the pathways were, that looked so narrow from where Zal would stand.

'It's all an optical illusion,' he'd said. 'It all is. The folks in the seats never really understand that we're forcing their point of view. If you stand *exactly here*, it'll look like this . . . Like those anamorphic peep-boxes Renaissance painters used to make, or those portraits that look like nothing but a slur of lines unless you look at them with a curved mirror.'

'Father took me to see half a dozen of those in Oxford,' agreed Emma with a smile. 'After King Charles I was executed, you know, his supporters would have anamorphics painted of him, to hang in their houses, to honor his memory without getting into trouble themselves. I was always fascinated by how they could *do* that.'

And she smiled at the memory. There'd been something both delightful and eerie, seeing those loops and streamers of light and dark paint suddenly meld into the sad features of the doomed king.

He was there all along, her father had said, to Emma's delighted ten-year-old squeals. *Like everything, you just need to look at it differently. You just need to know the secret.*

'It's easier if you've got a camera.' Zal led her, and the dogs, along the edge of the trench that would lie between his camera and the path, where galvanized trashcans stood, ready filled with chunks of wood and bushels of crumpled newspapers. Emma glimpsed Kitty's picture on one of them as they passed.

On the path itself Madge stood, feet apart, beefy arms folded, watching with narrowed eyes as Kitty – clothed in a simple skirt and sweater – practiced tripping, and the shirt-sleeved Praetorians thundered up behind waving their spears and swords.

'It's Madge's job, and Kitty's job, and *my* job, to make them not realize that what they're seeing, isn't what's really going on at all.'

As Emma walked back to Kitty's base camp – now pitched at the foot of the slope on which Rome was built and incorporating, as well as a beach umbrella, a tent that had clearly done service in an epic of the Crusades – she saw the massive dark bulk of Frank Pugh, standing on the path that led back to the main lot. Like Madge he stood with arms folded, and like Madge, seemed to be watching Kitty.

But whether in admiration, adoration, or bleak suspicion, Emma was too far off to tell. And by the time she'd reached the little cluster of chairs and make-up table, gramophone and vases (orchids today – from God alone knew who! – and a glorious exultation of yellow lilies), like Jim, the big man was gone.

'This is gonna be the greatest fire since Chicago!' exulted Madge, when she and Kitty returned to the camp and Ned Bergen's myrmidons moved in with the firehose wagons, to soak the dirt that surrounded the sprawl of columns and walls and 'abandoned' carts and market-baskets. There were, in fact, four 'burn' sets, this one and three smaller clusters of ruins at a respectful distance, against which Zal would film terrified extras fleeing, screaming, and falling under what looked like showers of flaming debris that in fact landed in pits of water eight or ten feet from their 'victims', while Kitty and Mr Crain sipped champagne at the Hotel Del Coronado.

And they'll come back, thought Emma, *on Monday for the special hearing . . .*

And on Wednesday, Aunt Estelle and Uncle David would arrive in San Pedro, and – Emma guessed – telephone the studio and ask her where she would like to meet them, and if she was packed to go.

And I'll tell them what?

She felt as if she'd barely had two minutes undistracted, to make up her mind.

What if the judge at the hearing remands Kitty for trial? What if her defense of: 'I got a note from a friend who was in trouble and went to meet that friend, who never showed up . . .' only increases Mr Pugh's suspicions – surely inflamed, by that time, by a feeble excuse of being sick over the weekend?

What kind of testimony would *he* give, regarding the gun, and who could gain access to Kitty's dressing room and under what circumstances?

And – perhaps most disquieting of all – how safe would Kitty be after that?

Always supposing he doesn't simply withdraw studio support and inform the judge that justice might take its course for all he cared.

He wouldn't endanger the picture . . .

But will he consider a star's tragic death as much of a publicity coup as the title of Goddess of the Silver Screen?

Why couldn't Aunt have written last October? When all this seemed so strange and uncomfortable, when I still thought Kitty was little more than a self-absorbed featherbrain? When I barely knew Zal?

Emma drew a deep breath, and went into the tent to get her own thermos of tea, Kitty's of coffee laced with rum, and the packet of sandwiches she'd prepared that morning. Leashed to the tent-poles, Chang Ming and Black Jasmine leaped to their feet, tails threshing. The leash leading into Buttercreme's box moved a little, as the tiny dog retreated further in disapproval of the entire process. *Let's wait and see what happens, before we make any decisions,* Emma told herself.

Kitty's costume hung from a portable rack, shimmering black and gold. Necklaces, earrings, rings glittered on a folding table. Outside, Emma heard Herr Volmort's slippery, reptilian voice greeting Madge and Kitty. 'Are you ready, Miss de la Rose?'

And she smiled, because he invariably sounded like the Grand Inquisitor politely steering his victim into the torture chamber. The kindest and most scholarly of men, his voice combined with that Middle-European accent would have made 'Mary had a little lamb' sound sinister.

And Kitty: 'Darling, can you bring me a robe from in there?'

Can I leave her, not knowing?

She didn't know.

At least, she reflected, gathering up the light cotton garment that would swathe Kitty for make-up, she wouldn't have to worry about the Praetorian Guards.

She'd gone over to Wardrobe early that afternoon, as soon as she and Kitty had arrived on the lot, and had confided in Millie Katz that she feared that whoever had shot Mr Festraw might have designs on Kitty as well. 'I know it's probably foolish,' she'd said, with a self-deprecating gesture. 'But I've heard some . . . some quite unbelievable stories about . . . well, about obsessed fans. Like that woman the other day who climbed over the wall of Mr Valentino's house and dove nude into his swimming pool . . .'

'Honeybunch,' Millie had sighed, 'compared to the stunts other women have pulled – *and* men! – that particular little mermaid was riding in the Sane and Respectable car with Grace Coolidge. Whatcha need?'

'I'd just like to make sure that you know who all the extras will be, during the burn filming tonight.'

Millie had checked. There were fifteen Praetorians and all their names were familiar to her, men who'd waltzed in ballrooms for Lubitsch or bled on DeMille's battlefields. 'This ain't a scene where anybody wants to be breaking in a new boy.'

One thing I don't have to worry about.

Two, actually, Emma reflected, as Kitty settled into her chair and closed her eyes for the little German to cold-cream her face. A call had come in for her to Kitty's dressing room shortly after their arrival on the lot, and Tony Cornero's unmistakable voice had said, 'Mrs Blackstone? I got somethin' for you that may help you, if you care to come by the club tomorrow at about four.'

She'd smiled a little at the young man's careful circumlocution – he clearly suspected that his telephone was tapped – but had thanked him, doubly glad that at least she'd have some better idea about Sid Gross's movements before going down to San Diego Saturday. There would be time, she reflected, while Kitty and Mr Crain were having their little seaside idyll for her to look over the list for anything that looked familiar, in terms of times and places . . .

And if worst came to worst, she could telephone Zal, and take the train back to Los Angeles if necessary.

Darkness stole over the hills, into the sky. When Ned Bergen walked past, Kitty asked, 'Can I set the fire?' and her dark eyes danced like an eager child's. A child who lives for the moment when she can set off a firecracker, and see the glory of its apotheosis.

Bergen glanced at Madge, who rolled her eyes.

'It'll take about ten minutes for everything to get cooking, once the fuses are lit.' The prop chief spoke like an indulgent father.

'You take Little Ned with you,' ordered Madge resignedly, 'and you get back here *on the double*. Heinrich's got to spray your face with sweat before you go.'

The fire was terrifying. Fourteen men were standing around with hoses just out of shot-line and the ground was saturated for yards in every direction. Nevertheless Emma struggled against a sense of panic, as if the blaze were a live thing, live and seeking a way to break free. The heat that streamed over her had an oily feel to it; the noise seemed to beat on her head, an uncontrolled animal roar. Her heart was in her throat as she watched Kitty flee along the path, stumbling in her torn rags of black and golden gauze, half-turning to gaze over her shoulder like a frightened beast. Emma had rewritten the scenario she'd been given last month as a melodrama of comeuppance. The Harlot of Babylon, immortalized in *Revelations*, had sent hundreds of Christians (and a few perfectly innocent and virtuous pagans) to their deaths, had had poor blameless little Philomela flogged in the arena and had made the noble Demetrius watch the deaths of his mother and sisters *after* he had given in to her lusts to save them . . .

This was the pay-off. The moment that God showed the evil Valerna what it felt like, to be pursued, to be terrified, to be alone.

She had pictured it differently while she was writing it, and wished that the fire wasn't so close to those fluttering tags of silk. (A week later, watching the dailies, she was aghast at how close the blaze appeared with Zal's forced perspective.) The third take, from a different angle with the infuriated Praetorians pounding along the path behind her, made Emma shiver, remembering that Sid Gross had walked about the lot in that armor with absolute impunity. It wouldn't take but a moment for one of them to spring forward, hurl Kitty into the blaze . . .

Stop it. Millie knows them all . . .

Three of them were very definitely Extra-Large . . .

STOP IT! Everything will be fine . . .

And everything was. Madge took different shots from different angles, Herr Volmort meticulously patted Kitty's face dry between takes, renewed her make-up with precise speed, dusted her with powder and then sprayed her with photogenic sweat, though by the end of each take her face dripped unattractively with the real thing. The director was determined to take full advantage of the burn – four times the size of the sets arranged for the close-ups with the extras – and it was nearly eleven before she scanned the crumbling inferno and ruled, 'That's it.'

'About fucking time.' Kitty accepted the thermos of orange

juice that Emma had brought to her between takes – with a straw in it, so as not to disarray the battered and terrified empress's immaculate lipstick. Standing with Kitty and Madge at the head of the path, Emma looked along that crooked track that Kitty had run, staggered, stumbled down a dozen times (and then another score for close-ups). It was a good ten feet wide and its sides glistened like amber oil where the flamelight caught the water that Ned's crew had sprayed between takes.

Emma still wasn't certain she'd have had the nerve to run down that slot between the flames.

Is that, too, part of 'It'?

She wondered if Kitty would have nightmares about it.

'Thank you, honey.' Kitty held out her hand to Madge. 'That couldn't have gone better! None of it could.' She smiled, warm as sunlight. 'What a shoot, hunh? Can I come tomorrow and see the dailies?'

'They won't be ready til Friday.' And, seeing Kitty's face fall, she added, 'You going out of town with Frank for a day or two, honey? I sure would,' she added, a schoolboy grin suddenly transforming the habitual grimness of her face. 'You tell me when, and I'll put on a special show for you.' Behind them, the strategically placed kliegs were going down. Ned and his minions were hosing the ruins, clouds of smoke billowing gray in the reflected glare of the work-lights, into the star-splattered sky.

Surrounded by tired Praetorians, Emma and Kitty followed the path back to the studio.

Claudite am rivos, pueri, Virgil had said, of the farmers finishing a day's hard work. *Close the sluices, boys. The fields have drunk enough.*

More lights were extinguished behind them, as if the night came closer, and followed them home.

SEVENTEEN

K itty slept late Friday morning, though Emma had instructions to wake her at noon. Her manicurist, Pearl, would arrive at two.

Emma herself was waked, as usual, by the gentle clatter of Pekinese toenails on the floor of her bedroom, at seven, the dogs having long ago learned who was in charge of the icebox. With the Pekes orbiting her feet, she washed, dressed, and descended to the kitchen, to mince up the cold chicken she'd cooked on Tuesday for precisely this purpose and mix it with biscuit cakes – Kitty had heard that canned meat for dogs was being sold but had reservations about what was actually in it.

As usual, Chang Ming and Black Jasmine wolfed down their rations and sat – trembling with impatience under Emma's watchful eye – while Buttercreme picked at the contents of her own dish at the opposite end of the kitchen.

What sort of arrangements would be on offer, Emma wondered, at the Hotel Del Coronado? The kitchen staff could certainly be bribed into storing shredded meat and dog biscuit, and presumably the Pekes would sleep in her room rather than in the suite shared by Kitty and Mr Crain.

I'll miss them. She shivered a little, remembering Mr Pugh standing on the pathway yesterday afternoon, watching Kitty rehearse without making a move to go to her.

Of course he wouldn't want to derail preparations for a scene that's costing I don't know how many thousands of dollars, and that can only be shot once . . .

With any luck, thought Emma, as she opened the kitchen door and carried Black Jasmine and Buttercreme down the tall steps to the yard below, there would be something in whatever Mr Cornero would give her this afternoon, which would prove who Mr Gross had met with. (Surely there wouldn't be a description of a clandestine rendezvous with Gloria Swanson after all?) It might well be that it had nothing whatsoever to do with Mr Pugh, and she could turn the information over to Zal, and return to Oxford with a clear heart.

If return to Oxford is what I want to do. And for a moment, instead of the uneven line of The Myrtles' roof, the glimmer of its windows in the dusk, she saw the sinking moon over the night-black Pacific. Heard the grind of tires following the sea-road north.

And for a moment it seemed to her – there in the twilight on Holywell Street – she glimpsed Jim in the gloaming behind her, lifting his hand to wave to her and then walking away into the dusk. And she knew there was someone else waiting for her, in the shadows of the porch.

When the three dogs had thoroughly explored the long grass around the scrubby orange trees, and pattered over to bid old Mrs Shang good-morning, Emma carried them back up to the service porch beside the kitchen and brushed them, which at this season involved almost a cupful of foxtails and clumps of shed undercoat the size of baby rabbits. Then, feeling a bit guilty because she knew she'd neglected her next project, she got out her stack of composition books, and for two hours, while birds chirped outside the open back door and now and then Mr Shang's clippers made a sword-like snick as he trimmed the bushes around the garage, she sank into the world of wild parties, social marriages, agonizing jealousies and passionate kisses – all freely cribbed from *Manon Lescaut*, with an occasional dash of Suetonius.

I'll have to turn this scenario over to Sam, she reflected. In between pouring drinks for ivory poachers and dodging German patrols in the Red Sea, had the scenarist ever heard of either *Manon Lescaut* or *The Lives of the Twelve Caesars*? *Well, he DOES quote a good deal of Shakespeare when he gets drunk . . .*

She knew she shouldn't really care whether Frank Pugh was left high and dry for a scenario or not. If he'd had Rex Festraw murdered, and had paid Mr Gross to try to murder her and Zal, it would serve him right . . .

But she couldn't bring herself to walk out on a project. And whether Mr Pugh had anything to do with these events or not, it wasn't fair to Kitty, or Madge, or whoever else was going to be connected with *Hot Potato*. (*Can I REALLY tell Aunt Estelle that my first professional work was an epic with that title?*)

At three, leaving Kitty in the hands of the birdlike little manicurist, Emma walked down Ivarene Street to Vine, to take the bus and then the streetcar along Sunset, to meet with Tony Cornero.

The Bel Giardino was quiet when she tapped at its door. It was opened by the enormous doorman, neatly buttoned into his burgundy uniform but with his cap askew. He bowed a trifle awkwardly, touched his cap, and said, 'Good afternoon, Mrs Blackstone,' in the slangy radio-Brooklynese that seemed to have come, factory-installed, on all of Mr Cornero's henchmen. Locking the door behind her, he led her upstairs. The big room itself was shadowy and nearly empty, save for a charwoman running an immense electric vacuum-cleaner over the snowy carpet that bordered the dancefloor, and the low mutter of a radio announcer's voice rattling off the narration for what sounded like a race of some kind. Horses? Dogs?

Pigs, perhaps? She'd have to ask Zal the details about that . . .

And where *was* Fresno?

'Mrs Blackstone.' Tony Cornero – and another man with his same sturdy build, and the suggestion of kinship in his chin and nose – rose from a corner table.

The other man said, 'I'll be down the cellar, Tony,' and bowed again to Emma before he left. Cornero held Emma's chair for her as she sat.

'This's the best we could do.' Returning to his own chair, the bootlegger took from among the neat stacks of papers on the table three sheets stapled together. 'Far as my boys could tell, sounds like Sid Gross is laying low.'

He held up his hand, snapped his fingers for the bartender: 'What'll you have, Mrs Blackstone? Champagne again?'

'Tea.' She smiled. 'If it's not inconvenient.'

'Louie!' he called out. 'Tea for the lady, and don't go tellin' me we ain't got any . . . Louie wouldn't know tea if the Queen of England spilled it in his lap.' He sipped his own drink, which smelled of gin and lime.

'Gross ain't been to his apartment and he hasn't been at his office since last Thursday. His girlfriend ain't seen him since the Monday before that. The Pasadena police found his car day before yesterday in a gully up in the Santa Susanna hills. The left front fender was scraped and dented, like he'd bumped it into another car, and the glovebox and trunk were cleared out.'

Emma paused, halfway down the first page of a list of sightings: Gross's apartment on Hope Street on the thirteenth – the Sunday before the murder. The café at the corner of Hope and Washington on the fourteenth for breakfast. The barbershop on West 23rd that same Monday afternoon. 'He would have gotten another, surely.' Whoever had assembled this had better informants than Colt Madison. Zal's wrecked Model-T had been hauled back to Foremost Productions the day after the attempt on their lives: Emma was fairly certain it was destined to go off a cliff or in front of a train in the next Wildcat Slim two-reeler. 'Can that be traced through the Motor Vehicles Department?'

'Sure could,' agreed the bootlegger. 'If Gross bought it under his own name, which I'll lay you five to one he didn't.'

Emma opened her mouth to speak her thought – that this seemed another case of someone having a great deal of money – and then closed it. Mr Crain had purchased the black Ford coupe for Zal, used, from one of his employees; it couldn't have cost more than a hundred dollars. The price, evidently, of a high-class bottle of wine. Yet the idea nagged at her thoughts, and with it, the sense that she could almost see what was really going on.

Like Zal's forced perspective. *It's all an optical illusion . . . We're forcing their point of view . . .*

A peep show, Mr Madison had said.

He was there all the time . . . you just need to know the secret . . .

She thought, *Yes. We're only seeing what's in the shot-lines. A Silver Screen Goddess award. A powerful man's jealousy. What's beyond those lines?*

But she said, 'Thank you for this,' then smiled at the bartender when he brought her a cup of tea which smelled vaguely of coffee grounds. 'Please let me know what it cost you to get this information, Mr Cornero. I know some of this' – she gestured with the papers, which included information, she could see running her eye down the first page, gleaned from cab drivers and the owner of the magazine-stand across the street from Sid Gross's apartment building – 'can't have come cheap.'

Cornero waved her question away. 'I'll settle that with Mr Crain,' he said. 'He's a real gent, Mr Crain – unlike that crooked cheap-ass son of his.'

Startled, Emma asked, 'Do you know his son?' From Kitty – and old Mr Crain – Emma had developed a mental picture that combined Uriah Heep with Cato the Censor: dour, stingy, and self-important in an oleaginous way. At least Cato the Censor wouldn't – as Kitty assured him that Young Mr Crain did (only he was nearing forty) – constantly write to his father hinting for money.

'I seen him.' The young bootlegger made a face. 'When I was back in New York, he'd come into the 300 Club to meet his business pals after hours, lookin' around him like he was at the zoo and couldn't wait to do his deals and scram.'

'A nightclub?' Emma almost laughed. 'And here he gives his father the impression he never leaves the sanctity of Long Island and his country club.'

'Country club my – uh – foot. You can do crooked stock deals at a country club as easy as you can at the 300, or anyplace in town . . . It's why you coulda knocked me over with a feather, when Selma downstairs told me she'd seen him at Doolittle's, last Wednesday night.'

'Doolittle's?'

Selma must be the kewpie-doll coat-check girl.

'Club over on Avocado Street, in Los Feliz.' Cornero shrugged. 'Quiet little place. Charlie Crawford owns it; Selma's dating one of the musicians there.'

Wednesday night. Emma flipped through to the last of the pages. *Drinks with Tim Crain, Doolittle's, nine p.m.* 'Are you sure? Is *she* sure?' Her heart was suddenly beating fast.

What they're seeing isn't really what's going on at all . . .
Ambrose Crain's son. *Here.*

'Yeah. Selma used to wait tables at the Quick and Easy, around the corner from the Crain Building on Fifth Avenue. She said for a guy that rich Crain was the world's lousiest tipper and treated the staff like garbage. She said the kitchen boys would take turns comin' up with the worst stuff they could drop in his food – I'm not even gonna tell you the stuff they made that crooked *mammalucco* eat.'

'Crooked?'

'Oh, hell, yeah, crooked,' said Cornero. 'I don't know whether poor old Mr Crain ever knew about it, but I know of at least twice, that his boy nearly got into felony territory, signing his old man's name to back stock deals that I know for sure were under the table.'

Emma sat for a long time, looking at that single typed line. *Drinks with Tim Crain, Doolittle's.* Last Wednesday at nine o'clock . . .

Here. In Los Angeles.
Meeting Sid Gross.

And feeling a cold certainty, as if she'd felt when those little bits of hands on pottery fragments had fallen into relationship with one another, those corners of robes, disembodied feet . . .

A column in Photo Play *a month ago.*

Kitty's voice. 'Did I tell you they struck oil on his Long Beach land? OCEANS of it, darling – this was last month . . . Standard Oil offered him a fortune for it . . .'

LOVE'S FATAL TRAGEDY . . .

Tony himself saying, *Unless he was secretly romancing some wealthy widow and her family wanted to rub him out . . .*

We're seeing what they want us to see.

The mournful dark eyes of King Charles I. *He's been there all along . . .*

Like Ned Bergen's minions, setting up a scene. Like Zal, forcing perspective.

'Thank you,' she said quietly. 'Thank you.'

She folded the papers and put them into her handbag,

finished her tea, and went down the stairs to catch the streetcar on Sunset Boulevard for home.

The dogs rushed to her in a frou-frou of flouncing fur and clattering toenails as she opened the door. It was late, nearly seven – home-going traffic had as usual blocked every inter-section along Sunset Boulevard and stopped the streetcar repeatedly – and the sky was filled with the glow of sunset light. Emma called out, 'Kitty?' but got no reply. In the kitchen, she saw at once that the dogs hadn't been fed. When they dashed in at her heels she stopped, taken aback, at the tiny spots of blood on the yellow tile of the kitchen floor. A second glance showed her that Chang Ming was limping. She knelt, and saw that under his long fur he had an abraded bruise on his right foreleg.

Cold to her heart, she ran upstairs.

Kitty's suitcase was gone.

Descending, she checked the living room – where the dogs' three wicker crates were still lined up neatly. With a sensation of the shaky cold spreading through the whole of her body, she almost ran through the kitchen and down the back steps to the gardener's cottage. The Shangs were in its tiny kitchen, preparing a skillet of vegetables and rice – *This what real Chinese eat*, Mr Shang had told her once. To her query, the old man said, 'Mr Crain man call, say, he and lady go away together, sudden. She not even wait to pack, he say. Like kids. Run off, be together alone.'

'When was this?' Emma asked.

The long eyebrows puckered over Shang's nose. 'Not so long. Six o'clock maybe?'

'And they phoned the cottage here?'

He nodded, and glanced at his wife for confirmation. 'Something wrong, Mrs Backston?'

Emma said softly, 'I don't know.' But as she climbed the stair to the kitchen again, she knew there was. *Setting up a scene. We're seeing what they want us to see.*

LOVE'S FATAL TRAGEDY . . .

Zal was at the lot already when she phoned.

Madge will kill him . . . Frank will kill him . . .

'Yeah?' He had an office the size of Kitty's upstairs bathroom, where he kept his lenses and his notes. She knew he was sitting at his cluttered desk, feet propped on the wastepaper basket.

'Zal,' she said quietly. 'I don't know what's happening, but I think something's happened to Kitty. I think . . . this sounds so stupid, but I think she may have been kidnapped.'

He didn't say, *Oh, come on!* Or, *Why would anybody . . .?*

'Who by?'

'Sid Gross,' said Emma. 'Working for Mr Crain's son. He – Timothy Crain – was in Los Angeles last Wednesday night, the day of Mr Festraw's murder. Mr Cornero's coat-check girl recognized him with Gross at some nightclub in Los Feliz. That was on the paper I got from Mr Cornero this afternoon. When I got home Kitty was gone, and one of the dogs is hurt – it looks as if he'd been kicked. Mr Shang tells me he got a telephone call, supposedly from one of Mr Crain's employees—'

'You at the house? I'll be there in ten minutes.'

She had no idea what he was going to say to Madge Burdon, and didn't ask. She barely had time to say, 'Thank you,' when he hung up.

EIGHTEEN

When she passed through the living room to fetch the first-aid kit from the bathroom, Emma halted, conscious again of the last, fading whiff of a half-familiar smell there. A smell that brought back something, some feeling of horror . . .

She came back into the kitchen, snipped Chang Ming's fur clear of the wound and daubed the abraded flesh with rubbing alcohol, a treatment the little dog bore with stoic patience. She manipulated his foreleg gently to make sure no bones had been broken, and indeed, once she'd set down their food bowls the limp almost disappeared. She returned to the living room, cringing at whatever that was . . .

. . . whatever that was . . .

Chloroform. The ambulances she'd driven from the Oxford station out to Bicester Hospital had reeked of it. Sometimes she still smelled it in her dreams.

I was right. I'm not making this up.

Headlights swept across the windows in the growing dusk. Zal said, 'What happened?' as Emma opened the door. 'You're sure it was Crain?'

'The woman who saw him was sure. She used to wait tables at a café where young Mr Crain had lunch in New York. She knew him by sight because he was such a bad customer. Mr Crain – Kitty's Mr Crain – and I spent Saturday evening together and his son's name came up in the conversation. I'm reasonably sure he would have said something, had he known his son was in town. The man who phoned the Shangs said Mr Crain and Kitty had decided, just like that, to run off on vacation together, but she'd never have left without feeding the dogs. And I honestly don't think she would have gone without them at all. In either case she'd have left me a note. And Chang Ming was hurt.' She stooped, to touch the red dog's head where he sat beside her ankle. 'Kicked, it looks like.'

Zal said, '*Momzer*. You phone Crain's place?'

'I was about to when you arrived. According to Mr Cornero, Crain the Younger has used his father's property more than once, as collateral on loans, without Mr Crain's knowledge. I suspect all this has something to do with that.'

'Why bring Kitty into it?'

'Because she's notorious,' said Emma quietly. 'Because she's the Goddess of the Silver Screen. Because she has "It". Her name has been plastered across every newspaper in the country for the past week and a half. So when Mr Crain – and his scandalous mistress – both turn up dead, nobody is going to run about investigating his son's financial activities.'

Zal's eyebrows went up, as if half admiring the scheme. 'Activities that'd come to light when Standard Oil runs a title check on the property that Daddy Crain's about to sell them?'

'Yes,' Emma said quietly. 'But only if Timothy Crain isn't the owner of them himself. Kitty is the obvious suspect in his murder – like the newspaper said, "Love's Fatal Tragedy". It's a story everyone will buy. But only if she's dead.'

Zal repeated the Yiddish word he'd used when informed of the presence of Rex Festraw in Kitty's dressing room last Wednesday. 'Makes sense. She's trashy, she's flashy, she's a "celluloid wanton" and thanks to the Pettingers and Thelma Turnbit, everybody in the country knows her name. You know where this Villa Whatever is?' he went on, crossing to the telephone niche. 'It's the only place where Gross and Junior could set up a show like that . . . if you're right. And I think you are.' He turned his head slightly, frowning. Sniffing.

'I think – I'm not sure – that what you smell is chloroform,' said Emma. 'And no, I'm not certain of any of this. But it makes sense. Kitty said the Villa was right on the edge of a forest, but I've never heard of a forest anywhere in two hundred miles . . .'

'There is actually one up in Big Bear. Or it could be Angeles National Forest – or any one of a whole string of national forests in the other direction, going up the coast. They might know at Crain's, if you've got the number – there's no phone at this Villa, is there?'

'Not hooked up.' She opened the drawer beneath the

telephone cabinet itself, with a whispered prayer of thanks
that one of the first things she'd done when entering her sister-
in-law's household last October had been to sort and arrange
its contents. 'Nor is the plumbing, evidently . . .'

'You got a California map?'

'In that cabinet.' She heard Zal dialing behind her as she
went up the stairs. A few minutes later, in the midst of digging
through the scented chaos of Kitty's bureau drawers, she heard
his voice, short questions spaced as if he were getting shorter
answers. When she came downstairs, empty-handed, he was
back in the living room, unfolding one of the California Auto
Club's enormous printed maps on the glass-and-chrome coffee
table, the dogs clustering around his feet as if he were unwrap-
ping a sandwich.

'No answer at his office.' He spoke without looking up.
'His butler says he got a call about six o'clock from a voice
he didn't recognize, saying, "This is Andy Wilkins, I'm an
old friend of Mr Crain's and he asked me to phone you and
let you know he'll be late getting home tonight. We met at
Joy's" – that's the drugstore across the street from Crain's
office on Highland – "and we're having dinner". Then he hung
up before the butler could ask him where, or could he speak
to Mr Crain. No soap on the Villa?'

She shook her head.

'This look familiar?' He held up a business card. On one side
was neatly printed the name, office address, and office telephone
number of Ambrose Crain. On the other, a firm, regular hand
she recognized had written: *100 Mint Canyon Road.*

Again she shook her head. 'It's Mr Crain's writing, though.'

'His butler said the Villa Foresta is on the edge of the Angeles
National Forest . . . Here we go.' He stabbed at the column of
infinitesimally tiny print at one side of the map, then scanned
the map itself.

'Kitty said it's about two hours' drive north of here.'

'Back-side of the mountains, then. This would be easier if
we knew what Kitty thinks she means when she says "north".'

Emma sat beside him on the couch, leaned around his arm.
Vast pale-green blocks of empty country, threaded with white
roads.

'Here we go. Mint Canyon Road – Christ, that's a distance. And if it turns out that's just the address of some lady who breeds Pekinese . . .' Zal paused, the map half folded-up again in his hands. 'Then I guess we'll have lost.' He scooped his cap from the coffee table where he'd dropped it, led the way out onto the porch, down the steps to the waiting car. Emma gathered her coat and handbag, locked the door behind her, descended as the last dove-blue darkness was deepening to indigo.

'Do you . . .?' she began as she got in, and stopped herself, self-conscious and wondering if she'd ever remotely thought that she'd be uttering the words . . .

Zal glanced at her, headlight glare slipping off the lenses of his glasses as he maneuvered the Ford up the steep drive.

'Do you have any kind of weapon?' She almost blushed: *I sound like someone in a blood-and-thunder novel . . .*

'Glovebox,' he said. 'It's Dirk Silver's.'

She opened it, only long enough to see that the automatic pistol was there.

'It's a Luger. I knew he kept one in his dressing room. God knows when it was last cleaned or fired, or whether he has a permit to carry the thing. I sure don't. It is loaded . . .' He braked halfway up the drive. 'Does Kitty have one? I'd rather have one that won't blow up in my hand. She had the gun Gross must have swiped from her dressing room to shoot Festraw with . . .'

'I've never heard her speak of another. Of course,' she added, 'I'd never heard her speak of the murder weapon, either . . . But I've just gone through her bureau looking for the address of the villa, and I didn't see one. If there's another in the house, I doubt I could find it in under two hours.'

He let in the clutch. Gravel spurted from the wheels as they lunged up the drive. 'That's our girl.'

'There's two ways of getting there.' The hills rose up around them. Spots of light amid trees that were no more than dark within darkness, where the Gloria Swansons and Rudolph Valentinos and Charlie Chaplins of the world sat on their terraces, looking down on the electric fires of Babylon, or out towards the endless sea. 'We can take this road northwest around the corner of the San Gabriels, then follow the Southern Pacific right-of-way back along the feet of the hills. That's about an hour, hour and a half at this time of night. Two hours in traffic. If we cut straight through the hills through Burbank and Altadena we can probably get there in forty-five minutes – if we don't blow a tire. That road is pretty primitive.'

Emma's heart gave a little lurch. 'What do you recommend?' The steadiness of her own voice surprised her. 'You say Mr Crain's butler got his call at about six, which must be shortly after Young Mr Crain secured his father's company in some way. It's . . .' She glanced at her watch. 'It's just after eight now. They have to have both of them there at the villa, and they have to do whatever they need to do, to set up the house to look like a love-nest killing.'

'If that's what's happening.'

'Do you think it is?'

'I do.' He was barely a shadow against the glare of his headlights. 'Mostly because Tim Crain's got the money to set up Festraw's murder, in order to make Kitty famous coast-to-coast as a woman who'd kill a lover.'

'And set it up in such a way that it *won't* get her put in jail. *That*,' agreed Emma, 'was clever. That the evidence was just enough to make all the newspapers, but would leave her still within his reach. He must have put detectives out to find Mr Festraw in New York, the minute he heard that the land he'd already signed over as collateral on some stock transaction was going to be sold and title-checked . . . He *would* be able to get that information, wouldn't he?'

'Oh, sure. If he follows market news and reports like Crain says he does . . . And if *I* were making hanky-panky with somebody else's real estate, you bet I'd have somebody in one of the brokerage houses keeping an eye on it. But we both could be wrong.'

'And we could be wrong about where this is all taking place,' said Emma quietly. 'Although I can't think of a place where Timothy Crain would have more control of the . . . the *set-dressing* of his father's murder by a scandalous woman. Our only alternative is to call the Los Angeles county sheriff . . .'

'Yeah, without a shred of proof and no idea where this is actually taking place, in four thousand square miles of LA county. They're gonna rush right out to thwart *that* crime.'

'Go through the hills.' She let her breath go in a little sigh. 'I think . . . I think we don't have any time to lose.'

The hillside homes disappeared in the dark. The lights of the village of Burbank among its orchards twinkled for a moment, then also were gone. The hills closed in around the little car, and when Emma wound the window down, the wind that flowed over them was redolent with the smells of dust and sagebrush. She could see the strip of ill-kept asphalt that looked barely newer than the ruined pavement that had led up Sycamore Canyon Saturday night, and wondered how robust the tires on the little Ford were.

And whether Sid Gross had anyone else with him.

At length she said, 'I'm sorry about calling you—'

'Herbie was dying for the chance to shoot. It's cut-and-dried stuff, extras running through the burning city screaming.'

'Even so—'

'Hey.' He took his hand from the wheel long enough to grasp her wrist. 'I love Kitty. She drives me nuts, but she's like a sister to me. And I couldn't let you . . .' He hesitated.

'There's nothing I could have done,' said Emma, 'if you hadn't come when I called.'

'I know. And I'm pretty sure you're right about what's going on. And when the newspapers came out about finding her body, I couldn't let you go through your life wondering if there was something you could have done.'

'Thank you.' There didn't seem to be much else to say. Around them the hills loomed taller, lightless as velvet under a velvet sky. There was still no sign whatsoever of a forest, but the pavement dwindled to little more than a graded track of broken asphalt, cut by watercourses and walled in by prickly shoulder-high brush, barely visible in the feeble gleam of the headlamps. Zal drove swiftly but carefully, the car swaying with the uneven roadbed but never jolting.

'Do you . . .?' Again she hesitated.

'Do I know how to shoot a gun?' She could hear the side-long flicker of his half-grin. And, more soberly, when she didn't reply: 'Or, do I think I can pull the trigger on another human being?' Silence for a time, and the soft grind of the tires on gravel. She remembered that he had spoken of dodging the draft. 'Can you shoot?'

Emma shook her head. 'Jim – my husband – offered to teach me, but I'm afraid I . . . I thought too much about what it would mean, to actually be ready to kill someone. And if one doesn't mean it, I don't expect one can be convincingly threatening in an emergency.'

'You'd be surprised.'

'That's what Jim said. *Have* you ever shot anyone?'

He said, 'Whoa,' and braked, cutting the headlights as another pair of far-off lights pin-pricked the blackness before him. In liquid moonlight Emma had the impression they'd come out on a wider road that curved down to their left, the direction from which the other car was coming. Uphill, she thought. Framed by the shoulders of the hills around them she had a dim sense of flat land beyond, and infinitely far off, a tiny salting of lights.

She kept silent, watching the car-lights approach. She recalled the headlights that Zal had mentioned seeing in their rear-vision mirror, twice or thrice on the twisty drive along the backbone of the Santa Monica hills, and the silent bulk of a car slipping away down Ivarene Street in the wake of Peggy's departure. Invisible in the blackness she could tell nothing of Zal's face. She herself felt curiously without fear.

We're dealing with people who calmly plan to kill Kitty and Mr Crain for money. Have been planning it for weeks. Had killed Mr Festraw the way a cook wrings a chicken's neck, because that's what's on the dinner menu . . . not that the man was any great loss. But she knew to the marrow of her bones that it wouldn't have mattered to these people – Sid Gross, and his employer Timothy Crain – if he had been. He was just a convenient piece of a convenient scheme.

How much money did one get in a murky business deal involving oil wells and stock futures, anyway?

Quite a bit, it sounded like.

She remembered the way Mr Crain had glanced aside when the subject of his son had arisen. *Even now, I find myself entangled in the past*, he had said. *Preoccupied by things I did wrong, or should have done differently . . .*

Concerning his son?

Heard in her mind Kitty's voice, casually speaking of an early swain in her chorus-dancing days. *Well, he was passionately in love with me but if his father'd cut him off he had no way – nothing – of making his own living. None of them do, you know. They can sell stocks but they can't wash dishes.*

She wondered if Mr Crain had given his son any ultimatum.

Kitty's in that car . . .

The headlights swung, disappeared around the shoulder of a hill. Her heart was pounding but she still didn't feel any fear. *How far is the villa from the main road? Did he see our headlights before Zal switched them off?*

Zal let in the clutch, guiding the car – carefully – by moonlight down the grade. In a startlingly matter-of-fact tone, Emma asked, 'Will they be able to hear us?'

'Depends on how many of them there are. If Junior's smart it'll be just him and Gross, unless he wants to be paying blackmail for the rest of his life. And if Gross is smart, he'll watch *his* back for the rest of *his* life. This may be the first time Junior's killed for gain. I've been told the second time's always easier.'

'Jim said that about war.'

Two stone plinths, barely visible in the gloom, marked a driveway that led downhill to the left. In the moonlight – only a few days past full – Emma could make out the brass numbers on one of the plinths: 100. As Zal turned the car between them she felt behind her breastbone the breathless sensation she'd had, just before her first piano recital. Chopin's second piano sonata. Her fingers – her wrists – twitched with the recollection: slow dark opening, then flickering notes like fire . . . *This is a stupid time to be remembering that . . .*

Across a shallow valley three enormous windows threw lakes of topaz out into the darkness. Zal cut the engine, steered the little Ford in silence over what felt like new paving, smooth and silent. Every molecule of Emma's flesh cringed, waiting for the sounds of shots that would tell her they were too late.

In moonlight and the residual glow from the windows, she saw there were two cars, parked in front of the three wide, shallow steps that ascended to a tiled terrace outside the windows. Trees made dark clouds beside the house, the only sign Emma had seen so far of the 'forest' of which everyone had spoken. In California, did two trees constitute a forest?

Why am I thinking this? If those men have guns I may be dead in the next ten minutes. WE may be dead . . . myself, Zal, Kitty, Mr Crain . . .

Poor Aunt Estelle will arrive to that news . . .

Through the windows she could see a couch, a chair, a long narrow refectory table, Renaissance antiques or very good fakes. A door of that big tapestried room opened and a thinnish, balding man came in, taller than Mr Crain but with enough resemblance to his sharp-featured face that she guessed at once that this was Timothy. He was speaking over his shoulder to someone in the dark of the hall.

A moment later a bigger man came in, tall, broad, and just the respectable side of fat. Emma remembered that 'XLarge' notation on Millie's costume log.

He was carrying Kitty in his arms.

She was unconscious, limp as a rag doll in the frock of wine-colored charmeuse she'd had on that afternoon, waiting for her manicurist. Gross – the man had to be Sid Gross, she could see the mole on his nose – dumped her into one of the chairs, and turned as Timothy crossed to the big carven fireplace, gesturing like a man giving instructions.

'You stay here.' Zal had stopped the car far back enough from the house that, hopefully, it wouldn't be seen from those great windows. *Not with the lamps on inside, it won't . . .*

He took the Luger from the glovebox, and in the darkness his voice was grim and steady. 'I'm going to check the other cars to see if there's another weapon in either of them, and then I'll see if there's a way into the house. You keep the doors locked and be ready to start up and get the hell out of here the minute there's trouble. Don't stick around waiting for me. They won't be able to find me in the hills. Starter-pedal on the floor here, button on the dash here . . . All right?'

She whispered, 'All right.'

He started to get out of the car, leaned back in, caught her by the shoulders and kissed her, hard. Then he slipped out and vanished almost at once into the darkness.

The three large windows framed the scene within like a triple proscenium arch. Evidently no drapes had yet been hung. Timothy Crain was still giving instructions in dumb-show; Gross nodded, then went out the door into the dark of the house once more. The millionaire's son went to the sofa, bent over it and with a visible effort dragged up the man who, up until that moment, had lain out of sight there. The whole scene was about thirty feet away but Emma recognized Ambrose Crain's slender form, gray suit, and white head lolling as his son propped him in a corner of the seat. Timothy studied his father for a moment – Emma wasn't close enough to see his expression – then changed his position, and turned to tip over the low, long coffee table in front of the couch. Emma saw that he was wearing gloves. When Sid Gross came back in, he was wearing them, too.

Gross bent to the humidor that had been on the coffee table, which had flown open when the table was upset, spilling cigars on the Persian carpet. Young Mr Crain – though Kitty was right, Emma thought, thirty-five at least, unhealthily pallid, the bare spot on his scalp blotchy with eczema – stepped over to him with a rebuke, and there was a brief argument. *It's got to look natural*, thought Emma. *It can't look as if a third – or a fourth – person was here . . .*

She was reminded again of Ned Bergen, arranging the empress's chamber for Marcus Maximus to stride in by moon-light . . .

When Gross handed Young Crain a small silver box, and Young Crain turned to calculate where it should fall if it were knocked off the table, the detective quickly stooped and helped himself to a half-dozen of the scattered cigars. (*Come ON, Zal, where are you . . .?*) Young Crain flipped the silver box open and dusted a little white powder on Kitty's chest, then dabbed the fingertips of her right hand in it (*You'll never get away with that, everyone in Hollywood knows she hasn't touched the stuff since February . . .*). With a flick of his hand he flung box and its remaining contents obliquely across the floor.

Star Slays Lover and Self in Dope Frenzy . . .

Of course he'll get away with it. Standard Oil's going to pay him millions for that Long Beach land.

Love's Fatal Tragedy . . .

Young Crain gave another curt order. Gross went to the decidedly un-Renaissance liquor cabinet behind a carved screen, came back with two glasses and a satchel. The satchel contained two nearly-empty bottles – by their shapes and color Emma guessed one was Gordon's gin, the other imported whiskey of some kind. Young Crain sprinkled whiskey over his father's body and the couch, sloshed the other glass with gin and dropped it on the floor.

Zal, where ARE you . . .?

Gross picked Kitty up, carried her to the side of the fireplace, laid her face-down on the floor. Both men stood back, considering the scene.

ZAL . . .!

Young Crain nodded briskly, dug in his pocket for an envelope and handed it to Gross. Gross counted what was in it, shoved it into the breast of his jacket, and took out a gun.

NINETEEN

Emma jammed the starter-pedal with her foot, hit the self-starter, yanked the car into gear and slammed the accelerator. The Ford roared into life – Gross and Young Crain snapping around like two characters in a play – and the little car bounced as it leaped up the shallow steps to the terrace . . .

Emma's foot rammed to the floorboards and she thought, *Now don't close your eyes or you'll run over poor Mr Crain . . .*

She hit the windows in an explosion of flying glass, slammed on the brake, and prayed that Zal was somewhere close by as she opened the door.

Gross brought the gun up and Young Crain swatted the weapon aside.

'Don't be silly,' said Emma, in the tone that had worked when one of Lawrence Pendergast's drunk and rampant friends had cornered her in the pantry. 'How are you going to account for a third corpse? Or a bloodstain on this carpet? They'll test the blood, you know,' she added, as Gross's gun wavered in his hand. Sam Wyatt had told her that much. 'They'll know it isn't either Mr Crain's or Miss de la Rose's.'

Gross looked at Young Crain. Emma could almost see a title-card, *'Wadda we do now, Boss?'* The wily Odysseus would have rolled his eyes in disgust.

'Mr Devine is already on his way back to Pasadena,' Emma went on, extemporizing from the dialog of every film she'd ever seen. 'Someone recognized you, Mr Crain, at Doolittle's Wednesday—'

The hall door opened and for an instant Emma's heart leapt to her throat, but it was, thank God, Zal, Luger in hand.

Gross's hands were already coming up in surrender when Young Crain lunged at him, almost tripping in the process, grabbed the gun he held, and fired at Zal. Zal ducked, and

Young Crain knocked the carved screen over into him, sending Zal's Luger flying. Young Crain spun, again almost over-balancing himself, and fired at Emma – who heard the clang of a bullet hit metal as she dodged behind the Ford's open door. As he turned back toward Zal, Kitty reared herself up unsteadily onto one hand, Zal's dropped Luger in the other.

Gross had already leaped behind the couch, and Timothy Crain turned and quite deliberately – at a distance of five feet – shot him. Then he bolted like a deer for the broken window and pelted into the night. Kitty fired after him – the police later found that bullet lodged in the ceiling – and Zal scrambled out from under the heavy screen, yet another gun in hand. ('Found it in the glovebox of Crain's car,' he told her later.)

Gross meanwhile had begun to sob, 'I'm hit! I'm hit! Oh, God!' and Emma, true to her VAD training, ran to his side. Zal ran to his other side and waved Emma back, searched the groaning detective for another weapon even as Kitty staggered to her feet and stumbled toward the windows, Luger held out at arm's length.

Emma caught her as she passed, her mind filled with bullets coming out of the dark, but Zal, tearing open Gross's coat to reveal a huge soak of blood over his right hip, said, 'He won't get far. Do the phones here work, Kit?'

'I don't . . .' She looked hazily around her. 'Where *are* we? Ambrose!' She fell to her knees beside the couch, gathered her elderly lover into her arms. 'Oh, Ambrose! Oh, my God, is he all right?'

Emma took the gun away from her. *We need an extra henchman*, she thought, as Gross continued to gasp and sob – he was quite clearly really injured, and not just faking in order to grab Emma as a hostage (which was how Sam Wyatt would have handled the scene . . .). Zal was pulling off his sweater, and then his shirt (prudently keeping hold of his gun); Emma tucked the Luger down into the couch cushions in such a way that even if it went off it would only shoot the floor, and pulling up her skirt, tore the flounce from her petticoat, which appeared to be much simpler to do in the movies than it was in actual fact . . . but perhaps that was because her hands had begun to shake.

Zal tore open the buckle of Gross's belt, undid his flies, and pulled his trousers down. He wadded sweater and shirt on either side of the streaming wounds in his hip and bound them tight with the strip of petticoat-silk. Emma meanwhile crossed to the liquor cabinet – miraculously still standing on its legs – and found another bottle of gin and three of Apollinaris water, as well as two small, neatly-folded bar towels.

'What happened to him?' Kitty looked up at her as she returned to the couch. 'Is he – Ambrose!' He stirred in her arms, as Emma soaked a towel with the water and applied it to his face. 'Oh,' she added, looking around her again. 'We must be at the villa! Thank you, dearest.' Emma had put three fingers of gin in the glass. Kitty took it from her hand, drank most of it, and poured the remainder between the old man's gray lips.

Mr Crain coughed. He whispered, 'Kitty . . .' and made a vague gesture with his hand.

'Gimme some of that water, Em.' Zal held out his hand. 'The phone, Kit – does it work?'

She brushed back her hair with the back of her wrist. 'I don't think so. That's one of the things we were waiting for. And – was that *Tim Crain*? Oh, Ambrose . . .' For a moment she turned distractedly back to the old man. Then: 'Was *he* behind it all? I didn't think he ever left New York! He'll be long gone—'

'Not really.' Zal finished giving his own patient some of the water, then helped him lie back again. 'Not if I can get to Palmdale fast enough. I disconnected the self-starter motors in both cars outside. Kitty' – he rose to his knees, looking over the back of the couch at her – 'are you OK? I mean, could you read a map while Emma drives? I think the closest hospital is Olive View – you feel all right, Mr Crain?'

The old man managed to say, 'I . . . I think so. Is that Kitty?' He groped for her hand, and shook his head woozily. 'Tim – My son . . . I – I thought he was here – I mean I thought he was at my office . . .'

'Get the map out of my car. What's left of my car.' Zal glanced ruefully at the Ford, sitting with four blown tires and its radiator hissing as water streamed from it onto the glass-strewn carpet. 'Easy come, easy go . . . You know Sylmar, Kit? Think you can get Emma there?'

'I can drive.' She lifted her chin proudly while steadying herself on a corner of the couch as she rose.

'Darling' – Emma had heard those words in that tone of voice before – 'we have no idea what Mr Gross might have injected you with after he chloroformed you. And if you'd had anything to drink—'

'Only some gin.' Kitty refilled the glass, and re-emptied it, with the virtuous air of one who has abstained all night. Then she looked down at the bosom of her dress, and brushed at the drift of white powder. 'And I'll *swear* I never took so much as a *sniff* of dope . . .' She turned, and hastily checked her reflection in the mirror. 'Oh,' she gasped. 'Oh, I look *terrible*—'

Zal was right, Emma reflected. Kitty never disappointed.

'Get me to a doctor,' whimpered Mr Gross, at Emma's feet. 'For the love of God, get me to a doctor—'

'It would serve you right if we *left* you here.' Kitty put a knee on the couch to look over the back of it at him. From her expression, Emma almost expected her to add, *Fools, where is your Redeemer now?* 'I mean, the police are going to be along—'

'Soon as I can get to Palmdale and call them,' said Zal. 'But I think . . .' He came around the couch and felt Crain's hands, something Emma had done already. They were ice-cold. 'I think Mr Crain, as well as First Murderer down here, should get looked at pretty quick. And I for one don't like the idea of leaving you ladies here with Junior running around loose out there in the dark. You don't happen to know if Junior knows anything about cars, do you, Kit?'

Mr Crain was unconscious again.

Feeling rather as if she'd blundered into one of those nursery riddles about fox, geese, and a bag of corn, Emma followed Zal out into the darkness, with the electric torch from the wrecked coupe in one hand and the Luger in the other. She divided her attention between the blackness of the hills beyond the glow of the villa's lights, and the stage-set brightness of the living room on the other side of the broken windows, half fearful that Timothy Crain would come springing out of the night with a gun in each fist and three previously unaccounted for henchmen at his heels. *If Sam were writing this, he would . . .*

The larger – and newer – of the two cars outside the villa was a long-nosed monster with a collapsible roof – fortunately in its raised position – velvet upholstery and gold-plated door-handles. Zal reconnected the starter, and drove it up the shallow steps onto the terrace, so that he and Emma could move Gross into it, using a tarpaulin which the plumbers had left on the bathroom floor as a makeshift stretcher. Kitty followed, pointing the Luger in all directions around her at the hills.

'We really do need a henchman . . .' Emma panted, as they gently maneuvered the wounded man into the back seat.

'If we had one,' returned Zal, 'he'd be in the kitchen even as we speak, making coffee.'

Mr Crain could be brought back to consciousness long enough to stagger to the car, but he was clearly under the influence of something.

'Which makes sense,' said Emma, 'if his son planned this to look like a . . . a murder-suicide during a drug-addled lover's quarrel. Don't they test a victim's blood and stomach contents?'

'If somebody hasn't slipped the coroner a thousand dollars they do,' agreed Zal. He fetched a pail, a rubber tube, and, after a little searching, a funnel from among the plumber's things in the bathroom, and siphoned the remaining gasoline from the disabled Ford, to pour into the tanks of both other vehicles. 'That should get you back to town all right. Take a left at the top of the drive, another left on the road when you get down out of the mountains, and follow that trail along the Southern Pacific tracks into Sylmar.'

Emma took a deep breath. 'All right.' *If Queen Boadicea could lead an army to sack Londinium, I can certainly cope with this.*

Zal helped her into the driver's seat, then leaned down again to kiss her lips. 'You OK?' His mustaches tasted of gasoline. Emma didn't care.

She nodded, not terribly certain whether this was true and wondering when the blood-rush of battle – which both Jim and Miles had told her about – was going to wear off, and what she'd do if this happened before they reached the hospital. Men she'd nursed in London had spoken of this, too: *Like as if somebody'd thrown a switch, miss*, was how one Devonshire man had put it, when she'd moved through the ward from bed to bed, making sure the men she'd ferried from the station were well and resting on the following day. And another had told her, *If we'd had a push on, an' come back to the trench, I knew I dasn't sit down 'til the whole show was over, for once I let mesel' get a bit cold I knew I'd never stand up again.*

'I think so. Yourself?'

And, when he'd nodded, she added, 'Thank you. I don't think I've ever been so glad to see anyone in my life.'

He kissed her again. 'Scipio Africanus has nothing on you, Em.' And, as Kitty clambered into the passenger seat with the Luger in one hand and the Auto Club roadmap in the other, 'See you ladies in Babylon.'

Two Los Angeles County sheriffs were waiting in the driveway when Emma drove up to Olive View Sanitarium, so she knew Zal had successfully reached a telephone. Olive View was a low building in the Spanish style that reminded her powerfully of the original hacienda back at Foremost Productions, and lit up like a Christmas tree. Kitty had fallen asleep within minutes of leaving the Villa Foresta. In between picking her way cautiously down the graded – but barely paved – road from the hills, and the scarcely-better 'trail' that paralleled the railway tracks, Emma had braked a half-dozen times to consult the Auto Club map by the light of Zal's electric torch. Even with the windows down she could smell, faintly, the scent of blood from the rear seat, and prayed that this was only seepage from Mr Gross's wounds and not a major hemorrhage (*Not that he doesn't deserve it . . . but still . . .*).

The car was eerily silent, the stars above the hills cold and steady in the bleached landscape of indigo and silver. The metallic awfulness of gasoline still lingered on her lips, and she shook her head a little, that Zal would have retained the presence of mind to check that after a drive of some eighty miles, there would still be enough fuel to get back to town.

Of course Zal would check.

It occurred to her how completely she trusted the man.

And, she reflected – if she read his voice and his words and his touch aright – how completely he trusted her. When she had telephoned the studio, it had never occurred to her – though she knew how dedicated was his commitment to his work – that he'd say, 'Em, we're about to start filming! Call the police.'

The brown-uniformed officer opened the car door for her, asked, 'Mrs Blackstone?' and two orderlies hastened from the hospital door with a wheeled stretcher. 'Is this Mr Gross?' He nodded toward the man being gently lifted from the back seat.

'Mr Sid Gross, yes,' said Emma. 'He attempted to murder me – and Miss de la Rose' – the men's eyes got big as they recognized Kitty, who raised her head and pushed the dark maelstrom of her hair from her face – 'earlier this evening. Mr Crain as well.' Another orderly was helping the groggy millionaire to stand. 'I believe he's been drugged, as well as chloroformed earlier this evening.'

'Drugged, hell.' Kitty rubbed her forehead with a look of agony in her eyes as she climbed from the front seat of the car. Emma noted with relief that she'd already brushed the cocaine from her frock. Questions about *that* would be all they'd need. 'I feel like I've had about half a bottle of gin poured down my throat, darling – and I didn't even enjoy it. I don't even *remember* it. *Please* don't tell us we're under arrest,' she added, widening those beautiful eyes at the nearest sheriff.

He capitulated with the speed of the leading man in any one of her past fifteen films. 'Not arrest, m'am – Miss de la Rose. But we do need to ask you some questions, and probably the Los Angeles Police will be along to ask you some more . . . and you really should see a doctor—'

'And don't try to tell anyone anything,' warned Emma, 'until you're talking to the sheriffs. Oh, dear,' she added. 'I wonder if anyone's thought to call Mr Fishbein?'

And she realized as she said it that she had definitely been in Hollywood too long.

What had begun as a tiring afternoon turned into a very, very long night. It seemed to Emma that she had taken the streetcar along Sunset Boulevard to the Bel Giardino in some other

year – or some other lifetime. Part of this, she realized at about
one o'clock in the morning, was simply the effect of hunger.
When Zal walked into the sanitarium's small lounge bearing
a greasy paper sack of sandwiches from a railroad workers'
bar in Palmdale, she flung herself into his arms, kissed him,
and almost wept.

'Wow,' said Zal. 'This works better than booze!'

Conrad Fishbein came in fifteen minutes later – pink and
cheerful with his hair combed and his beard trimmed – trailed
by Al Spiegelmann, who looked as if he'd been pulled, still
damp, out of the bottom of a laundry bag. Both men stared
hungrily at the sandwich she and Zal had been saving for Kitty,
until Emma rose and went into the corridor, found the little
cluster of nurses and orderlies chattering excitedly at the nurses'
station, and asked, 'Is there any possibility that the kitchen
could be opened up? The police are going to be here shortly,
and it looks like we may be here for quite some time. Of
course,' she added, 'it goes without saying that Mr Crain will
reimburse the hospital for whatever inconvenience this causes
you.'

By the time the police arrived, an orderly had brought in a
tray of vegetarian sandwiches (healthful but nowhere near as
good as the ones from Rennie's Railway Café) and enough
coffee to revive the American Expeditionary Force.

Emma told her story to the sheriff's deputies and then to
Detective Meyer, and produced from her handbag (which she
had managed to keep with her through mayhem, destruction,
vehicular assault and attempted murder) the papers Tony
Cornero had given her what seemed like a hundred and fifty
years ago at the Bel. 'I had reason to suspect that Mr Sid
Gross was the driver of a car that attempted to run myself
and Mr Rokatansky off the coast highway Saturday night,'
she said. 'I was told that the car itself was found by the
Pasadena police in the Santa Susanna mountains. Mr Cornero
had very kindly offered to use his resources to find out what
he could.'

'We know all about Sid Gross, m'am.' Avram Meyer fished
a pack of cigarettes from his pocket, then replaced it a little
self-consciously. 'He came out from under ether singin' like

a canary. But I'd like to get your story before I tell you what his is.'

'You don't have to answer anything, Mrs Blackstone,' said Spiegelmann, around a mouthful of Swiss cheese and whole-meal bread. 'And I would like it to go on record that it was Mr Crain, Senior, who hired Mr Cornero, on the recommendation of a private detective, and that Mrs Blackstone had no previous connection or acquaintance with Mr Cornero or any of his associates.'

'So noted,' agreed Meyer, as Mr Spiegelmann rather ostentatiously fished for something – a billfold, perhaps? – in his breast pocket, and Emma made herself look as innocent as she knew how. 'Can I have one of those sandwiches?'

And in fact, though she felt a little odd about it under the circumstances, the story she told was the unvarnished truth: how she had recalled Mr Crain's remarks about his son never leaving New York; how a remark made by someone at the Bel Giardino – she did not recall who (*Well, REASONABLY unvarnished, anyway . . .*) – seemed to indicate that the younger Mr Crain might easily have been involved in financial chicanery with his father's oil property in Signal Hill; how she had returned to the house at seven to find Miss de la Rose gone, one of the dogs injured, and the air smelling faintly of chloroform, an odor she recognized from her days driving an ambulance during the War.

'It occurred to me, you see,' she said, 'that if anything happened to Mr Crain, the first person to be suspected would of course be his son – particularly if this was not the first time he'd used his father's property as collateral for his own financial speculations. But if his father were linked with a notorious screen star, who would even then be on trial for the murder of her ex-husband – particularly if Miss de la Rose were found dead at the scene herself, with a gun in her hand – no one would so much as glance at his son's dealings. Particularly,' she added, 'if he could produce witnesses that he was in New York at the time.'

Meyer's smile slowly widened in his villainous Van Dyke. 'Well, aren't you the clever girl – m'am,' he added. 'From what Gross has coughed up so far, you guessed it pretty much

down the line: he's the one who got onto the Foremost lot the
week before last and swiped the gun and the stationery from
Miss de la Rose's dressing room. And he's the one who plugged
Festraw, the minute Festraw was done takin' that dressing-
room phone call from Tim Crain. He knew all about Stan the
Mark payin' for Festraw to come out to LA . . .'

'Did Mr Festraw actually intend to blackmail Miss de la
Rose?' asked Emma curiously.

'Sounds like he thought that was what the whole thing was
about, yeah,' agreed the detective. 'Crain using Festraw to put
the squeeze on Miss de la Rose. Festraw didn't know a thing
about the letters – Gross planted those in the dressing room,
and on Festraw, after Festraw was dead . . . and in Festraw's
room . . .'

'Sounds like Gross had a lot to say for himself,' remarked
Fishbein, without losing his perpetual, friendly smile.

Meyer scratched a corner of his mustache. 'I'd be talkative
too, if after all my trouble my boss turned around and plugged
me on general principles. You mind if we take this, Mrs
Blackstone?' He held up the stapled sheets Cornero had given
her.

Spiegelmann reached across and plucked them from his
hand. 'Our office will have a copy for you in the morning,
Detective Meyer.'

Emma wondered if Tony Cornero's secretary had made a
carbon-paper copy of the list, and how much of a battle there
would be if Spiegelmann's copy turned out to contain information different from the original . . .

And then gave it up. She had to let it out of her hands
sometime, and couldn't imagine how anyone could profit from
exonerating either Crain or Gross. And she felt, simply, too
tired to try to untangle further conspiracies that may or may
not have existed.

'Mr Spiegelmann, Mr Fishbein – you may want to be with
me while I talk to Mr Rokatansky and Miss de la Rose. If
you don't mind, Mrs Blackstone . . .' He paused on the way
to the door, turned back. 'Oh, Mr Rokatansky said to give you
this. It's from the sanitarium's library.'

He handed her a copy of Macauley's *Lays of Ancient Rome*.

TWENTY

Emma finished the night in one of the sanatorium's rooms reserved for the families of patients.

Waking late the following afternoon, she was informed by Nurse Alvarez that Mr Crain's servants had appeared with a large touring car at eight, and had carried off Mr Crain – much improved by sleep and saline draughts – Miss de la Rose, and Mr Spiegelmann back to Los Angeles. But, said Nurse Alvarez, Miss de la Rose had telephoned only an hour ago, begging everyone's pardon for not remembering that Mrs Blackstone was still asleep at the sanatorium, and would they please give her whatever she asked for – and of course bill Foremost Productions for whatever inconvenience this might entail – and ask Mrs Blackstone to telephone her at Mr Crain's – or at her house – or at Foremost Productions – when she woke up?

She could just imagine Kitty getting out of the car at the house, looking at the dogs, and gasping, *Oh, nertz! We forgot Emma!*

As Zal had said, *That's our girl.*

If I go back to Oxford, Emma reflected with a sigh, *at least people will remember where they left me . . .*

But the whole idea seemed a very long way off.

She was consuming tea and toast in the shade of the cloister garden, feeling rather like Odysseus having a quiet dinner with King Alcinous and reading Macaulay's long, deliciously scholarly preface, when Zal appeared.

'There are times,' he said as he crossed the flagstones in the mild California sun, 'when I want to dunk Kitty in the rain barrel. Only Kitty would forget you were here – after you saved her life . . .'

Emma smiled, marked her place and stood. 'Did you think she wouldn't?'

'As my mother would say,' sighed Zal, '*oi gevalt*. You OK?'

They kissed. It felt as natural as smiling.

They kissed again, and stood for a long time, arms around each other, sprinkled with the dappling of pepper-tree shade. *I could have been killed last night*, thought Emma. *Or last Saturday. Zal could have been killed.*

Aunt Estelle will be here on Wednesday.

Her breath went out in a little sigh.

She said, 'I knew you'd come. Thank you. And thank you for the Macaulay—'

'It was that or Lady Paget's *Colloquies With An Unseen Friend.*'

Emma shuddered. That congeries of spiritualism, the hollow earth theory, and speculations upon the fate of Atlantis had been a favorite of Mrs Pendergast and she had been obliged to read it aloud not once but several times.

'Thank you for looking.' Emma sat again, Zal drawing up the other wicker chair. 'It wouldn't even have occurred to me that a sanatorium must have a library – at least it wouldn't have, last night. Will you have coffee? Kitty telephoned earlier this morning and told the staff here to send Mr Pugh a bill for all their inconvenience – which included accidentally leaving me behind – so they're falling over themselves to be of service to me . . . Is that more sandwiches?' She nodded toward the paper sack he'd set down beside the chair.

'Underwear,' he said. 'And a hairbrush, and a clean blouse, from Make-Up and Wardrobe – I think this was on screen in *Sparkin' in the Dark*. Millie Katz put them together when I stopped by the studio this morning to make sure the cameras are set for the retakes tomorrow. And, Madge asked me to ask you to please rewrite scenes eighty-three through eighty-seven and have St Peter actually marry Philomela and Demetrius on-screen, so people won't think they're up to anything they shouldn't be. And she needs this by tomorrow night. They caught Tim Crain.'

Emma drew a deep breath. 'Did they? Good.' Nurse Alvarez – who seemed to have been appointed (or appointed herself) guest liaison – appeared under the archways of the patio's little cloister, and crossed to them.

'Can I get you anything, Mr Rokatansky?'

'Coffee, if you would, thank you, m'am. Mounted sheriffs picked him up just north of Granite Mountain, and I guess he was almost happy to be taken in, til he found out he was under arrest. I gather he started out denying he was Timothy Crain – they found his driving license and business cards in his wallet – and then pretended he had amnesia. Meyer tell you what he got out of Gross?'

Emma nodded. 'Once we knew Gross had met with Crain it was fairly obvious what was going on. If he hadn't tried to run us off the highway I'm not sure we'd ever have known Gross was in it.'

'Well, I gather that was the one thing Gross was worried about – that Kitty would start comparing notes with Eliot Jordan about that so-called rendezvous in the film room, and start inquiries on her own. Gross figured if something went wrong, he'd be the guy to take the fall – but if Kitty died in a car smash-up, it would queer Crain's deal but leave Gross safe. Nice people.'

He shook his head, and ran his fingers along the cover of the *Lays of Ancient Rome*.

'Nicer than the Romans,' Emma pointed out.

Zal looked up and grinned. 'Meyer told me this morning they've already traced the money Stan Markham in New York sent to the Winterdon back to Junior's account, and the cost of his train ticket out here as well. I guess Junior was putting through a deal for controlling shares of Iron State Copper, that his dad had already turned down. The Long Beach property was his security. You were right – that's what this was all about.' And after a moment he added, 'That, and getting his hands on Dad's money once and for all.'

Quietly, Emma asked, 'How is Mr Crain taking it?'

'He's leaving for New York in the morning,' said Zal. 'With his lawyer, Kitty says, to see if there's anything he can do for the ex-Mrs Crain. He's also meeting with the accountants who're going to go over his son's books with a nit comb. And signing the papers to cut Junior out of his will. And consulting with Cornero's PI about how to find out whether the ex-Mrs Crain was in on it as well.'

Emma winced. 'Whether she was or she wasn't, that will
be hard.'

'I feel bad for the guy.' Zal made a small gesture, helpless
in the face of another man's pain. 'According to Meyer, Crain
Senior never saw this coming. He said he'd clashed with his
son a couple of times, and knew that Junior had stuck his hand
in the till once or twice, and had some bad debts. But you
don't think . . . Christ, you don't expect something like this.
Not from your son. And maybe your wife.'

*Do you do that, Mrs Blackstone? Want to go back and do
a second take . . .?*

'*You* don't,' said Emma softly. 'And *I* don't. And I'm sure
that young Mr Crain felt totally justified, because of his
father's affair with – as my aunt would say – a "cinema
performer".'

Zal sighed a little, and whispered, 'Jesus. Crain says –
according to Meyer – that Junior met him just outside the
Commercial Exchange Building, as he was coming out at five.
I guess the soda jerk in the drugstore across the street can testify
that Junior waited at a table beside the telephone there for forty
minutes, until it rang. He jumped up like a jack-in-the-box,
answered it, and went straight out the door and across the street,
so I'm guessing somebody in the building had been paid off to
play chicky. Crain says Junior was all over himself about how
glad he was he'd caught dear old Dad, and he had to talk to
him, and he'd give Dad a ride home.'

He smiled his thanks to Nurse Alvarez, who came out at
that point with a cup of coffee, some sugar and a little pitcher
of cream on a tray. 'I appreciate it, thank you, m'am. And
thank you – all of you – for putting up with that whole inva-
sion last night.'

'This is a hospital,' said the nurse. 'Most of our patients
are tuberculosis cases, and *very* quiet. But we're here to help.'
Leaning closer, she whispered, 'Everybody was *thrilled*. And
Miss de la Rose signed autographs, for the entire crew,
including the kitchen staff.'

As she went back into the shadows of the cloister, Zal said,
'I'm gonna talk to Crain and make sure he writes these nice
people a great big check. Maybe they didn't save *his* life, but

they could well have saved Gross's . . . and it's Gross who's gonna put Junior behind bars for the rest of his life. Crain says Junior pulled into the driveway of one of those twisty canyon drives above Sunset, got into the back seat with him, whipped out an oilskin wrapper of chloroform rags and slapped it over his face, and that was the last thing Crain knew until he woke up in the hospital. I guess Junior poured about half a bottle of cognac down his throat when he was half-conscious, so the booze would show up in the autopsy. Nice boy. The funnel was still under the seat, with his fingerprints all over it. Thought of everything.'

Emma shivered. 'So Gross was watching the house all that time?'

Zal nodded. 'Like I said, he was afraid that if Kitty – or you, because he knew you were part of her household – figured out there was a conspiracy to get her out of the way right at that time, the cops might start looking below the surface, the way you started to. I mean, if Kitty's husband turns up dead and Madge Burdon, Darlene Golden, Socrates the Elephant and thirty-seven extras all have proof of where she was at the time, so what? It's her not being able to say where she was, that smears the whole thing all over every newspaper in the state.'

Emma nodded slowly. 'It had to be notorious,' she agreed quietly. 'It had to be a scandal. Kitty *had* to be the obvious suspect. And she had to keep her mouth shut about where she really was. Gross knew about Eliot, I take it?'

'Oh, yeah. Gross did a lot of work around the studios. It was a good plan.' Zal stirred sugar into his coffee. 'It would have worked, if you'd kept your nose out of it.'

And no one would have cared, thought Emma. *Not really.*

Yes, there would have been TREMENDOUS hoopla in the papers, and Temptress of Babylon *would have done land-office business in theaters because of the scandal and murder and tragedy* . . . But in a year, or six months, or maybe just a few weeks, Foremost would have a new top star, and Mr Pugh would have a new mistress, and the cinema-going public would sigh and forget. If Camille de la Rose disappears – the way Martha Mansfield and Olive Thomas disappeared – there's always Gloria Swanson and Theda Bara and Colleen Moore and all the other Goddesses of the Silver Screen.

And I'd read the news in The Times *in the breakfast parlor of my quiet home in Oxford and think, Oh, how terrible! I knew her . . .*

Or alternately, Aunt Estelle would arrive Wednesday and make enquiries at the studio and be told, *We're so sorry, Mrs Blackstone was involved in some sort of accident Friday night . . .*

And Aunt Estelle would cry a little and get on the train for New York and . . .

And what?

And nothing.

Emma rested her forehead on her knuckles, suddenly weary with the crushing weariness of last night, and last Wednesday, and six months of brushing Pekinese and sorting out Kitty's checkbook and watching her bring home every good-looking stuntman and saxophone player in Hollywood, and wondering who was going to tamper with evidence and why . . .

A warm hand rested on her back. 'Come on,' said Zal quietly. 'Let me get you home.'

'You love this man,' said Madge Burdon. 'You lust after him the way you lust after Eliot Jordan and Ricky Dix and that stunt-rider last week at Anita Tempest's party. And here's this mealy-mouthed psalm-singin' Christian prissy-pants all over Demetrius like a cheap suit—'

'Phillymelly ain't no prissy-pants!' yelled Darlene, and cracked her gum. 'She's a woman of . . . of passion and fire, sensuous and unforgettable—'

Emma had the impression she'd read those descriptive words in one of the film magazines, only they'd been applied to someone other than Darlene's character.

'Oh, nertz! Demetrius forgets all about her for about seventy-two scenes,' Kitty retorted.

'That's what I want to see, girls!' cried Madge. 'I wanna see sparks fly! You run up that staircase like it's your man's soul you're saving from that Babylonian slut! Kitty, I want to see jealousy and contempt in every muscle of your body!'

The marble-and-gold staircase had been reassembled yesterday, just after someone had taken a belated look at the dailies of scene fifty-six and noticed a coffee cup on the bottom step. Given the amount of champagne which Kitty had consumed last night after the dismissal of the Special Hearing – and the very small hour at which she had returned home that morning – Emma reflected that she looked quite good, standing in the royal box with poor Mr Perkins, dog-sick with the hangover of the century, kneeling in chains at her feet.

Emma, who had celebrated much more circumspectly with Zal at the house, had to admit to feeling a bit sleepy herself.

The Rothstein Boys crashed into the middle of Tchaikovsky's 'Marche Slave', and Darlene hurled herself up the stair as if she planned to tear out her rival's hair, rather than fling her arms around her agonized beloved, at the top.

She didn't get the chance to do either. Just as she reached the thirtieth of the thirty-two golden steps, Kitty flung up her hand in a gesture of passion and jealousy, took half a step back, and tripped on the side of the throne.

'Cut!' Madge yelled, as the empress caught her balance. 'You OK, Kit?'

'I'm *so* sorry,' Kitty apologized. 'That was so clumsy of me. I'm just a little . . . tired this afternoon.' She smiled sweetly, as if everyone knew why she was just a little tired.

Beside her, Emma was aware of Frank Pugh standing just behind the cluster of chairs and dog boxes, watching the scene with a fatuous smile illuminating his face. 'Poor kid,' he said. 'It's all my fault. I shouldn't have kept us out so late—'

'Oh, Mr Pugh.' Emma raised her eyes to him, just as if she hadn't spent a good portion of the previous week wondering if he were a murderer . . . and just as if she didn't still think him capable of it. 'After the strain of the last few weeks, you know, I wouldn't be surprised if Kitty's all the better off for being able to relax as she did.'

He beamed, as Darlene stomped down the thirty marble steps to the arena's sands, and took her place like a passionate, sensuous, and unforgettable runner on the blocks. 'D'you think so, Duchess?'

Languidly, Kitty turned her gaze towards the studio chief

and gave him a look of smoldering allure, instants before
Madge yelled, 'Camera! Action!' and the 'Marche Slave'
blazed forth once more.

Galvanized with rage, Darlene charged up the stairs. Kitty
lifted her hand in a gesture of passion and jealousy, took half
a step forward, and stepped on Demetrius' chains, causing
him to sprawl headlong.

'Cut!' yelled Madge.

'I've seldom seen her so . . . so *happy* as she was when she
came in last night,' said Emma. *No harm in laying it on with
a trowel.* She was fairly certain that Kitty had.

Mr Pugh almost rolled over onto his back and purred.

The morning's new issue of *Screen Stories* lay on the
make-up table, glorified with the face of Camille de la Rose
in the crown of the Empress of Babylon. *THE GODDESS OF
THE SILVER SCREEN*, shrieked the letterhead. *The Queen of
'It', the Cat's Pajamas, the One and the Only . . .*

Enough to disgruntle anyone, thought Emma, even were it
not plain to everyone in the studio that Mr Pugh had accepted
Kitty's explanation that all those nasty stories about her having
dinner at the Coconut Grove with other men were the productions of Mrs Turnbit and her vile ilk. They were all part of
the horrible plot to use Kitty as a cat's-paw in a scheme that
involved murder and stock fraud and oil wells on Signal Hill
and had nothing to do with genuine romance . . .

If what exists between Kitty and Mr Crain IS genuine . . .

'Take four!' shouted Madge. 'Action!'

'Marche Slave' thundered into life. Darlene dashed with
unflagging malice but a certain diminution of vitality up the
thirty-two marble steps . . . and Kitty turned her head sharply,
as if at some noise from elsewhere in Stage One, where Ned
Devine's crew were hammering together flats which tomorrow
(God willing) would be the palatial living room of the wealthy
Shepherd family, whose son has risked all to marry the raven-
haired 'hot potato' Cincinnati Wilder, the chorus girl with the
heart of gold.

Over a dinner of Chinese leftovers and bootleg champagne
in the kitchen, after their return from the Los Angeles County
Courts building yesterday, she and Zal had come up with seven

or eight completely improbable conclusions to *Hot Potato*, in between toasting the dismissal of charges against Kitty Flint, a.k.a. Camille de la Rose, a.k.a. Mrs Chava Festraw . . .

And maybe one or two toasts, Emma reflected, to the fact that she and Zal hadn't been killed themselves in the process.

During take seven – with Darlene visibly laboring up the steps yet again (Kitty had dropped one of her bracelets) – Emma picked her way through the clusters of light stands on the edge of the new set, to the trestle tables by the door, in quest of cups and her tea thermos and water for the dogs. *Aunt Estelle should be calling me tomorrow*, she reflected, but her heart felt curiously calm. *You HAVE run away with the gypsies*, Zal had said to her, in the velvet darkness of the highway beside an ocean turned to liquid silver by the moon.

And she recalled Mr Crain, paraphrasing Cafavy's poem: *Ithaca will not make you rich; it's the road that makes you rich.*

Dodging Laestrygonians and bootleggers, Cyclopes and crooked cops . . .

But I don't belong here, she thought. *And I could have been killed, Friday night, while my right work, my true work, lies undone back in Oxford . . .*

Do I ever get to make it back to Ithaca?

Or return to my tower of Shalott?

'Emma?'

She stopped halfway to the trestles with their serried ranks of coffee cups and thermoses.

She had forgotten how much Aunt Estelle's voice sounded like her mother's.

Or had put it out of her thoughts, she reflected, for four agonizing years.

The scent of Guerlain's sandalwood in the dimness, like the whisper of a ghost.

And there she was. Taller than Mother, and stouter. Mother had been the more beautiful of the sisters, but the bone structure that Emma had known all her life was there, and the smile was the same.

I can go home! For two weeks she had known it, but the

reality of it was like waking from a dream, to find the Emperor Claudius' Etruscan–Latin Lexicon clasped in her arms.

I can go home . . .

Turning her head she saw Zal Rokatansky, his cap turned backwards so the bill wouldn't scrape the take-up reel, cranking gently while the wicked Valerna tore the gentle, Christian, and somewhat winded Philomela from Demetrius's arms, and hurled her to the ground. 'Get your meathooks off him, bitch!' cried the empress, a command which would appear on the title-card as: *Unhand one whom your better has chosen, wench!*

And the thought came to her, *But then I will lose THIS home.*

As if the words – like the face of Charles I – had been there all along.

Then Estelle was in her arms, saying, 'Oh, Emma, darling!' and Emma clasped her close, the familiar scent that dusted her clothing, whispered from her hair – silk-fine and netted close in a tidy snood, still the mousy hue somewhere between brown sugar and barley-straw, like Emma's own. *Mother's had begun to turn . . . It would all be silver by now . . .*

She whispered, 'Aunt . . .' and began to cry. She knew perfectly well that her tears were for the home she was losing, as much as for the one she knew now she would choose.

'Oh, darling!' Estelle Vambrace was weeping also. 'Oh, dearest! Oh, you look so much like Sarah . . . David, doesn't she look like Sarah?'

Uncle David – so much like a caricature of a colonial official, in his London tailoring and close-clipped mustache that Emma almost laughed through her tears – muttered an inaudible assent and held out an awkward hand. Emma grasped it. 'So glad,' she said. 'So glad!'

'They said at the office that we should find you here.' Estelle's rich contralto was her own, not Mother's, with a volume that rivaled Madge's. 'Good heavens, is that how they film cinema shows?' She looked out through the great doors into the gardens. 'How extraordinary! Is that a *woman*?' She stared at Madge Burdon in disapproval and didn't even trouble to lower her voice.

Emma sank hers to a conspiratorial whisper. 'Everyone in Hollywood wants to know that.'

She took them by the hand – this respectable British couple, daughter and son of Victoria's empire, as her own parents had been – and led them across to the doors.

Madge yelled, 'Cut! Elmore, what the hell was that? You defeat frikkin' Marcus Maximus in hand-to-hand combat and then you go trip on your own frikkin' chains?'

Fuming (and panting) Darlene descended the stairs yet again . . .

Herr Volmort bustled over to her to dust powder and touch up paint; Zal crossed to the door, shaking his head. Kitty descended behind Darlene, looking as innocent as if she hadn't just made her rival run up a very long flight of stairs seven times and clearly planned to do it at least eight more.

'Mr Zal Rokatansky,' said Emma, 'Miss Camille de la Rose – these are my dear Aunt Estelle and Uncle David. They're on their way through to New York, to take the *Ravenna* back home to Britain next week. They most kindly stopped here to visit with me on their way.'

There was a momentary shocked pause, as Aunt Estelle and Uncle David stared at her. It came to Emma that neither her aunt nor her uncle had remotely contemplated even the possibility that she would not fall, sobbing with gratitude, into their arms and then run home to pack her bag.

That she would not choose to leave.

Zal's eyes touched hers, and she saw his shoulders relax. If he could have found an appropriate way to do so he'd have taken her hand. But behind the thick glass of his spectacle-lenses, his glance said everything. Then he turned to ask Uncle David something about India, true and genuine in a way that made up for every ersatz screen kiss and false-fronted set. Kitty cried, in her sweet little-girl voice, 'Oh, darling, you can't let your Aunt and Uncle take a *cab* to the station! Tomorrow you take the Packard and drive them.'

And Emma said, 'Of course. Thank you.'

As Kitty turned back to Herr Volmort and his powders, and Madge summoned Zal for a conference about the lights, Aunt Estelle drew Emma aside. 'Dearest,' she said – and she sounded both disapproving and dismayed, 'surely you'll be coming with us! We've already wired the American Line asking for accommodations for five on the voyage.'

It took Emma a moment to realize that each of them had a body-servant, probably Indian, who would form the nucleus of the Oxford household.

'I'm so sorry.' She almost laughed with the sudden clarity of her relief, but knew they wouldn't understand. 'There was no way I could get in touch with you . . .'

Appalled, Aunt Estelle turned to survey Kitty, in her elaborate shreds of jewels and gauze, her Pekinese pattering eagerly around her sandaled feet. Looked past her at the arena, where prop men smoked in their shirt-sleeves as they raked sand and shifted historically inaccurate statues, and the Nubians of the empress's retinue – glistening with cocoa butter – clustered around the casting ads in the back of *Variety* (which also – prominently – bore Camille de la Rose's name).

'You can't actually say that you prefer living in this place!' She gazed round-eyed as the glittering Goddess of the Silver Screen, the temptress of Babylon, accepted a cigarette from Frank, and let him escort her to the make-up table, past the fulminating Darlene, her Pekinese trailing behind.

Her aunt didn't, Emma observed, even seem to notice Zal, or the way Zal's eyes touched her own as he returned to his camera.

Jim standing in the deepening twilight of Holywell Street, bidding her go on ahead of him. Miles smiling at her as she climbed the steps of The Myrtles once again.

But Jim was gone. Miles was gone.

The road will make you rich.

And there were other things ahead.

Gently, she said, 'Thank you – more than I can ever say – for your offer to take me back. To let me make a home with you. I'll never forget that kindness.' She took her aunt's hands.

The scent of her mother's perfume.

'But I will stay. I have . . . my life here, now.'

Uncle David was peering out into the arena, as Zal checked the light meters, and Darlene, at the bottom of the endless marble stair yet again, tried to look as if she didn't know exactly what Kitty was up to. 'Deuced interesting! What are they doing now?'

Emma hugged her aunt again. 'And I will drive you down to the train station tomorrow – Miss de la Rose has the most shockingly enormous car. Where are you staying, darling? I can take you there now, and come back for you this evening, to take you out to dinner – did you just arrive?'

'Last night.' Aunt Estelle looked around with distaste as Ned the Lesser, in his undershirt and with a cigarette dangling from his lip, brushed past her with a papier-mâché bronze clock for the *Hot Potato* set.

And very quietly, as his wife's attention was diverted, Uncle David asked, 'You're sure, my dear?'

Emma smiled. 'I'm sure.' She had never felt more sure of anything in her life.

Estelle sighed, and shook her head. 'What your mother would say I can't think!'

Emma didn't reply, as she led them toward the outer doors of the stage. But in her heart she knew exactly what her mother would say.

And what her father would say.

And Jim.

Whatever makes you happy.

The bravura strains of Tchaikovsky swelled from the set behind her, and she stepped out into the mild California sunshine.